John Ward
June '83

CHRISTIE'S REVIEW
OF THE SEASON 1983

CHRISTIE'S REVIEW OF THE SEASON 1983

Edited by John Herbert

PHAIDON · CHRISTIE'S
OXFORD

Distributed through Phaidon · Christie's Ltd
Littlegate House, St Ebbe's Street, Oxford OX1 1SQ

British Library Cataloguing in Publication Data

Christie's review of the season.—1983
  1. Art—Periodicals
  705   N9
  ISBN 0-7148-8008-6

Distributed in USA and dependencies by Salem House,
99 Main Street, Salem, NH 03079

Design and layout by Norman Ball
Phototypeset in CRTronic Baskerville by
Logos Design, Datchet, Berkshire

Printed and bound in The Netherlands by
Drukkerij Onkenhout b.v., Hilversum

ENDPAPERS: JOHN WARD, R.A.: *Christie's Sale at Godmersham Park*
Signed and dated June 83
Pen, ink and watercolour
12½ x 18½ in. (31.75 x 46.99 cm)

FRONTISPIECE: Kees van Dongen:
Aux Courses
Sold 21.3.83 in London for £172,800 ($255,744)
Record auction price for a work by the artist

**All prices include the buyer's premium where
applicable. The currency equivalents given
throughout the book are based on the rate of
exchange ruling at the time of the sale**

CONTENTS

Gold lever watch with
enamel portrait of
Napoleon I
Signed *Robin à Paris*
1¾ in. (4.4 cm)
in diameter
Sold 23.3.83 in
New York for $5,500
(£3,691)

Mr John Lumley, Director of Impressionist and Modern Pictures and Sculpture, selling Piet Mondrian's *Composition with Red, Blue and Yellow* from the collection of Mr and Mrs Armand P. Bartos, of New York for the record auction price of £1,512,000 ($2,328,480).

Foreword

JOHN A. FLOYD, *Chairman*

The pictures and works of art reproduced in the following pages illustrate far better than I can in words that the 1982-83 season has been a very encouraging one for Christie's. The sales total was £229.4 million, 33 per cent up on the previous year when the art market, like every other aspect of our economy, was hit by the world-wide recession. Last autumn there was a resurgence in the market to which I drew attention in the Company's interim statement. This has not only continued but increased.

The increase in sales has been most marked in the United Kingdom, reflecting the amount of highly important works of art sent in for sale from abroad. The improvement in London at King Street is also a direct consequence of a number of important initiatives taken during the past two years. The reduction in buyer's premium and concentration on fewer and more important sales have resulted in attracting more buyers and sellers from all over the world, as well as containing costs.

The word 'record' has almost ceased to have any meaning – one price exceeds another so quickly – but it has certainly been Christie's most successful season ever and the prices achieved world-wide show that the market is continuing to improve. This is good news for all those involved in the British fine art market, the economic importance of which has been underlined recently by the Committee of Invisible Exports' authoritative report. This showed that in 1980-81 the art market contributed, on a conservative assessment, over £50 million in commissions and services to Britain's overseas earnings and for the season under review the sum is likely to be considerably increased.

One reason for the continued strength of the London market, in spite of the increasing importance of that in New York, is that the auctioneers' terms of sale in London for foreign vendors are the lowest in the world; there is also the essential complementary element to the auctioneers' role which is the existence of the largest number of experienced fine art dealers in the world.

Even with salerooms in America (£91.9 million turnover this year) and others in Europe, all of which produce overseas earnings, Christie's continues to attract to London a very considerable quantity of works of art from abroad; in 1982-83 it was no less than 30 per cent of our London sales.

Some of the modern paintings from the collection of Mr and Mrs Armand P. Bartos, of New York, on view before the sale. The 16 works sold for a total of £4,079,800 ($6,282,290)

The importance of the London art market to Britain's economy seems sometimes to be lost on our legislators and others who should know better, because of the concern over Britain's art heritage. Everyone associated with the London art market is mindful about this subject and Christie's is no exception. Since 1956, over £40 million worth of highly important pictures and works of art, including £11 million in the current year, have passed into museums all over the country as a result of sales negotiated by Christie's on behalf of private collectors. Consequently there should be less wild talk about auctioneers and certainly no insults. Everyone should realise that we take a responsible view of the whole problem.

Introduction - Art in Diversity

HUON MALLALIEU

It would be interesting to know what the first James Christie would have had to say about a collection of 16 printed items relating to human freaks and their role in entertainment. He was no mean entertainer himself – although certainly no freak – and his skills in cajolery allied to his business flair made him and his firm household names. However it is doubtful if even he, for all his powers of 'specious oratory', could have elicited the 19th century equivalent of the £3,900 which was made by the collection when it was offered at Christie's South Kensington recently. He was, of course, willing and able to sell almost anything, from a Rembrandt to a field of standing hay, from the silver candelabra of the fallen French aristocracy to a collection of horse brasses. Although inevitably his successors have to try to exercise some sort of discrimination at the lower end of the market, since a lot, however fascinating, should at least cover the costs of cataloguing it, one of the most remarkable aspects of the business is the extraordinary diversity of the objects which go under the hammer each year.

Naturally enough the headlines are most often taken up with the most expensive items, and with 'auction record prices' – although except in near contemporary fields these have often been rendered virtually meaningless by the changing values of currency. While the price of $1,210,000 paid in New York for De Kooning's *Two Women* of 1954-55 is informative as it made it currently the most expensive contemporary painting, a 'record' £45,000 for a lovely oil sketch by Whistler only serves to emphasise the extreme rarity in market terms of the artist's major works. This point was made with some force in February 1983, when a 1935 £1,000 note was sold for £6,800. At first glance one might think that this was an admirable return on the initial outlay, but alas, not so, since £1,000 in 1935 represents £20,000 in modern currency.

Much more impressive from a financial point of view, and also valuable as an indication of changing fashions, was the fate of Carl Haag's watercolour of the Holy Rock in the Mosque of Omar, Mount Moriah, Jerusalem, which was painted in 1891. Haag was a Bavarian who settled in England and made himself a distinguished, if not particularly innovative, member of the British watercolour school, specialising in the then fashionable Orientalist subjects. He must also have been a considerable diplomat to have won permission to paint inside the Mosque, a task in which previous artists had failed. In about 1970, when such subjects were no longer in vogue the watercolour visited Christie's and made a respectable 85 gns. Since then the political and economic worlds, and with them the artistic, have changed greatly, and on its return to the saleroom in November, 1982, it was bid to £48,000.

In the same period Christie's too has changed, perhaps more than in all the previous history of the firm. Then the American offices were little more than forwarding posts, and of the other overseas stations only Geneva, then as now an important centre for the sale of jewels, could be

The Japanese art collector Shigeki Kameyama surrounded by some of his treasures in his Tokyo home after his return from buying Piet Mondrian's *Composition with Red, Blue and Yellow* for £1,512,000 ($2,328,480). He is holding a copy of Christie's Forthcoming Sales Magazine which features the picture on the front cover. (See illustration page 143)

Photograph by courtesy of Associated Press.

considered to be in the same business league as London. Now London and New York stand as twin pillars in a truly multi-national empire. The same decade has seen a diversification of the business itself, with the founding of Christie's Contemporary Art and the Christie's Fine Arts Course. The firm establishment of Christie's South Kensington in London and Christie's & Edmiston's in Glasgow has made it possible once again to cater for a wider – only the over-fastidious would say lesser – range of interests than had become practical at King Street.

These places are constant reminders that the auctioning of art and antiques is and should be fun as well as big business. In a sardonic swipe at nostalgia Byron held that 'all times that are old were good', and today it often seems that all artefacts that are old are art. While it is not the province of the auctioneer to form taste and foster fashions in the way that both critic and dealer must, it is the mark of a good auctioneer to mirror the prevailing collecting fashions and to encourage them to grow and flourish.

Age and association confer dignity, and rags and bones are no longer the exclusive preserve of the totter. Both age and aesthetics would account for the £2,000 that was paid at South Kensington for a nightcap of about 1600 embroidered in bright coloured silks and gold thread with flowers and strawberries, but association alone must excuse the otherwise somewhat purient interest shown in the long johns of Edward VII and the stockings of his mother. Evidence of a new phase in the collecting of old clothes is provided by five pairs of 1972 platform shoes which were sold recently for £30.

While the buyer of two Belfast sinks at £1 in the contents sale held by Christie's & Edmiston's at Guthrie Castle in May doubtless had a practical use for them, perhaps as features of a garden, the distinction between the useful but old fashioned and the obsolete but aesthetic is a hard one to draw, and it is constantly shifting. One would like to imagine the purchaser of an 1870's 'Alberta' sewing machine with mother of pearl inlay using it to repair a collection of Victorian dresses, preferably by the light of an oil lamp. More probably it is now only an object of admiration for itself rather than for its function, like the Victorian gilt brass and ivory fishing reel which another purchaser bought purely as a work of art, he being no fisherman.

Some years ago, after a fire at the Glasgow School of Art, a studio couch by C.R. Mackintosh which had been slightly damaged, was abandoned for the dustman. Before the next collection, however, it was spotted and taken away by a Clydeside boatbuilder. It was a useful seat, but on the last of two or three occasions when the yard had been flooded and the couch had set off for the Atlantic he debated whether to let it float away, but decided to fish it out again and to try to sell it. It brought him a tidy sum and when it has been repaired it will doubtless have a string across it to prevent anyone from sitting on it in the future.

A further example can be taken from yet another Scottish sale, the remarkable auction of scientific books which raised £210,000 for the Royal Society of Edinburgh on June 10, 1983.

One of a pair of
George I petit point
cushion covers
26 x 17½ in. (66 x
44.5 cm)
Sold 6.6.83 at
Godmersham Park for
£15,120 ($23,889)

Among them were 23 volumes of lithographed marine charts dating from 1822-69. Charts have a particularly short life as works of reference, sometimes becoming outdated and even hazardous to use within months of issue. These did not appear to have been used at all, and with a further revolution of time had been transformed into works of art. Thus the unexpected price of £32,000.

The saleroom is indeed a great leveller. A draft of the closing bars of the String Quartet in G Major (K.516) in Mozart's hand may jostle with a pile of old London bus tickets or a letter from Karl Marx to his doctor. One month a 1943 Spitfire Mk. IX, credited with four kills, and one of only 15 still flying, may sell for £260,0000. Another month, a Dickin Medal – the animals' V.C. – presented in 1944 to Mercury, a carrier pigeon, may reach £5,000.

All this, taken together with such run of the mill items as Gainsboroughs, Mondrians, Regency mahogany pedestal partners' desks, 163-piece famille rose armorial part dinner, tea and coffee services, the Pierpont Morgan silver collection, Weisweiler consoles dessertes, handfuls of Turners and heaps of Durers, demands an even greater degree of flexibility and mental agility on the part of experts and cataloguers. However, a firm that can casually call up expertise on such esoteric subjects as early racing cars, wild flowers, heraldry and the digging of lakes should be able to meet the challenge of the collecting passions of the future, however bizarre.

Negotiated Sales

CHRISTOPHER R. PONTER, LL.B.

One of the highlights of the year was the highly successful transfer, at a gross valuation of £4 million, of the Godman collection of Oriental porcelain in lieu of tax, and this collection will now find a permanent home in the British Museum (see article page 390). In addition, Christie's have continued to benefit their clients with a number of other private treaty transactions during 1983, of which mention can only be made of a few.

The Earls of Derby have always had a close association with the Walker Art Gallery, Liverpool, and it is pleasing to report that the Gallery's efforts to raise the special net price of over £1 million to acquire Lord Derby's painting by Nicolas Poussin of *The Ashes of Phocion collected by his Widow* (1648) has ensured that the painting remains at Merseyside.

Two Gainsborough portraits of men prominent in musical society of the late 18th century were also sold by private treaty – that of John Joseph Merlin to Kenwood for a net sum of £44,800, and another of Johann Christian Bach (seventh son of the great composer) to the National Portrait Gallery for a slightly greater net sum.

The National Museum of Wales has ended its search for an important Claude painting by acquiring from the Allendale Trustees a very fine painting of *St. Philip Baptising the Eunuch*.

Of the other works of art and manuscripts negotiated to public collections during the year, mention should be made of the rare example of a Verzelini Goblet accepted by the Office of Arts and Libraries in lieu of a net tax liability amounting to £52,750. The Victoria and Albert Museum acquired by private treaty an important Ivory Crucifix by David le Marchand, one of only three known religious works by this sculptor better known for his portraits of early 18th century British worthies. The gross value was in the region of £35,000.

During the year celebrating the 500th anniversary of the birth of Raphael (1483-1520) it is satisfying to record that Christie's succesfully negotiated the sale to the National Gallery of Raphael's panel of *St. John the Baptist Preaching* (c.1505). This is the only surviving part of the predella originally beneath the main altarpiece *The Ansidei Madonna* which had been acquired by the Gallery in 1885, and is among the earliest authentic paintings by Raphael to have been imported into this country.

NICOLAS POUSSIN: *The Ashes of Phocion Collected by his Widow*
Oil on canvas
46 x 69½ in. (116 x 176 cm)

Courtesy Walker Art Gallery, Liverpool

CLAUDE GELÉE, called LORRAINE: *St. Philip Baptising the Eunuch*
Oil on canvas
33 x 54 in. (84 x 137 cm)

Courtesy National Museum of Wales, Cardiff

15

Above

RAFFAELLO SANZIO,
called RAPHAEL: *St. John
the Baptist Preaching*
Tempera on panel
9 x 20¾ in.
(23 x 53 cm)

Far left

Late 17th or early
18th century English
ivory Corpus Christi
Signed by David
le Marchant
15½ x 10½ in.
(39.5 x 27 cm)

Left

Elizabethan Goblet
By Giacomo
Verzelini, engraved by
Anthony de Lisle
Dated 1586
6½ in. (16.5 cm) high

PICTURES, DRAWINGS AND PRINTS

LUCA GIORDANO: *Hercules on the Funeral Pyre, with Philoctetes Kindling the Flames*
Signed JORDANUS
Oil on canvas
45 x 113½ in. (114.3 x 288.3 cm)
Sold 10.12.82 in London for £34,560 ($55,987)

LORENZO DI NICCOLO: *Madonna and Child with St. John the Evangelist, St. Louis of Toulouse and Angels*
Tempera on panel
37¼ x 21 in. (94 x 53 cm)
Sold for $71,500 (£44,687)

NICCOLO GIOLFINO: *Coronation of Darius Hystaspes*
One of three cassone panels
Tempera on panel
10 x 12½ in. (25.5 x 31 cm)
The three sold for a total of $104,500 (£65,312)

All sold 10.6.83 in New York

ALESSANDRO DI MARIANO
FILIPEPI, called SANDRO
BOTTICELLI: *Portrait of Giovanni
di Pierfrancesco de'Medici*
Tempera on panel
23 x 15½ in. (58.5 x 39.2 cm)
Sold 10.12.82 in London for
£810,000 ($1,312,200)
By order of the Trustees of the
late Lady Merton
The sitter, Giovanni di
Pierfrancesco de'Medici (1467-
1498) was described as
'giovane, bellissimo, di valore e
di spirito...'; Filippino Lippi
included his portrait in the
Uffizi *Adoration of the Magi* of
1496. He is holding a *trecento*
Sienese medallion, apparently
of St. John the Evangelist, that
presumably originally formed
part of the frame of an
altarpiece

GIULIANO BUGIARDINI:
*The Madonna and Child
with the Infant St.
John the Baptist*
Tempera on panel
44 x 34 in.
(111.7 x 86.3 cm)
Sold 10.12.82 in
London for £66,960
($108,475)
From the collection of
the Stirlings of Keir
Acquired by Charles
Stirling in Italy
*c.*1820-25, this
masterpiece of
Bugiardini's early
maturity shows the
influence of Fra
Bartolommeo; like
Bugiardini's
comparable pictures
at Allentown and in
the Florence Accademia,
it may be dated about
1520

PIERFRANCESCO DI
JACOPO FOSCHI: *Portrait
of Bartolomeo Compagni*
Inscribed and dated
1549
Tempera on panel
40½ x 30½ in.
(103 x 82.5 cm)
Sold 10.12.82 in
London for £45,360
($73,483)
From the collection of
the Stirlings of Keir
Formerly
misattributed to
Pontormo, this
characteristic work by
Foschi was purchased
by Charles Stirling in
Italy before 1826

BERNARDINO LUINI:
*Portrait of a
Young Woman*
Oil on panel
transferred to canvas
13¾ x 10¾ in.
(35 x 27.3 cm)
Sold 10.12.82 in
London for £75,600
($122,472)
Possibly a fragment of
a larger work of after
1525. The pose and
type derive from
Leonardo, perhaps
from a drawing for
Leda and the Swan.

Opposite

BARTOLOMÉ ESTEBAN
MURILLO: *Young Girl
Raising her Veil*
Oil on canvas
20½ x 15½ in.
(52.4 x 39.4 cm)
Sold 15.4.83 in
London for £378,000
($582,120)
In the 18th
century a pendant to
the *Peasant Boy* now in
the National Gallery.
By 1844 it formed part
of the Holford
Collection, and
fetched 5,600 gns. at
the Holford sale at
Christie's in 1928

GIOVANNI ANTONIO CANAL, IL CANALETTO: *The Piazza di San Giovanni in Laterano, Rome*
Oil on canvas
25 x 38¾ in. (63.5 x 98.5 cm)
Sold 10.12.82 in London for £172,800 ($279,936)
By order of the Trustees of the late Sir Clifford Curzon, C.B.E.
The picture appears to be based on a drawing by the artist, who is known to have visited Rome as a young man in 1719. A very similar view occurs in a drawing in the British Museum.

FRANCESCO GUARDI: *The Bacino di San Marco, Venice*
Oil on canvas
21 x 33½ in. (53.3 x 85 cm)
Sold 10.12.82 in London for £118,500 ($191,970)
By order of the Trustees of the late Sir Clifford Curzon, C.B.E.
This picture is generally considered to be the pendant to the signed *Canale della Giudecca with the Zattere* in the Berlin Museum

HUBERT ROBERT: *La Source du Temple de Vesta;* and *Le Repos dans le Parc*
Oil on canvas
97 x 47 in. (246.5 x 120 cm)
Both sold 10.6.83 in New York for a total of $286,000 (£178,750)

JAN CORNELISZ.
VERMEYEN: *Portrait of
a Man*
Oil on panel
29½ x 24½ in.
(74.9 x 62.2 cm)
Sold 10.12.82 in
London for £140,000
($226,800)
From the collection of
the Earl of Pembroke
and Montgomery
Already at Wilton at
the end of the 18th
century and for long
thought to be the work
of Holbein, this is a
typical example
of the portrait style of
the Netherlandish artist
J.C. Vermeyen

Opposite

SIR ANTHONY VAN DYCK: *Portrait of Thomas Howard, 2nd Earl of Arundel (1585-1646)*
Oil on canvas
44 x 31½ in. (113 x 80 cm)
Sold 8.7.83 in London for £496,800 ($779,976)
From the collection of Rebecca Pollard Logan
Painted by Van Dyck during his brief visit to England in 1620-21

HENDRICK TERBRUGGHEN: *Scene of Mercenary Love*
Bears monogram
Oil on canvas
29¼ x 35 in. (74.3 x 89.2 cm)
Sold 8.7.83 in London for £86,400 ($135,648)

JAN VAN KESSEL: *Still Life of Flowers*
Signed
Oil on canvas
22¾ x 15¾ in.
(57.5 x 40 cm)
Sold 15.4.83 in London for
£51,840 ($79,837)

SALOMON VAN RUYSDAEL: *Nymwegen Castle and the River Waal*
Signed with initials and dated 1652
Oil on panel
27½ x 36¼ in. (69.8 x 92 cm)
Sold 8.7.83 in London for £496,800 ($779,976)
By order of the Trustees of the Earl of Listowel Will Trust
From the collection formed by Lord Ennismore, lst Earl of Listowel, between 1800 and 1815 for Kingston House, Knightsbridge

PHILIPS WOUWERMAN: *Departure of a Hawking Party*
Signed in monogram and with initial
Oil on panel
19 x 25¼ in. (48.2 x 63.9 cm)
Sold 8.7.83 in London for £135,000 ($211,950)
In the de Rothschild collection, London in the 19th century,
this fine example of Wouwerman's work was sold by Captain
Ernest Duveen at Christie's in 1925, when it fetched 600 gns.

Opposite

JACOB ISAAKSZ. VAN RUISDAEL: *A Winter Landscape with
Peasants Gathering Firewood*
Signed
Oil on canvas
14¼ x 12½ in. (36.2 x 31.7 cm)
Sold 15.4.83 in London for £129,600 ($199,584)
One of Ruisdael's few winter landscapes, this delicately
executed work was once in the Braamcamp and Six
collections, Amsterdam

The Fenwick Oil-Sketches and Constable's 'Salisbury Cathedral from the Meadows'

IAN FLEMING-WILLIAMS

During his lifetime Constable sold or otherwise disposed of only a small proportion of his landscape paintings. At the time of his death, in March 1837, the greater part of his life's work was still under his roof, much of it – the oil-sketches for instance – unknown to any but the family and a few close friends. The following year, to raise funds for his seven orphaned children, Constable's collection of prints and drawings and two hundred of his oils, including such masterworks as *Salisbury Cathedral from the Meadows*, *Brighton Pier* and *The Leaping Horse*, were auctioned at Foster's. The three were sold, fetching respectively £110.5s., £45.3s. and £52.10s., but many items at the sale were withdrawn, having failed to reach their reserves. These, with the rest of the collection – still numerically the greater part of Constable's output – remained with the family. A substantial portion subsequently passed down to the next generation, but towards the end of their lives, in the 1870s and '80s, the surviving children began to dispose of their share of the inheritance. Mostly, it was sold by auction, at Christie's, but they were by no means tight-fisted with their possessions and Charles, Lionel and Isobel gave away examples of their father's work most generously to various friends – sometimes in quite large batches.

A number of these gifts are recorded. One such group, some 20 or 30 drawings given by Charles Constable to his friend Caton Thompson, was lost during the Second World War when a London depository was blitzed. From time to time, however, there comes to light an hitherto unknown work or group of works that one or another of the children had presented to a friend. We have recently had an example of this — the five handsome oil-sketches that Isobel Constable gave to her friend Alice Fenwick, daughter of H.P. Ashby, a landscape painter who had known Constable in the 1830s. Consisting of two dated and three datable works, *Stoke-by-Nayland (of 30 July 1816)*, *Willy Lott's House with Rainbow* (1 October 1812), a Brighton *Study of Sea and Sky*, *Salisbury Cathedral from the Meadows* and *Salisbury Cathedral from Long Bridge*, all five were quite unknown when they were brought in for examination to the Tate Gallery and were seen by Leslie Parris in April 1981. Not unexpectedly, the four last named created a considerable amount of interest when they came up for sale at Christie's in November 1982.

The discovery of the two Fenwick Salisbury views was of particular interest to scholars as it brought very near to completion the set of studies Constable made for the last of his great six-footers, *Salisbury Cathedral from the Meadows* (a). From these studies and from a reading of the Correspondence it is now possible to attempt a reconstruction of the probable chain of events that led up to the final painting.

In 1829 Constable twice stayed with his friends the Fishers at Salisbury: in July for about three weeks, and in November for a slightly longer period. During the July visit he painted a number of views from the Fishers' house in the Close and made several drawings of the cathedral from afar, including, it would seem, the Mellon and Fitzwilliam studies we shall shortly be discussing. In the letters John Fisher wrote between these visits there are several interesting references. Constable was apparently planning to work on a rather larger scale than usual on his next visit, for in August Fisher reported that 'the great easel' had arrived '& waits his office' and then continued: 'Pray do not let it be long before you come & begin your work. I am quite sure the "Church under a cloud" is the best subject you can take. It will be an amazing advantage to go every day & look afresh at your material drawn from nature herself'. On

JOHN CONSTABLE, R.A.:
*Salisbury Cathedral from
Long Bridge*
7¼ x 11 in.
(18 x 27.9 cm)
Sold 19.11.82 in London
for £324,000 ($518,400)
Equals the world record
auction price for a
finished work by
Constable achieved in
July, 1982

JOHN CONSTABLE, R.A.:
*Salisbury Cathedral from the
Meadows*
7¾ x 11 in.
(19.5 x 27.9 cm)
Sold 19.11.82 in London
for £216,000 ($345,600)

3 September Fisher told Constable how he yearned to see him tranquilly at work on his next great picture and lectured him quite severely on the need to make a start in good time. 'Now come & work', he concluded, '& don't talk about it.' In a third letter, of 21 October, Fisher begged him to come soon, for, as he said, the trees were already naked. Constable appears to have complied. In a letter of the 24th his brother, Abram, said he thought there was a chance of the weather being fine for the journey.

This autumnal, second visit is commemorated by six dated drawings. The first a pen and watercolour study of cattle and pollarded willows in the Victoria and Albert Museum was begun on 13 November. The second, a stormy watercolour of Fisherton Mill in the British Museum, dated 19 November, was taken from quite near the viewpoint he chose for the final painting. On the 23rd, towards the end of his stay, he made yet another pencil sketch of the cathedral from across the fields, this time from the south. 26 November is inscribed on the last of the dated drawings, a pencil study of trees and cottages in the Fondazione Horne. There are no details of Constable's return to London. He is next to be found receiving his Diploma at the Royal Academy on 10 December.

The following works are relevant to a study of the preparatory work for *Salisbury Cathedral from the Meadows*: four pencil drawings of the cathedral, three from the north west – *Salisbury Cathedral from the Meadows (with a cart)* (b) in the Mellon collection, *Salisbury Cathedral from the Meadows (with an angler)* (c) in the Fitzwilliam Museum, and a drawing of the same subject dated '11 1829' with a man and a dog in the foreground, in the Lady Lever Art Gallery, Port Sunlight (d) – and the one from the south, the study dated 23 November, at one time in the Gregory collection (present whereabouts unknown; repr. *Illustrated London News*, 16 July, 1949, p.99); next, three oil-sketches, the 7 by 11 inch Fenwick pair, *Salisbury Cathedral from the Meadows* and *Salibsury Cathedral from Long Bridge*, and a larger, 14 by 20 inch version at the Tate; and finally, but, in the opinion of the present writer, only possibly, the full-size oil painting of the subject at the Guildhall Art Gallery (repr. B. Taylor, *Constable, Paintings, Drawings and Watercolours*, 1973, pl.148).

The cathedral was the subject of some of Constable's finest drawings and paintings. From a distance, looking down from the surrounding hills or from across the almost enveloping water-meadows, with its spire darting up into the sky like a needle, as Constable himself described it, the building appears to have had a particularly strong appeal for him; especially when the clouds, lit or in shadow, contrasted with the alternating lights and shadows passing across the tower and spire. On occasion his patron, Bishop Fisher, had cause to complain of his fascination '[if] Constable would but leave out his black clouds!', he had chuntered. The Church under black clouds, a theme with more than one level of meaning, had evidently been discussed as a possible subject for Constable's next big picture when he was staying with John Fisher in July, and from Fisher's letter of 9 August it looks as if Constable was intending to make a start on a scale demanding a big easel on his return to Salisbury. That visit materialised in late October or early November.

Probably with this major work in mind Constable had sketched the cathedral at a distance from several viewpoints in July, but it was the drawings he made that month to the north west, close by and beyond Fisherton Mill, (the Fitzwilliam (c) and Mellon (d) studies) that provided him with the material he wanted — the former supplying the compositional setting, the latter secondary elements such as the carts or waggons and the pollarded willow. In the Fenwick paintings we see him developing these views a stage further. In the *Salisbury Cathedral from Long Bridge* he retains every feature in the Fitzwilliam drawing (while slightly remodelling the footbridge), but with vigorous brushwork and contrasting effects of chiaroscuro begins to build up a more powerful, highly charged image. In the other Fenwick oil-sketch he is to be seen experimenting with the staffage, removing the further waggon in the Mellon drawing and tucking the other one away temporarily in the corner.

The third drawing of the cathedral from the north west, the Port Sunlight pencil study (d), is of a different character from the other two. Dated '11 1829' (November would seem to be the most likely missing word) and lined diagonally for transfer, it is clearly a compositional sketch, a preparatory work for the Tate Gallery's *Salisbury Cathedral from the Meadows*, a sketch on canvas ruled with identical pencil diagonals (e). These two studies, combining elements from the

(a)

(b)

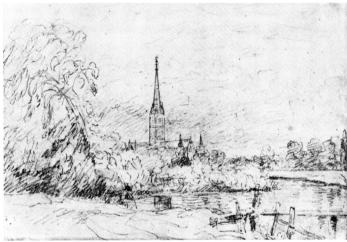

(c)

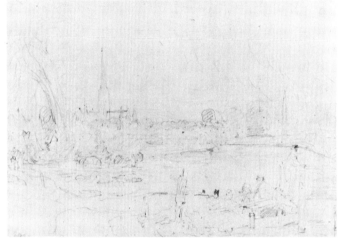

(d)

(e)

(a) *Salisbury Cathedral from the Meadows*
Oil on canvas
59¾ x 74¾ in.
(151.8 x 189.9 cm)
Private Collection

(b) *Salisbury Cathedral from the Meadows (with a cart)*
Pencil
9¼ x 13⅜ in.
(23.4 x 33.9 cm)
From the collection of Mr and Mrs Paul Mellon

(c) *Salisbury Cathedral from the Meadows (with an angler)*
Pencil on paper watermarked 1822
9¼ x 13⅛ in.
(23.5 x 33.2 cm)
Fitzwilliam Museum, Cambridge

(d) *Salisbury Cathedral from the Meadows*
Pencil, inscr. '11. 1829'
9¼ x 13¼ in.
(23.5 x 33.7 cm)
Lady Lever Art Gallery, Port Sunlight

(e) *Salisbury Cathedral from the Meadows*
Oil on canvas
14⅜ x 20⅛ in.
(36.5 x 51.1 cm)
Tate Gallery

other four, with a new emphasis on foreground incident — the single horse in the drawing replaced by a full team in the Tate composition — and a fresh idea, the dog following his master across the footbridge, represent the next stage in the development of the composition; a development that leads us on to the seventh and penultimate work in series, the Guildhall painting.

There is a division of opinion over this work, as there has been over one or two of the other full-size versions of Constable's major compositions. Beneath the visible painted surface of one of these difficult paintings, the *White Horse* in the National Gallery, Washington, an x-ray photograph has revealed under-painting very probably from Constable's hand, suggesting that perhaps, in order to render it marketable, a later 19th century hand has been at work. It is possibly that the Guildhall picture (from which some later paint has already been removed), is also an original full-size sketch by Constable worked over by another hand. As we have seen, the subject of his next big picture, the Church under a cloud, had already been under discussion when Constable was staying with Fisher in July, and the various pencil studies of the cathedral at a distance made during that stay appear to have been part of his initial search for the right motif. The Fenwick sketches, the Port Sunlight pencil composition and the Tate painting represent further stages in the collecting and development of the material. The next stage would have been a start on the final picture, or – as it was most often Constable's practice to walk the course, as it were, beforehand – a start on a trial, full-size canvas. For either Constable would have needed a large, studio easel. The dispatch of the 'great easel' in August must surely indicate an intention to begin just such a work when he returned to Salisbury in the autumn. With the likelihood of there having been a large sketch for *Salisbury Cathedral from the Meadow*, one cannot ignore the possibility that the Guildhall painting is, or was, the work in question.

As a coda, there is the question of the pencil sketch Constable made towards the end of his second stay, on 23 November. This is a view of the cathedral from the south, from quite a different viewpoint, and were it not for one feature would have no direct bearing on our subject. But there is one important, indeed one central element in the final picture that is to be found in none of the preparatory works we have been considering – the rainbow. Constable had his back to the sun when making his drawing on 23 November and as he worked, with hardly more than three strokes of his pencil, noted a rainbow, an effect that must have made a colourful and dramatic contrast with the cathedral spire deep in shadow. Was it this observation, this sign of dark giving place to light, that inspired the inclusion of the rainbow in *Salisbury Cathedral from the Meadows*?

JOHN CONSTABLE, R.A.: *Study for 'The Young Waltonians'*
Inscribed and dated 1811 on reverse
Oil on panel
7¼ x 5⅝ in.
(18.3 x 14.5 cm)
Sold 19.11.82 in London for £86,400 ($138,240)
The finished picture, exhibited in 1820, was sold at Christie's 20.6.51 for 42,000 gns and is now in a private collection

JOHN MICHAEL WRIGHT: *Portrait of Miss May*
Oil on canvas
40 x 42 in. (101.6 x 106.6 cm)
Sold 15.7.83 in London for £48,600 ($76,788)
From the Godmersham Park Collection

SIR PETER LELY: *Portrait of Lord and Lady Dacre*
c. 1650
With coat of arms and inscribed
Oil on canvas
49¼ x 67¼ in. (125.1 x 170.8 cm)
Sold 19.11.82 in London for £54,000 ($86,400)
From the collection of The Hon. Lady Ford
First recorded at Belhus, Essex, by Horace Walpole

THOMAS
GAINSBOROUGH, R.A.:
Portrait of Mr and Mrs
Carter of Ballingdon
House, Bulmer, Essex
Oil on canvas
35½ x 27¼ in.
(90.1 x 69.2 cm)
Sold 22.4.83 in
London for £140,400
($216,216)
The sitters' daughter
Frances married
Robert Andrews in
1748: Gainsborough's
celebrated picture of
the young couple is in
the National Gallery

This portrait was
apparently sold by the
Andrews family in
1920 for £105, and
came for sale as a
result of a photograph
being sent to us from
New Zealand

Opposite

WILLIAM HOGARTH:
Portrait of The Rt. Hon.
Richard Mounteney, 1st
Baron of the Exchequer in
Ireland (1701-1768)
Oil on canvas
29 x 24½ in.
73.6 x 62.2 cm)
Sold 22.4.83 in
London for £64,800
($99,792)

ARTHUR DEVIS: *The Till Family*
c. 1750-1751
Oil on canvas
42 x 58 in. (106.6 x 147.2 cm)
Sold 15.7.83 in London for £91,800 ($142,290)
Previously sold at Christie's 26.5.33 for £200
From the Godmersham Park Collection

Opposite

ARTHUR DEVIS: *Portrait of the Rev. H. Say and his Wife*
Signed and dated 1752
Oil on canvas
32½ x 27½ in. (82.5 x 68.5 cm)
Sold 15.7.83 in London for £102,600 ($159,030)
Record auction price for a work by the artist
From the Godmersham Park Collection

ROBERT HEALY: *The Duke of Leinster Skating with Friends and Lady Louisa's Dog, 'Hibou'*
Signed and dated 1768
Charcoal heightened with white on paper
21¼ x 29¼ in. (54 x 74.3 cm)
Sold 15.7.83 in London for £51,840 ($80,352)
From the collection of The Hon. Desmond Guinness
One of a series of drawings executed by the artist for Tom Conolly of Castledown in 1768-9.
Conolly's wife, Lady Louisa, was the sister of the Duchess of Leinster

THOMAS ROBERTS: *The Duke and Duchess of Leinster Walking by the Sheet of Water at Carton, Co. Kildare*
Oil on canvas
44½ x 60 in. (113 x 153 cm)
Sold 15.7.83 in London for £62,640 ($97,092)
From the collection of The Hon. Desmond Guinness
This is one of four canvases executed for the 1st Duke of Leinster: the demesne at Carton was one of
the outstanding landscape gardening projects of the 18th century in Ireland

JOHN WOOTTON: *The Round Course at Newmarket*
Oil on canvas
23½ x 80 in.
(59.6 x 200 cm)
Sold 22.4.83 in London for
£48,000 ($73,920)

JOHN DALBY: *Full Cry*
Signed
Oil on canvas
9¼ x 15 in. (23.5 x 38.1 cm)
This is one of a set of four pictures
All sold 10.6.83 in New York for $110,000 (£68,750)
From the collection of Donald W. Tynion

GEORGE STUBBS, A.R.A.: *Fanny, the Favourite Spaniel of Mrs Musters*
Signed and dated 1778
Oil on panel
23½ x 27½ in. (59.6 x 69.8 cm)
Sold 15.7.83 in London for £64,800 ($100,440)
Fanny is the dog in the portrait of Mrs Musters by Sir Joshua Reynolds

BEN MARSHALL: *Ispwell Lass*
Signed and dated 1805
Oil on canvas
33⅞ x 40¼ in. (86.1 x 101.6 cm)
Sold 10.6.83 in New York for $253,000 (£158,125)

JOHN MARTIN: *Belshazzar's Feast*
Signed and dated 1820
Oil on canvas
63 x 98 in. (160 x 249 cm)
Sold 15.7.83 in London for £108,000 ($167,400)
Record auction price for a work by the artist

FREDERIC, LORD LEIGHTON, P.R.A.: *Nausicaa*
c. 1878
Oil on canvas
57½ x 26½ in. (146 x 67 cm)
Sold 24.6.83 in London for £226,800 ($340,200)
Record auction price for a work by the artist
This subject to taken from the eighth book of Homer's Odyssey.
Nausicaa finds Odysseus shipwrecked on a beach and invites him
back to her father's palace. The moment captured in this picture
is Nausicaa's reactions to Odysseus's victory in the games with
the Phaeocians. 'Now Nausicaa, in all her heaven-sent beauty,
was standing by one of the pillars that supported the massive
roof. Filled with admiration as her eyes fell on Odysseus, she
greeted him warmly'

JAMES JOSEPH TISSOT: *The Garden Bench*
1882
Signed
Oil on canvas
39 x 56 in. (99.5 x 142.5 cm)
Sold 24.6.83 in London for £561,000 ($842,400)
Record auction price for a work by the artist and any Victorian picture
Tissot's mistress, Mrs Kathleen Newton, and her children are depicted on the garden bench, presumably in Grove End Road.
Mrs Newton died of consumption on 9 November, 1882, and Tissot immediately returned to Paris. This was the end of his
English period, and the present picture bridges the transition, having been painted in England but exhibited in France. Not
surprisingly, it was of considerable sentimental value to the artist and he retained it in his possession until his death

DAVID ROBERTS, R.A.: *The Island of Philae, Nubia*
Signed and dated 1843
Oil on canvas
30¼ x 60½ in (76.8 x 153.7 cm)
Sold 18.3.83 in London for £75,600 ($114,156)
Record auction price for a work by the artist

JOHN WILLIAM WATERHOUSE, R.A.: *Ophelia*
Signed
Oil on canvas
49 x 29 in. (124.4 x 73.6 cm)
Sold 26.11.82 in London for £81,000
($128,790)
Record auction price for a work by the artist

GEORGE INNESS: *New England Valley*
Signed and dated 1878
Oil on canvas
30⅜ x 45 in. (77.2 x 114.4 cm)
Sold 3.12.82 in New York for $132,000 (£79,518)

FITZ HUGH LANE: *Blue Hill, Maine*
Oil on canvas
20⅛ x 30 in. (51 x 76.2 cm)
Sold 3.6.83 in New York for $352,000 (£220,000)

FREDERICK CHILDE HASSAM: *Summer Evening*
Signed and dated 1886
Oil on canvas
12⅛ x 20¼ in. (30.7 x 51.4 cm)
Sold 3.11.82 in New York for $154,000 (£96,250)

JOHN SINGER SARGENT: *Portrait of Mrs Ernest G. Raphael*
Signed and dated 1905
Oil on canvas
64½ x 44¾ in.
(163.8 x 113.7 cm)
Sold 3.6.83 in New York for
$330,000 (£206,250)
From the collection of the late
Cyril Raphael
Mrs Ernest Raphael was the
daughter of Reuben Sassoon,
friend of Edward VII. She
married Ernest Raphael on
May 1, 1893, and the brooch
she is wearing is, according to
family tradition, from the
Collection of Empress
Eugénie. The brooch was
sold at Christie's 7.6.83 in
New York for $34,100
(£21,446)

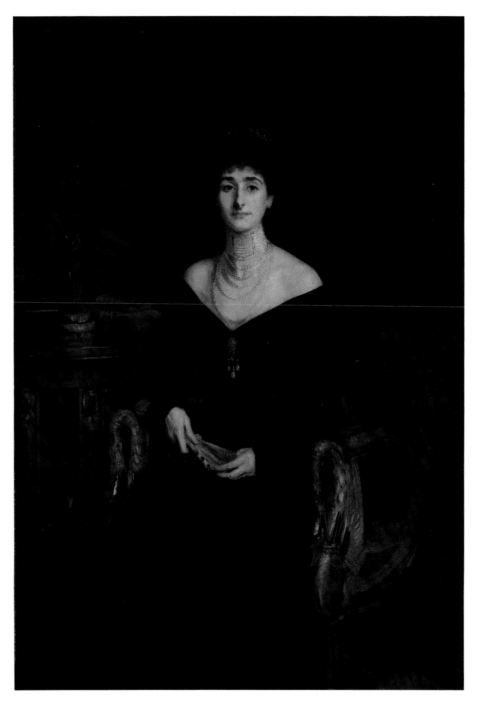

WILLIAM J. GLACKENS: *From Under Willows*
c. 1914
Signed, inscribed with title on stretcher
Oil on canvas
25¼ x 31¼ in. (64.2 x 79.4 cm)
Sold 3.6.83 in New York for $352,000 (£200,000)
This painting was purchased directly from the artist in 1920

Opposite

WALTER UFER: *The Bakers*
Signed
Oil on canvas
50¼ x 50¼ in.
(127.6 x 127.6 cm)
Sold 16.10.82 in Houston for
$374,000 (£200,000)
Record auction price for a work
by the artist

American works on paper

JAY CANTOR

A number of interesting tendencies emerged in the major sales of American paintings held in New York during the 1982-83 season. Not only did the Hudson River School continue to attract serious competitive interest, but increasing interest was seen in the American Impressionist, early Modernist and Regionalist circles. Perhaps most surprising in these trends was the strong showing for works on paper and indeed many of the record prices of the season were made by drawings and watercolours.

Christie's was fortunate in being able to offer major works by the two foremost artist of the 19th and early 20th centuries, Winslow Homer and Thomas Eakins. In the case of *Sponge Boats, Key West*, an extraordinarily accomplished work demonstrating Homer's mature mastery of the watercolour medium, the $561,000 (£337,951) selling price was not only a record for a watercolour by the artist, but also for any American watercolour. *Sponge Boats, Key West* was part of a consignment of five watercolours and drawings by Homer from the Estate of Mrs. Dunbar Bostwick, the granddaughter of the pioneering collector, Mrs H.O. Havermeyer and the daughter of another significant collector, Mrs. J. Watson Webb, the founder of Shelburne Museum in Vermont. A second Homer watercolour, *At Anchor*, also exceeded the previous record for the artist selling at $330,000 (£206,250). Homer's early maturity, reached during his stay along the English coast at Tynemouth and Cullercoats in 1881 and 1882, produced another important Bostwick picture; the drawing, *Blyth Sands*, represents the stoic dedication of fisherman's wives facing the intense rage of the sea as they search for evidence of the return of their husbands from their perilous occupations. The pitting of man against nature first realized in these drawings remained a significant theme throughout Homer's career. Homer's work showed increasing influence of Japanese prints so important to later 19th century painters, and another work on paper by a contemporary, *Geisha At Her Toilet* by Robert Frederick Blum, actually resulted from a visit to Japan in 1890. Blum produced a major oil from his Japanese sojourn sold by Christie's in June 1982 for $473,000 (£261,325) and, not surprisingly, his small pastel, a masterwork by the artist in the medium, reached an equally significant price when knocked down for $104,500 (£62,951).

The exploration of the American scene and a dedication to close observation coupled with an almost manic effort of simplification and abstraction have been a constant *leitmotif* of American art since its rather primitive beginnings. Grant Wood's coy rendering of *Adolescence* in his drawing of 1932 not only made a record price for the artist, but provided a witty synopsis of the intense exploration of the vernacular carried out by American regionalist artists during the serious self-questioning engendered by the Great Depression. Estimated at $8,000-12,000, this drawing soared to a stunning $143,000 (£90,506), more than doubling the previous record for the artist.

WINSLOW HOMER: *Sponge Boats, Key West*
Signed and dated 1903
Watercolour and pencil on paper
14 x 21⅞ in. (35.5 x 55.5 cm)
Sold 3.11.82 in New York for $561,000 (£350,625)
Record auction price for an American watercolour, and for a work by the artist

Contemporary realism, coupled with an interest in the historical past were also significant concerns of Thomas Eakins whose watercolor *Spinning* was sold along with two oils in Christie's June 3rd sale for the benefit of the Estate of the artist's neice, Rebecca Macdowell Garrett. *Spinning*, which shows the artist's sister Mary dressed in historical costume working at the spinning wheel, was executed in the early 1870s when historical consciousness aroused by the approaching centennial of American Independence provided an exciting range of subject matter for contemporary painters.

The $550,000 (£348,100) not only established a new price level for any work by the artist, but also amply demonstrated the considerable revaluation of an artist who though largely ignored in his own lifetime has come to be considered one of the giants of the history of American painting.

American watercolours and drawings have during the past season arrived at a level of serious consideration by collectors and museums and underscored the long overdue re-evaluation of the considerable achievement of American artists.

THOMAS COWPERTHWAIT EAKINS:
Spinning
Signed and dated 1881
Watercolour on paper
15⅝ x 10⅝ in. (39.8 x 27 cm)
Sold 3.6.83 in New York for
$550,000 (£343,750)

ROBERT FREDERICK
BLUM: *Geisha at Her Toilet*
Stamped with artist's stamp
Pastel on paper laid on board
14⅛ x 11⅝ in.
(36 x 29.5 cm)
Sold 3.12.82 in New York for $104,000
(£62,951)

GRANT WOOD: *Adolescence*
Signed and dated 1933
Ink wash, pencil and white chalk on paper
laid down on board
24½ x 14½ in. (62.3 x 37 cm)
Sold 18.3.83 in New York for $143,000
(£94,078)
Record auction price for a 20th century
American drawing and a work by the
artist

Above

PAUL HOWARD MANSHIP: *Diana*
Inscribed PAUL MANSHIP 1921
© and No 3
Bronze
37½ in. (95.3 cm) high
Sold for $77,000 (£48,734)

Right

HIRAM POWERS: *Greek Slave*
Signed H. POWERS. Sculp
Marble
46 in. (117 cm) high
Sold for $198,000 (£125,316)
Both sold 3.6.83 in New York

JEAN FRANÇOIS MILLET: *La Becquée*
1859
Signed
Black chalk and pastel
27⅞ x 10¾ in. (32.8 x 27.3 cm)
Sold 27.5.83 in New York for $247,500 (£153,726)

Both sold by order of the Executors of
the Estate of Florence E. Dickerman

JEAN FRANÇOIS MILLET: *La Femme au Puits*
c. 1866
Signed
Black chalk and pastel on paper laid down on canvas
11¼ x 8¾ in. (28.5 x 22.3 cm)
Sold 27.5.83 in New York for $258,580 (£160,559)

JULES ADOLPHE AIMÉ LOUIS BRETON: *Le Départ pour les Champs*
Signed and dated 1857
Oil on canvas
29 x 49½ in. (73.6 x 126 cm)
Sold 26.11.82 in London for £48,600 ($77,274)
Record auction price for a work by the artist

GUSTAVE BAUERNFEIND: *Jerusalem from the Mount of Olives*
Signed and dated 1902
Oil on canvas
51½ x 79 in. (131 x 201 cm)
Sold 26.11.82 in London for £70,200 ($105,300)
Record auction price for a work by the artist

CARL HAAG: *The Holy Rock, Summit of Mount Moriah, Jerusalem*
Signed, inscribed and dated 1891
Watercolour heightened with white
39¼ x 22 in. (101 x 56 cm)
Sold 25.11.82 in London for £51,840
($82,426)
Record auction price for a work by the artist
Previously sold at Christie's 21.10.69 for
85 gns

At the request of Queen Victoria the Sultan gave Carl Haag permission to paint the Holy Rock and admit him to the Harem es Shereef. No other artist had ever been permitted to enter this holy place, which to the Mahommedans is second only to the Kaaba in Mecca in sanctity.

ANDERS LEONARD ZORN: *I Fria Luften*
Signed and dated '88
Canvas laid down on board
22 x 31⅛ in. (55.9 x 80.6 cm)
Sold 26.11.82 in London for £48,600 ($77,274)

HEINRICH VON ZUGEL: *Roadside Conversation*
Signed
Oil on panel
17½ x 28¾ in. (44.5 x 73 cm)
Sold 27.10.82 in New York for $99,000 (£61,875)
From the collection of Mr Edward S. Barnard

A Raphael drawing reinstated

NOËL ANNESLEY

Enthusiasts for Old Master Drawings are frequently heard to bemoan the ever dwindling supply of fine drawings on the market, and to make comparisons with the opportunities enjoyed by earlier generations of collectors. There is truth in such plaints, and yet the series of sales organized at Christie's last season might almost have been designed to show (they were not!) that at all levels of price an abundance of material is still available. While any season that boasts important sheets by great artists, Raphael, Rembrandt (four), Rubens (three) and Veronese must be considered remarkable, perhaps more encouraging still was the sheer variety of fine draughtsmen represented, and often in generous numbers. The Tiepolos, those prolific breeders of drawings, were represented by no less than 22 examples, of which 13 were by Giovanni Battista, including *The Meeting of Anthony and Cleopatra*, one of his most beautiful creations. Other Italians like the Zuccari, Francesco Salviati, Castiglione, Salvator Rosa, Stefano della Bella, Guercino and Piranesi were to be had in fine examples, as were the French masters, Boucher, Fragonard and Hubert Robert. Britain, for so long the traditional source of supply for drawings, now takes second place to the Americas and to continental Europe, yet London remains the centre of activities in the field.

The event that caused the most interest was the dispersal, in December, of a small but choice group of drawings formed by a continental collector chiefly active in the 40s and the early 50s. The focal points of the sale were two: the marvellous and well known Rubens sheet of studies after Titian, one of the most evocative expressions of his admiration for his Venetian predecessor; and the *Christ in Glory*, a chalk study, in the 19th century and earlier a famous Raphael, but neglected in recent times since its 'demotion' by Oskar Fischel, doyen of Raphael scholars, in the 1890s. It belonged to the extraordinary group of Raphael drawings assembled by Sir Thomas Lawrence. After the British Government had so short-sightedly failed to acquire the whole collection on favourable terms after Lawrence's death in 1830, Samuel Woodburn, his art dealer and friend, bought it himself and arranged a sequence of 10 Exhibitions between May 1835 and July 1836 to display the greatest treasures. That devoted to Raphael was number 9, and this drawing was described in the catalogue thus 'no.56. THE ALMIGHTY. – with extended arms; being the upper part of the celebrated picture called the *Five Saints*, now at Parma, which is engraved by Marc Antonio Raimondi. This highly interesting study is executed in black and white chalk, and is in perfect preservation'. Woodburn initially hoped that the Exhibitions would be bought *en bloc* by the Government or by a single collector (those of Claude and Rembrandt went to William Esdaile; of the Carracci and Giulio Romano to the Earl of Ellesmere), but in 1838 he made a selection for the Prince of Orange, later King William II of Holland, of no less than 52 from the 100 (catalogued) Raphael drawings, 59 of the 100 Michelangelos that formed the final Exhibition, and much else. The Prince is recorded as the owner of the *Christ in Glory* under the reproduction (no.18; in reverse) in Woodburn's *Lawrence Gallery*, published in 1841.

Much of King William's collection was dispersed in 1850 and this drawing passed to his son-in-law, the Grand Duke Carl Alexander von Saxen-Weimar-Eisenbach, and thence to the Weimar Museum, where it remained until the 1930s. It is worth recalling here that the remainder of the drawings from the Raphael and Michelangelo Exhibitions were acquired by Oxford University in 1842 and are now the chief glory of the Ashmolean Museum.

Lawrence was the leading drawings connoisseur of his time but it was inevitable that some of the attributions in the

RAFFAELLO SANZIO, called RAPHAEL:
Christ in Glory
Inscribed 'Raphaello da Urbino fe'
Black chalk and wash and white chalk on
pale grey preparation, watermark large
crossed arrows (apparently Briquet 6294,
1520), the sheet extended at the sides
8¾ x 7 in. (22.3 x 17.7 cm)
Sold 9.12.82 in London for
£205,200 ($328,320)
Record auction price for a drawing by the
artist
Now in the J. Paul Getty Museum, Malibu,
California

Exhibitions should have been questioned and on occasion rejected in subsequent studies; nor should one expect to find unanimity of opinion in the particular case of Raphael who not only ran a large and extremely productive studio but had the ability to inspire his most gifted pupils to a deceptively close imitation of his own work. In the late Parma altarpiece, for which this drawing served as a study, there is a certain coarseness of execution suggesting the hand of Giulio Romano, and following the 'exclusionist' tendency to associate preparatory drawings for studio productions with the artists (often not securely identifiable) who painted them, Fischel reattributed the drawing also to Giulio: as such it remained classified until its recent reappearance. But Raphael, so fluent as draughtsman and inventor, continued to produce the designs for studio commissions until his premature death. A fresh appraisal of this drawing's quality, both of conception and of execution, and its close connection with other undoubtedly autograph examples of Raphael's late style, led us to seek support for its return to the master, and we were gratified to find that this view had already been reached by at least two modern scholars, and now enjoys general currency.

PAOLO CALIARI, IL VERONESE:
Studies of Ganymede and of the Last Supper
Inscribed. 'Ganimede rapitto da Giove'
Pen and brown ink, brown wash
11⅛ x 7½ in. (28.8 x 19.2 cm)
Sold 9.12.82 in London for £91,800 ($146,880)
Record auction price for a drawing by the artist
From the collection of Mrs H.M. Calmann
No picture of Ganymede by Veronese is recorded, and it is thus likely that these studies, and that on a sheet of studies in the Morgan Library, relate to the *Jupiter Crowning Germany* formerly at Berlin. This was one of the series of four canvases executed in the 1570s for a ceiling in the Fondaco dei Tedeschi, Venice. This sheet is of particular interest as the study of the *Last Supper* establishes that the altarpiece of the subject in the Cappella del Sacramento of the church of San Zilian at Venice was designed by Veronese.

FEDERICO ZUCCARO: *The Submission of the Emperor Frederick Barbarossa to Pope Alexander III*
Black chalk, pen and brown ink, brown wash, on two attached sheets
21¾ x 21⅜ in. (55.4 x 53 cm)
Sold 12.4.83 in London for £38,880 ($58,320)
Record auction price for a drawing by the artist
Formerly in the collections of Sir Peter Lely and Sir William Forbes.
Federico was commissioned in 1582 to paint one of the series of historical scenes in the Sala del Gran Consiglio of the Doge's Palace, Venice, the previous decoration having been destroyed in the fire of 1577. The picture was finished only in 1603, and this drawing is one of the more elaborate of the studies to survive.

SALVATOR ROSA: *The Dream of Aeneas*
Black and white chalk
12¾ x 8¾ in.
(32.4 x 22.2 cm)
Sold 12.4.83 in London for
£16,200 ($24,300)
Formerly in the collection of
Sir William Forbes
A *modello* for the artist's etching
(Bartsch 23), probably
made soon after 1662. The
picture of the subject, from
the Northwick Park
Collection and sold in these
Rooms, 28.5.65, lot 34, is
now in the Metropolitan
Museum

BERNARDINO BARBATELLI, IL POCCETTI: *The Death of the Beati Uguccione and Sostegno*
Inscribed 'Pocetti' twice, black chalk, brush and brown ink, brown and grey wash heightened with white, squared in red chalk
10¾ x 10⅜ in. (27.3 x 41.4 cm)
Sold 5.7.83 in London for £14,580 ($22,599)
Poccetti frescoed 14 of the 18 lunettes of the Chiostro Grande, in the Church of Santissima Annunziata, Florence between
1604 and his death in 1612. These scenes illustrated the history of the founders of the Monastery of Monte Senario di Maria.
This drawing is an early project for no.21 in the series: a later composition design, corresponding closely with the fresco, is in the
Uffizi.

GIOVANNI BATTISTA
TIEPOLO: *The Meeting of
Anthony and Cleopatra*
Black chalk, pen and
brown ink, brown
wash
13 x 10⅛ in.
(33 x 25.6 cm)
Sold 12.4.83 in
London for £60,480
($90,720)
Record auction price
for a drawing by the
artist
A related drawing is
in the Metropolitan
Museum. Both are
connected with an oil
sketch in the
Wrightsman
Collection, which
itself served as a study
for the large picture of
1747 at
Arkhangelskoye
near Moscow

GIOVANNI BATTISTA
TIEPOLO: *Bust of Palma
Giovane*
Red and white chalk
on blue paper,
watermark three
crescents
11⅝ x 7⅞ in.
(29.5 x 22.6 cm)
Sold 9.12.82 in
London for £18,360
($29,376)
One of a series of
studies taken from
Vittoria's terracotta
bust of Palma, now at
Vienna, and probably
drawn about 1743

FRANÇOIS BOUCHER: *Sleeping Baby*
Black, red and white chalk, green and yellow watercolour on pale grey paper
9⅛ x 11½ in. (231 x 290 cm)
Sold 9.12.82 in London for £30,240 ($48,384)
Previously sold at Christie's 9.6.44 for 260 gns.
From the collection of the late Sir Clifford Curzon, C.B.E.

JEAN HONORÉ
FRAGONARD: *The
Sacrifice of the Rose*
Black chalk, grey and
touches of brown, red
and yellow wash
17⅛ x 13⅛ in.
(43.4 x 33.2 cm)
Sold 5.7.83 in London
for £28,080 ($43,524)
From the collection of
Desmond Browne,
Esq, and previously in
the collections of H.
Walferdin and the
Baron de Neuflize
The Sacrifice of the
Rose, an allegory of
the ecstasy of love,
was painted by
Fragonard on at least
five occasions. The
present drawing is a
study for the first of
these pictures, datable
about 1770

SIR PETER PAUL RUBENS: *Female Nude and female Heads, after Titian*
Black and red chalk and traces of white chalk on light grey-brown paper
17⅝ x 11¼ in. (44.8 x 28.6 cm)
Sold 9.12.82 in London for £108,000 ($172,800)
Record auction price for a drawing by the artist
Formerly in the collection of P.H. Lankrink
Now in the J. Paul Getty Museum, Malibu, California
These studies were taken from three pictures by Titian, the *Venus and Adonis* of 1554 and the *Diana and Callisto* and *Diana and Actaeon* of 1559, all of which Rubens would have seen in the Spanish royal collections on his visit to Spain in 1628. While the first is still in the Prado, the others are now lent by the Duke of Sutherland to the National Gallery of Scotland

SIR PETER PAUL RUBENS: *The Assumption*
Black chalk, pen and grey-brown ink,
grey-brown wash
11⅜ x 7½ in. (29.8 x 18.9 cm)
Sold 12.4.83 in London for £51,840
($77,760)
Formerly in the collections of
T. Philipe and Sir William Forbes
Engraved for the *Breviarium Romanum*
and the *Missale Romanum* published in
1614
Now in the J. Paul Getty Museum,
Malibu, California

REMBRANDT HARMENSZ. VAN RIJN: *Christ and the Canaanite Woman*
Pen, brush and brown ink, slight use of white for corrections
7⅞ x 11 in. (19.9 x 27.9 cm)
Sold 12.4.83 in London for £108,000 ($162,000)
From the collections of Jonathan Richardson, Thomas Hudson, Sir Joshua Reynolds and the Morritt family
Probably drawn in the late 1640s, this sheet, from so many distinguished collections, illustrates the passage in St Matthew, XV,
21-8: 'And behold a woman of Canaan came out of the same coasts, and cried unto Him, saying, "Have mercy on me, O Lord, thou
Son of David; my daughter is grievously vexed with a devil." '
Now in the J. Paul Getty Museum, Malibu, California

REMBRANDT HARMENSZ. VAN RIJN: *Two Studies of the Head of a Turbaned Man*
Pen and brown ink
3¼ x 3⅛ in. (8.2 x 7.8 cm)
Sold 22.11.82 in Amsterdam for D.fl.145,600 (£10,293)
From the collection of the late Mrs E. Meyer, and formerly in the collection of J.P. Heseltine
Studies for one of the elders in the Mauritshuis *Susannah and the Elders* of 1637

HANS BOL: *Parable of the Good Samaritan*
Signed with monogram, bodycolour on vellum laid on panel
5⅜ in. (13.7 cm) in diameter
Sold 12.4.83 in London for £9,720 ($14,580)

English Portrait Drawings: from Lely to Constable

ROBIN GRIFFITH-JONES

The exhibition *Sir Peter Lely* at the National Portrait Gallery in 1978 brought together a group of drawings that revealed for the first time the full sensitivity of Lely's draughtsmanship. Among the most memorable was *Portrait of a Girl, probably Elizabeth Seymour, Countess of Ailesbury*, from the late 1650s, her hair in ringlets, her left hand raised to a bow of ribbon at her bosom, a landscape lightly sketched beyond. Formerly in the collection of Sir Joshua Reynolds (whose stamp can be seen, lower left), and one of the few Lely drawings still in private hands, it would have been a highlight of any sale, and on 29 March it secured the highest price of the morning at £39,960 ($58,741). Thus it became the most expensive English drawing sold at auction, doubling the record set here only five months earlier with the sale of Constable's *Captain Allen, Cousin of the Artist* (£18,900; $30,807): made in London in January 1818, this compares strikingly in pose and mood – and features – with Constable's only other finished portrait known in pencil, the self-portrait of 1806.

The brilliant tradition of English portrait painting at the end of the 18th century is delicately reflected in the pastellists and draughtsmen of the period. This season has been exceptionally rich in such drawings: Catherine Read's *The Hon. George and William Rice, c.*1773 (£1,026; $1,672); a pair of drawings by Ozias Humphry of *Georgiana, Duchess of Devonshire*, 1782, and her closest friend and successor as Duchess, *Lady Elizabeth Foster* – the former based on Gainsborough's portrait not exhibited until the following year (£1,620; $2,640); Angelica Kauffmann's *Self Portrait as Hope*, related to the painting in the Academy of St. Luke, Rome, to which the artist was elected in 1785 (£972; $1,584); and above all an outstanding group assembled by Mr and Mrs Robert Tritton for Godmersham Park – two rare studies by Charles Grignion (£3,186; $4,970), John Smart's *Captain Kidd, Madras* (£2,160; $3,369), a small pair by Chinnery (£3,888; $6,065), four delightful ovals by John Downman (with a top price of £4,104 ($6,402) far exceeding the previous auction record for a drawing by Downman), and, finest of all, Hugh Douglas Hamilton's pastel of *The Rev. William Rose as a young Man, in academic dress, reading to his parents*, 1775, acquired by Mrs Tritton after its sale here in 1945 by the sitter's descendant, Mrs Rose, for 75 gns.; on 14 June this fetched £6,264 ($9,772).

SIR PETER LELY: *Portrait of a Girl,*
probably Elizabeth Seymour,
Countess of Ailesbury
Signed
Black, red and white chalk on
grey-brown paper
11⅛ x 7¾ in. (28.3 x 19.7cm)
Sold 29.3.83 in London for
£39,960 ($58,741)
Record auction price for an
English drawing

HUGH DOUGLAS HAMILTON: *The Rev.*
William Rose as a Young Man, in academic
dress, reading to his parents
Signed and dated 1775
15 x 19 in. (38.1 x 48.3 cm)
Sold 14.6.83 in London for £6,264
($9,772)
Previously sold at Christie's 12.10.45
for 75 gns.
From the Godmersham Park Collection

THOMAS GAINSBOROUGH, R.A.: *Sheep by a*
Lane on a Wooded Heath
Black chalk and stump heightened with
white
11 x 14¾ in. (27.9 x 37.5 cm)
Sold 14.6.83 in London for £19,440
($30,326)
From the collection of E.A. Mott, Esq

JOHN CONSTABLE, R.A.: *Dedham: The Old Lecture House seen across Long Meadow from Black Brook*
Signed and dated 1800
Pen and brown ink and watercolour with touches of white heightening
13 x 18⅛ in. (33 x 46 cm)
Sold 29.3.83 in London for £16,200 ($22,680)
This watercolour was a gift from the artist to Maria Sophia Newman, daughter of the Rev. Samuel Newman, Rector and Lecturer of Dedham, on her marriage to Lt. Col. Harcourt Master, 52nd Regiment, 6 March 1800, and was sold by her great-great-grand-daughters

JOHN CONSTABLE, R.A.: *Portrait of Captain Allen, Cousin of the Artist*
Signed and dated 1818
Pencil
12 x 8 in. (30.5 x 20.3 cm)
Sold 16.11.82 in London for £18,900 ($30,807)
From the collection of the late P.A. Wells, Esq

JOSEPH MALLORD WILLIAM TURNER, R.A.: *Tamworth Castle, Staffordshire*
Watercolour
11½ x 17½ in. (29.2 x 44.5 cm)
Sold 14.6.83 in London for £75,600 ($117,936)
Engraved by J.T. Willmore, 1832, for Turner's *Picturesque Views in England and Wales*, pt.XV, no.4.
Previously sold at Christie's 30.4.37 for 660 gns.

JOSEPH MALLORD
WILLIAM TURNER, R.A.:
Berwick-on-Tweed
Watercolour
3⅜ x 5⅞ in.
(8.6 x 14.9 cm)
Sold 14.6.83 in London for
£45,360 ($70,761)
From the collection of
Mr William P. Wood,
Pennsylvania
Commissioned by
Sir Walter Scott and his
publisher Robert Cadell,
and engraved by W.
Miller, 1833, for *Scott's
Poetical Works*, vol.XII,
frontispiece

JOSEPH MALLORD
WILLIAM TURNER, R.A.:
The Falls of Schaffhausen
Pencil, pen and red and
brown ink and
watercolour
9 x 11⅜ in.
(22.9 x 28.9 cm)
Sold 16.11.82 in London
for £49,680 ($79,488)
From the collection of
R.H. Bishop, Esq. and
Mrs A.M. Le Bon Olive
An unrecorded sheet from
a series of Schaffhausen
views probably datable to
Turner's tour of 1841

THOMAS SHOTTER BOYS:
Greenwich: Figures in the Park below the Observatory
Signed and dated 1830
Watercolour
7 x 9⅞ in. (17.8 x 25.1 cm)
Sold 16.11.82 in London for
£15,120 ($24,192)
From the collection of the late
Mrs W.E. Finn

PAUL SANDBY, R.A.:
Reading Abbey Gate
Bodycolour
11⅛ x 16 in. (28.3 x 40.6 cm)
Sold 29.3.83 in London for
£10,800 ($15,120)

CHARLES ROBERTSON:
A Story-Teller, Morocco
Signed with
monogram and dated
1883
Watercolour
heightened with white
23½ x 50¾ in.
(59.7 x 128.9 cm)
Sold 19.7.83 in
London for £15,120
($23,738)

SIR LAWRENCE ALMA-
TADEMA, O.M., R.A.:
Egyptian Chess Players
Signed and dated 1868
Watercolour
15 x 21¾ in.
(38.1 x 55.2 cm)
Sold 10.5.83 in
London for £16,200
($25,596)
Formerly in the
collection of Henry
Stacy Marks, R.A.,
and sold at Christie's
five times since 1875

ARTHUR RACKHAM:
Little Miss Muffet
Signed and dated 12
Pen and black ink and
watercolour
10¾ x 7¼ in.
(27.3 x 18.4 cm)
Sold 23.2.83 in
New York for
$13,200 (£8,571)
One of Rackham's
illustrations to the
nursery rhymes *Mother
Goose*, published by
William Heinemann,
1913

Above left
SIMEON SOLOMON: *Shadrach, Meshach and Abednego
in the Burning Fiery Furnace*
Signed with monogram and dated 1863
Watercolour heightened with white and
gum arabic
13 x 9 in. (33 x 22.9 cm)
Sold 1.3.83 in London for £9,720 ($14,580)

Left

ARCHIBALD THORBURN: *Blackgame Packing*
Signed and dated 1910
Watercolour heightened with white
11 x 15¼ in. (27.9 x 38.7 cm)
Sold 26.10.82 in London for £10,260 ($16,416)
Record auction price for a work by the artist
From the collection of Miss H. Ingham

JEAN BAPTISTE ISABEY:
The Artist's Room at Plombières
Inscribed 'ma chambre a
Plombières en 1820'
Pencil and watercolour
6¼ x 8⅜ in. (15.8 x 21.4 cm)
Sold 14.12.82 in London for
£5,940 ($9,504)

SIR JAMES PENNETHORNE:
Design for the Albert Memorial,
Hyde Park, London
Pen and grey ink and
watercolour
25½ x 38 in.
(64.8 x 96.5 cm)
Sold 14.6.83 in London for
£4,320 ($6,739)
One of a group of designs by
Pennethorne sold from the
collection of his great-
grandson

JACOPO DE'BARBARI: *Triton and Nereid*
(Bartsch 24; Hind 21)
Engraving
S. 5 x 7⅛ in.(12.7 x 19.2 cm)
Sold 21.4.83 in London for £21,600 ($32,400)
Hind records only nine impressions of this very rare print, datable to *c.* 1504, all of which are in public collections

Right

ALBRECHT DÜRER:
The Standard Bearer
(Bartsch 87; Meder, Hollstein 92)
Engraving
P. 4½ x 2¾ in. (11.4 x 7 cm)
Sold 21.4.83 in London for £4,320
($6,480)

Far right

ALBRECHT ALTDORFER: *Christ on the Cross*
(Bartsch 8; Hollstein 9)
Engraving
P. 5¾ x 3⅞ in. (14.6 x 9.9 cm)
Sold 21.4.83 in London for £7,020
($10,530)
By order of the Executors of
the late Dr Felix Somary

Right

ALBRECHT DÜRER: *Adam and Eve*
(Bartsch, Meder, Hollstein 1)
Engraving, a very early Meder II
impression
Sold 16.11.82 in New York for
$33,000 (£19,880)

Far right

MARTIN SCHONGAUER: *Christ on the Cross with four Angels*
(Bartsch 25; Lehrs 14)
Engraving
S. 11½ x 7¾ in. (29.1 x 19.8 cm)
Sold 21.4.83 in London for
£18,360 ($27,540)

REMBRANDT HARMENSZ. VAN RIJN: *The Woman with the Arrow (Venus and Cupid?)* (Bartsch, Hollstein 202; Hind 303) Etching with drypoint and burin, second state (of three) Sold 16.11.82 in New York for $66,000 (£39,759)

Opposite right

LORENZO TIEPOLO: *The Immaculate Conception*, after G.B. Tiepolo (Bermudez, p.46, as G.B. Tiepolo; Nagler, p.100, 1, 6, as G.B. Tiepolo; De Vesme p.393, no.7; Rizzi 257) Etching P. 12½ x 8½ in. (31.8 x 20.9 cm) Sold 21.4.83 in London for £5,940 ($8,910) This extremely rare and possibly unique etching had not been seen by De Vesme and Rizzi, the most recent cataloguers of the Tiepolos' etchings and had been misattributed to Giovanni Battista in an early 19th century listing by Bermudez. Classified as anonymous while in the Stirling-Maxwell collection, it was recognized by Christie's as the work of Lorenzo Tiepolo.

Opposite far right

WILLIAM BLAKE: *Little Tom the Sailor* (Russell 18; Binyon 347-8; Bindman 384) Relief etchings with engraving on pewter, the headpiece and tailpiece extensively handcoloured Overall P. 18⅝ x 6¼ in (47.3 x 15.9 cm) Sold 21.4.83 in London for £14,040 ($21,060) Sir Geoffrey Keynes had not seen this particular impression at the time of his article in *The Book Collector*, 1968, in which he records only eight impressions. This one, which he saw at a later date, last appeared at Christie's on 8 Feb 1893 as the property of Mrs Steele, and sold with 12 other 'pewtertypes' for £1.4.0.

Ernst Ludwig Kirchner and the Spirit of Die Brücke

JAMES ROUNDELL

Germany has contributed three major movements to the art of 20th century Europe, those known as Bauhaus, Der Blaue Reiter and Die Brücke. The first two were from their inception intellectual and internationalist movements with influence far beyond the frontiers of Germany. Die Brücke, by contrast, was intensely national in identity. All three groups had two characteristics in common, their rejection of Impressionism and their origins in the post-Impressionist art of France and Austria. The Bauhaus artists were inspired by the pioneering examples of Cubism, Orphism and Futurism to examine and analyse the functions and components of form. Der Blaue Reiter fused the mystical ideals of Russian peasant art with the subordination of the object to purity of line and colour, displayed in Viennese and Munich Jugendstil, in the move towards abstract art as an expression of inner vision. For the artists of Die Brücke, however, direct visual perception remained the stimulus for their creativity. Their art, and that of contemporary German artists influenced by them, has become known by the wider term German Expressionism. Appreciation of their achievements was confined to Germany before the Second World War, and the appearance of, and high prices attained by, major examples of their graphic art in London during the past year confirms the recent quickening of the post-war assessment that their contribution to Modern Art is a vital and original one.

Die Brücke was founded in Dresden in 1906. The four founder members – Ernst Ludwig Kirchner, Erich Heckel, Karl Schmidt-Rottluff and Fritz Bleyl – all belonged to the architectural faculty of the Dresden Institute of Technology. As painters they were self-taught. The group stood for the unity of youth against the traditionalist art establishment. The aim was to inject a contemporary vitality into art by the expression of inner passionate responses to visual stimuli rather than by the 'faithful' reproduction of nature as exemplified by Impressionist and traditionalist German styles. In order to publicize their aims and to inform their active and passive associates (some 68 in 1910) the Brücke artists created and published annual portfolios and exhibition catalogues which revolutionized book design in Germany. The single most revolutionary portfolio was the 1910 Galerie Arnold exhibition catalogue (the copy sold on 2 Dec., 1982, originally belonged to Gustav Schiefler, one of the 'passive' members of Die Brücke as well as the cataloguer of, amongst others, Kirchner's graphic work). The concept was of a portfolio totally cohesive in design and execution. The primitive typeface together with the irregular spacing and uneven margins matched the style of the woodcut illustrations. The catalogue also emphasised the communal identity of the group's style by the device that each artist execute woodcuts from the paintings of another. The two-dimensional planes and stark chiaroscuro of the woodcuts illustrate the group's debt to the prints of Félix Vallotton. The form

ERNST LUDWIG
KIRCHNER: *Leipziger
Strasse, Kreuzung, Berlin*
(Schiefler 260; Dube
250 II/III)
Lithograph, 1914,
signed and inscribed
'Handdruck' in brown
crayon
L. 23½ x 20 in.
(59.5 x 50.8 cm)
Sold 2.12.82 in
London for £48,600
($77,760)

G. HEYM: *Umbra Vitae, München, Kurt Wolf Verlag, 1924* (Dube, etchings 461, woodcuts 759-807, 61) One etching and 50 woodcuts, the cover, endpapers and frontispiece printed in colours, copy 1 of 10 on Japan, with the extra etching of the author S. 9⅛ x 6¼ in. (23.5 x 16 cm) Sold 2.5.83 in New York for $19,800 (£13,200)

and facial features of the figures allied with the deliberate roughness of technique display the group's awareness of primitive and oriental art. Kirchner continued the design concept of the Galerie Arnold catalogue in other, later, book projects. One of the most notable was his production of Georg Heym's *Umbra Vitae* in 1924. The copy sold on 3 May 1983, in New York originally belonged to Heinrich Stinnes, one of the earliest major collectors of German Expressionist art.

Following the unity of Die Brücke artistically and intellectually in the years 1908-10, the move from Dresden to Berlin in 1911 began the development of each member's personal style which led to the group's eventual break-up in 1913. Strangely it was Kirchner's *Chronik der Kunstlergemeinschaft Brücke* in 1913 that precipitated the break by its rather personal interpretation of their ideals and history. Kirchner spent the summer of 1913 on the Baltic island of Fehmarn where he became inspired by the force of nature and the concept of man's unity with his surroundings. The merging of the rhythms of the nude form with those of the landscape can be seen in his lithograph *Badende in Wellen* (London, 30 June 1983, lot 140). This lyricism gave way to a preoccupation with the rhythms of the city in a series of pictures and prints executed in Berlin in 1914. The lithograph *Leipziger Strasse, Kreuzung* is a supreme example of Kirchner's graphic output at this time which has since come to be regarded as the highpoint of his art and the essence of German Expressionism. The fashioning of the composition by means of diagonals and verticals delineated with an almost brutal force and

Right

ERNST LUDWIG
KIRCHNER, ERICH
HECKEL AND OTHERS:
*Catalogue of the Brücke
Exhibition at Galerie
Arnold, Dresden,
Schlosstrasse,
Sept 1910*
(Bolliger-Kornfeld 41)
Woodcuts, 1910, title
woodcut and set of
nineteen plates with
text, published by
H. Niescher, Dresden,
1910
S. 9¼ x 7⅜ in.
(23.5 x 18.5 cm)
Sold 2.12.82 in
London for £5,940
($9,682)

Far right

K.G. BRÜCKE: *Austellung
der Künstlergruppe
Brücke in Galerie
Commeter, Hamburg,
Hermannstrasse, 1912*
(Bolliger-Kornfeld 42)
Woodcuts, 1912, cover
woodcut, text with ten
original plates and six
reproductive plates,
printed by
A. Littmann
S. 10 x 8 in.
(25.5 x 20.3 cm)
Sold 30.6.83 in
London for £10,260
($15,800)
Sold by order of the
Executor of the late
Eric Morris, Esq.

sense of nervous energy captures vividly the vibrancy and tension of the last months of pre-First World War Berlin. The spiky, Gothic forms, inspired by Kirchner's study of wood carvings from the Middle Ages, are here given a truly contemporary expression of excitement.

Kirchner's woodcut *Porträt Otto Mueller* was executed in 1915 after the break up of Die Brücke, but is still a Brücke print in style and content. Mueller joined Die Brücke in 1910 and became a close friend of Kirchner, sharing his fellow-artist's interest in primitive, Egyptian and Oceanic cultures, as indicated in this portrait by the hieroglyphic motifs of a cat and two eyes. The use of blue and brown in a non-descriptive, emotive fashion reflects Kirchner's assimilation of Fauve art. The work of the other major Brücke artists – Mueller, Heckel and Schmidt-Rottluff – seldom has the sense of urgency and vitality communicated through this portrait and in many of Kirchner's other pre-1920 graphic works. Of the group it was Heckel perhaps who came closest to Kirchner's work in some of his woodcuts, for example, the *Akt am Strande* of 1913 (the impression sold in London on 30 June 1983, was rendered more dramatic by the artist's own handcolouring).

It is to artists usually considered outside the inner circle of Brücke art that one must turn for a comparable expression of passion in art. Emile Nolde was a member of the group for fifteen months in 1906/7 and during this time the colours of his palette were liberated and he learnt the techniques of lithography and woodcut. To these media he brought a distinctive Nordic religious power of expression allied to a painterly style of execution. The 'Impressionist' artist Lovis Corinth was another whose style was radically altered by his exposure to Die Brücke and he went on to create some of the most forceful depictions of landscape in German art. While Die Brücke was also concerned with the struggle of peasant existence this found its most expressive manifestation in the etchings, woodcuts and lithographs of Käthe Kollwitz. Following the passionate creativity and optimistic idealism of Die Brücke and their contemporaries came a reaction in 1920s Germany when artists became chiefly concerned with depictions of social degradation and depression. However the spirit of excitement displayed by Die Brücke has recently found a contemporary echo in the work of Die Neuen Wilden.

OTTO MUELLER: *Lagernde Zigeunerfamilie mit Ziege* (Karsch 166)
Lithograph printed in colours, 1926-7, third state (of four), with Heckel's pencil signature on the reverse
L. 27½ x 19⅞ in. (70 x 50.4 cm)
Sold 2.12.82 in London for £14,040 ($22,464)

ERNST LUDWIG KIRCHNER: *Porträt Otto Mueller* (Schiefler 220; Dube 251 a l IV)
Woodcut printed in black, red-brown and royal blue, 1915, signed and inscribed 'Probedruck' in pencil
L. 13⅝ x 12 in. (36 x 30.5 cm)
Sold 2.12.82 in London for £22,680 ($36,288)
Formerly in the collection of Gustav Schiefler, cataloguer of Kirchner's prints
Now in the collection of The British Museum

MARC CHAGALL: *Selbstbildnis mit Grimasse* (Kornfeld 43 VI b)
Etching with aquatint, extensively handcoloured, 1924-5, signed in pencil, numbered 81/100
P. 14⅝ x 10¾ in. (37.3 x 27.4 cm)
Sold 2:12.82 in London for £19,440 ($31,104)
Record auction price for a print by the artist
Only a few impressions from the edition of 100 were handcoloured and were presented by the artist as gifts.

EDWARD MUNCH: *Das Kranke Mädchen* (Schiefler 59)
Lithograph printed in colours, the drawing stone in the second state (of three), signed in orange pencil and inscribed 'No.1 II 2' in blue pencil
L. 16⅝ x 22½ in. (42.2 x 57 cm)
Sold 16.11.82 in New York for $61,600 (£37,108)

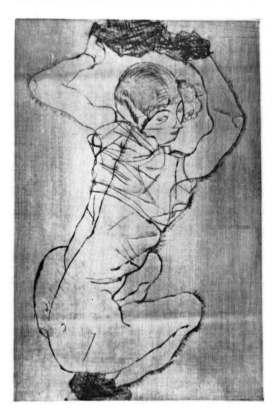

Above

CAMILLE PISSARRO: *Effet de Pluie*
(Delteil 24)
Soft-ground etching with aquatint
and drypoint, 1879, fifth state (of
six), one of only three impressions
of this state
P. 6¼ x 8⅜ in. (15.8 x 21.1 cm)
Sold 2.12.82 in London for £9,072
($14,515)
Formerly in the collection of Félix
Bracquemond: from a group of 33
prints by Pissarro
The influence of Degas on
Pissarro's etching technique is
evident in this print. Degas also
pulled some impressions of this
print in other states

Above right

EDGAR DEGAS: *Femme Nue Debout, à sa
Toilette* (Delteil 65; Adhémar 63)
Lithograph, *c.* 1890, third state
(of four), signed in pencil
L. 13 x 9⅝ in.
(33 x 24.6 cm)
Sold 2.12.82 in London for
£14,580 ($23,328)

Right

EGON SCHIELE: *Kauernde* (Kallir 6a)
Drypoint, 1914, one of only a very
few impressions printed before
the plate was steelfaced, signed
and dated in pencil
P. 18⅞ x 12½ in. (47.8 x 31.9
cm)
Sold 2.12.82 in London for
£18,360 ($29,376)
Record auction price for a
print by the artist

JACQUES VILLON: *Les Cartes ou La Réussite* (Auberty & Perussaux 44; Ginestet & Pouillon E76)
Aquatint with hard and soft-ground etching printed in colours, 1903, signed in brown crayon, numbered 18/25
P. 13¾ x 17⅝ in. (34.9 x 44.8 cm)
Sold 16.11.82 in New York for $44,000 (£26,506)
Another impression of this print was sold 2.12.82 in London for £27,000 ($44,199)

PIERRE BONNARD: *La Petite Blanchisseuse* (Roger-Marx 42; Bouvet 40; Johnson, Vollard, 11)
Lithograph printed in colours, 1896, signed in pencil and numbered 'No 13', from the edition of 100 printed by A. Clot for A. Vollard, L'Album des Peintres-Graveurs, 1896
L. 11½ x 7¾ in. (29.3 x 19.6 cm)
Sold 2.12.82 in London for £19,440 ($31,104)
A hand-coloured proof impression was sold 30.6.83 in London

WASSILY KANDINSKY: *Das Rosa Segel* (Roethel 8)
Woodcut printed in colours with a light application of gold, 1903,
the very rare second state (of three), signed and inscribed
'HOLZSCHNITT (Handdruck)' in pen and red ink on the original
mount, and on the reverse '8 – Einsame Fahrt' in red crayon
L. 5 x 11¾ in. (12.7 x 29.9 cm)
Sold 2.12.82 in London for £19,440 ($31,104)

PAUL GAUGUIN: *Portrait de Stéphane Mallarmé* (Guérin 13; Agustoni 14)
Etching extensively worked up with pen and black ink and brown
and grey wash, 1891, Agustoni's first state (of three) before Guérin's
first state, the only known impression of this state
S. 5⅞ x 4½ in. (15 x 11.4 cm)
Sold 2.12.82 in London for £20,520 ($32,832)
Record auction price for a print by the artist

ODILON REDON: *Arbre* (Mellerio 120)
Lithograph, 1892, dated in pencil,
from the edition of only 25,
printed by Becquet, Paris
L. 18¾ x 12⅝ in.
(47.5 x 31.9 cm)
Sold 2.12.82 in London for
£22,680 ($36,288)

VINCENT VAN GOGH: *Dans le Verger* (de la Faille 1659)
Pen transfer lithograph extensively worked up in pen and ink, 1883, a very fine impression of this extremely rare print (only three other impressions are recorded)
L. 8½ x 11 in. (21.7 x 28 cm)
Sold 2.12.82 in London for £30,240 ($48,384)
Record auction price for a print by the artist
From the collection of Mrs T.J. Tiemstra-D'Audretsch

HENRI DE TOULOUSE-LAUTREC: *Partie de Campagne, ou La Charrette Anglaise* (Delteil 219; Adhémar 322; Adriani & Wittrock 216; Johnson, Vollard, 143)
Lithograph printed in colours, 1897, third (final) state, signed in pencil and dedicated 'à Ancourt', printed by A. Clot, an impression apart from the numbered edition of 100 published by A. Vollard in L'Album d'Estampes Originales de la Galerie Vollard, 1897
S. 15⅝ x 20 in. (39.7 x 51 cm)
Sold 2.12.82 in London for £30,240 ($48,384)

HENRI DE TOULOUSE-
LAUTREC: *Elles*
(Delteil 179-89;
Adhémar 200-10;
Adriani & Wittrock
177-87)
Lithographs printed
in colours, 1896,
cover, frontispiece and
set of 10 lithographs,
the cover signed in
pencil by the artist,
signed by the
publisher, G. Pellet
and with his stamps,
numbered 87 from the
edition of 100, the
frontispiece and set of
ten lithographs all
with the red stamp
and numbered
Overall
S. 21⅝ x 16⅞ in.
(55 x 42.8 cm)
Sold 16.11.82 in
New York for
$220,000 (£132,530)

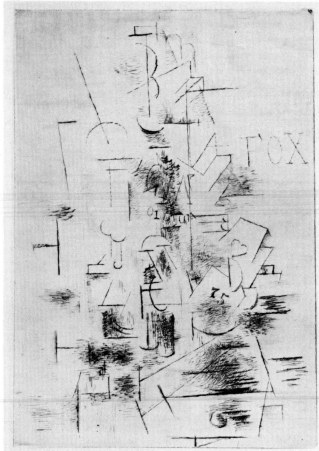

Above
PABLO PICASSO: *Nature Morte, Bouteille (Vie Marc)*
(Geiser 33b; Bloch 24)
Drypoint, 1912, signed in pencil, numbered
'No. 5', from the edition 100 printed by Delâtre
for D.H. Kahnweiler, published 1912
P. 19¾ x 12 in. (50 x 30.6 cm)
Sold 2.12.82 in London for £16,416 ($26,266)
Purchased by The National Gallery of Australia

Above right
GEORGES BRAQUE: *Fox* (Engelberts, Hatje 5;
Vallier 6)
Drypoint, 1911, signed in pencil, numbered
'No. 5', from the edition of 100 printed by Delâtre
for D.H. Kahnweiler, published 1912
P. 21⅝ x 15 in.
(55 x 38 cm)
Sold 2.12.82 in London for £14,040 ($22,464)
Record auction price for a print by the artist

116

JASPER JOHNS:
False Start I (Field 10)
Lithograph printed in
colours, 1962, signed
'Jasper' and inscribed
'artist's proof' (the
edition was 38), with
the ULAE blindstamp
L. 17⅝ x 13¾ in.
(44.8 x 34.9 cm)
Sold 14.10.82 in
New York for $13,200
(£7,620)
From the collection of
The Robert C. Skull
Foundation for the
Arts, Inc.

Opposite

GIORGIO MORANDI: *Natura Morta*
(Vitali 74)
Etching, 1930, first state (of two),
signed in pencil
on the support sheet,
numbered 8/30
P. 9⅜ x 11⅜ in (23.8 x 29 cm)
Sold 30.6.83 in London for
£8,640 ($13,306)

Wild Turkey

JOHN JAMES AUDUBON: *Wild Turkey, Male*, Plate I
from The Birds of America, by
W.H. Lizars and R. Havell
Coloured engraving with
aquatint, published by Audubon,
c. 1827
Sold 15.10.82 in Houston for
$35,200 (£20,346)
From a group of 434 Audubon
prints (lacking only plate 136)
in a double elephant folio
which realised a total of
$1,541,265 (£890,904)

BARON L.A.G. BACLER
D'ALBE: *Le Mont Blanc Vu
au Dessus de la Vallée de
Sallanche*
Coloured etching, signed
in pen and black ink by
the artist and dated 1789,
with dedication to
Le Prince de Piémont,
published by the artist at
Sallanche
S. 17¾ x 25⅛ in.
(45 x 63.8 cm)
Sold 7.6.83 in London for
£6,480 ($10,238)

HENRI L'EVÊQUE: *Vue de
Genève prise des Eaux Vives*
Coloured etching,
published *c.*1770
P. 14½ x 21¾ in.
(36.8 x 55.2 cm)
Sold 7.6.83 in London for
£14,040 ($22,310)

CAMILLE PISSARRO: *Le Boulevard Montmartre, Matin Brumeux*
Signed and dated 97
Oil on canvas
21⅝ x 25½ in. (55 x 65 cm)
Sold 29.11.82 in London for £334,800 ($539,028)
One of a series of pictures of the Boulevard Montmartre painted from an upper window of the Grand Hôtel de Russie

BERTHE MORISOT: *Avant le Théâtre*
c. 1875
Signed
Oil on canvas
22⅛ x 12⅛ in. (57.2 x 30.8 cm)
Sold 17.5.83 in New York for $253,000 (£162,179)
Record auction price for a work by the artist
From the collection of Mrs Edward G. Robinson

MARY CASSATT:
Reading 'Le Figaro'
c. 1883
Signed
Oil on canvas
39¾ x 32 in.
(101 x 81.3 cm)
Sold 17.5.83 in
New York for
$1,100,000 (£705,128)
Record auction price
for an American
Impressionist picture
A portrait of the
artist's mother

Opposite

CAMILLE PISSARRO:
Bouquet de Fleurs,
Chrysanthèmes dans un
Vase Chinois
c. 1870
Oil on canvas
25⅝ x 19⅞ in.
(60 x 50.5 cm)
Sold 17.5.83 in
New York for
$308,000 (£197,435)

EDGAR DEGAS: *Danseuses à la Barre*
Signed and indistinctly inscribed
Pastel
26 x 20⅛ in.
(66 x 51 cm)
Sold 3.11.82 in
New York for
$1,045,000 (£618,343)
From the collection of
the late Mrs Dunbar
W. Bostwick

EDGAR DEGAS: *Danseuses au Repos*
Signed and dated 1874
Oil and gouache on paper laid
down on canvas
18⅛ x 12¾ in. (46 x 32.5 cm)
Sold 3.11.82 in New York for
$1,320,000 (£781,065)
From the collection of the late
Mrs Dunbar W. Bostwick

PAUL CÉZANNE: *Paysage d'Ile de France*
Oil on canvas
21½ x 25⅝ in. (54 x 65 cm)
Sold 3.11.82 in New York for $726,000 (£429,586)
From the collection of the late Aaron W. Davis

Opposite

PAUL GAUGUIN: *Jeune Bretonne*
Signed with initials and dated 89
Oil on canvas
18⅛ x 14⅞ in. (46 x 38 cm)
Sold 17.5.83 in New York for $660,000 (£423,076)

PIERRE BONNARD: *Matinée* or
Les Confitures
1915
Signed
Oil on canvas
49 x 32¼ in. (124.5 x 82.5 cm)
Sold 29.11.82 in London for
£259,200 ($414,720)
The figure is Marthe, the artist's
wife

Opposite

PIERRE BONNARD: *L'Indolente*
c. 1899
Stamped signature
Oil on canvas
34¼ x 40¾ in. (87 x 104 cm)
Sold 27.6.83 in London for
£302,400 ($471,744)
Record auction price for a work
by the artist

Modern pictures

PAUL SIGNAC: *Les Andelys; L'Ile à Lucas*
Signed and dated 86
Oil on canvas
26 x 17½ in.
(66 x 44.5 cm)
Sold 21.3.83 in
London for £172,800
($260,928)

GEORG TAPPERT:
Zwei Akte in einen
Landschaft
1910
Signed
Oil on canvas
57⅞ x 48⅜ in.
(149.5 x 123 cm)
Sold 18.5.83 in
New York for
$187,000 (£119,871)
Record auction price
for a work by the artist
From the collection of
Mrs Jean Howard

ERICH HECKEL:
Akt (Dresden)
1910
Oil on canvas
31½ x 27½ in.
(80 x 70 cm)
Sold 27.6.83 in
London for £162,000
($252,720)
Record auction price
for a work by the artist
On the reverse is a
painting *Stilleben mit
Pflanzen* executed
1920

ALEXEJ JAWLENSKY:
*Junges Mädchen mit
grünen Augen*
1910-1911
Signed
Oil on board
21¼ x 19½ in.
(54 x 49.5 cm)
Sold 27.6.83 in
London for £172,800
($269,568)

PAUL KLEE: *Keramisch-mystisch (in der Art eines Stillebens)*
Signed, numbered B8 and dated 1925
Oil on board.
13 x 18¾ in. (33 x 47.4 cm)
Sold 21.3.83 in London for £388,800 ($587,088)
Record auction price for a work by the artist

Opposite

LYONEL FEININGER: *Gelmeroda III*
c. 1913-1915
Signed
Oil on canvas
39⅞ x 31½ in. (100 x 80 cm)
Sold 3.11.82 in New York for $242,000 (£142,353)

GEORGE GROSZ: *Das Paar*
c. 1917-1920
Signed
Watercolour
22½ x 18 in. (57.5 x 46 cm)
Sold 28.6.83 in London for
£41,040 ($64,022)

CONRAD FELIXMÜLLER: *Der Tod des Dichters Walter Rheiner*
Signed and dated 1925
Oil on canvas
73 x 51 in. (185.5 x 129.5 cm)
Sold 29.11.82 in London for £145,800 ($232,960)
Record auction price for a work by the artist
On the reverse is a painting *Kunstfreunde III* executed in 1939
Walter Rheiner, born in Cologne in 1895, committed suicide in Berlin in 1925 by throwing himself from a window. He was a poet of the *Dresdner Sezession* and published several small books of poetry before his death, the most notable of which was *Das Tonende Herz* in 1918. The Akademie der Künste in West Berlin houses all the Rheiner archives.

DIEGO RIVERA: *Retrato de Ramon Gomez de la Serna*
Signed with initials and dated '15
Oil on canvas
43 x 35½ in.
(109 x 90 cm)
Sold 17.5.83 in New York for $308,000 (£197,435)
Record auction price for a work by the artist
Previously sold at Christie's, London, 24.6.56 for £5,513

Opposite

FERNAND LÉGER:
Esquisse pour 'La Ville'
Signed and dated 19
Oil on canvas laid down on board
31⅞ x 25⅝ in.
(81 x 65 cm)
Sold 26.6.83 in London for £378,000 ($589,680)
From the collection of Mr and Mrs Armand P. Bartos of New York
'La Ville' for which this is a study is now in the A.E. Gallatin Collection, Philadelphia Museum of Art

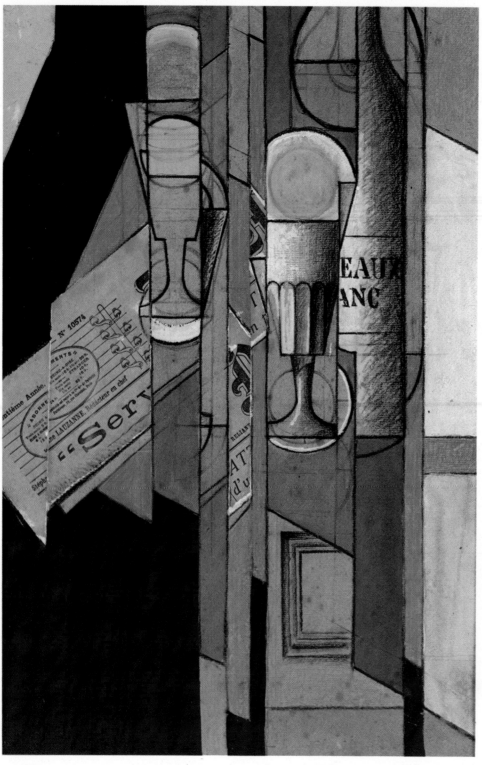

JUAN GRIS: *Verres, Journal et Bouteille de Vin*
1913
Collage, gouache, watercolour, coloured chalks and charcoal
17¾ x 11⅞ in. (45 x 29.5 cm)
Sold 27.6.83 in London for £172,800 ($269,568)
Record auction price for a work by the artist
From the collection of Mr and Mrs Armand P. Bartos of New York

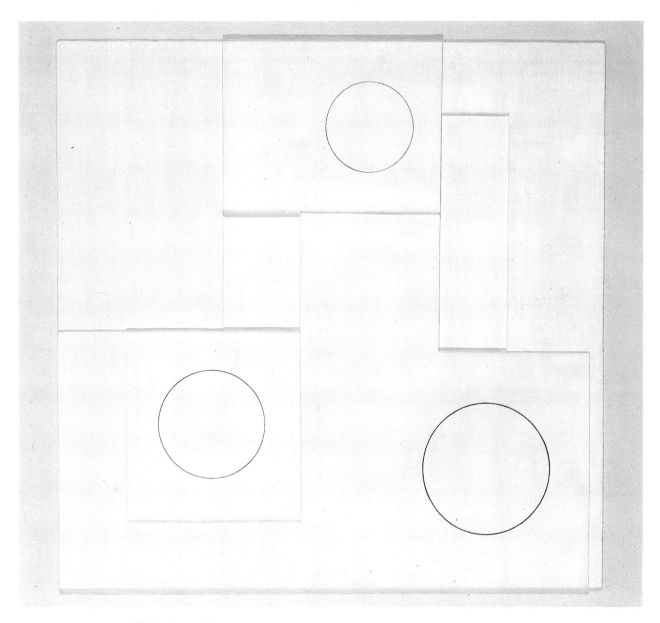

BEN NICHOLSON, O.M.: *1938 (white relief)*
Signed, inscribed with artist's address and dated 1938 on the reverse
Oil and pencil on carved board
22⅜ x 23¼ in. (57 x 59 cm)
Sold 27.6.83 in London for £81,000 ($126,360)
From the collection of Mr and Mrs Armand P. Bartos of New York
One of two white reliefs by Nicholson sold at Christie's, London during the year for the same price

PIET MONDRIAN:
Composition with Red and Blue
Signed with initials and dated 39-41
Oil on canvas
17¼ x 13 in.
(43.5 x 33 cm)
Sold 27.6.83 in London for £561,600 ($876,096)
From the collection of Mr and Mrs Armand P. Bartos of New York
This picture was started in 1939 in London and completed in 1941 in New York

PIET MONDRIAN: *Composition with Red, Blue and Yellow*
Signed with initials and dated 30
Oil on canvas
20⅛ x 20⅛ in. (51 x 51 cm)
Sold 27.6.83 in London for £1,512,000 ($2,328,480)
Record auction price for a work by the artist and for any abstract work of art
From the collection of Mr and Mrs Armand P. Bartos of New York

PABLO PICASSO: *Femmes et Enfants au bord de la Mer*
1932
Signed
Oil on canvas
31⅞ x 39⅜ in. (81 x 100 cm)
Sold 17.5.83 in New York for $1,089,000 (£698,076)

JOAN MIRÓ: *Le Port*
Signed, inscribed and dated 2.7.45 on the reverse
Oil on canvas
51¼ x 63¾ in. (130 x162 cm)
Sold 27.6.83 in London for £961,200 ($1,480,248)
Record auction price for a work by the artist and for that of any living painter
From the collection of Mr and Mrs Armand P. Bartos of New York

SALVADOR DALI: *Dormeuse, Cheval, Lion invisibles*
Signed and dated 1930
Oil on canvas
23¾ x 27⅝ in. (60.5 x 70.2)
Sold 21.3.83 in London for £432,000 ($652,320)

Opposite

RENÉ MAGRITTE: *Le Bouquet tout fait*
Signed, inscribed with title and dated 1957 on the reverse
Oil on canvas
64⅛ x 51⅛ in. (163 x 130.5 cm)
Sold 3.11.82 in New York for $308,000 (£181,176)

ALBERTO GIACOMETTI: *Femme de Venise II*
1956
Signed, inscribed 'Susse Fondeur Paris' and
numbered 1/6
Painted bronze
47⅝ in. (121 cm) high
Sold 3.11.82 in New York for $429,000 (£252,353)
Record auction price for a work by the artist

DAVID SMITH: *2 Doors*
Signed, inscribed with title and
dated 4-24-1964
Polished steel
110½ x 93½ x 17½ in.
(281 x 237.5 x 44.5 cm)
Sold 10.11.82 in New York for
$572,000 (£357,500)
Record auction price for a work
by the artist and for any 20th
century American sculpture
From the collection of
Dr and Mrs Joseph A. Gosman of
New York

JACKSON POLLOCK: *Untitled*
Signed and dated May 1943
Oil and gouache on paper
22¾ x 29 in. (58 x 73.5 cm)
Sold 10.5.83 in New York for
$165,000 (£105,769)
From the collection of
Mrs Davidson Taylor

Opposite

ROBERT RAUSCHENBERG: *Studio Painting*
Signed, inscribed with title and 'one of 2 panels connected with
string and bag, R.R.', and dated 1960-61 on the reverse of the right panel
Oil, fabric, paper, rope, metal pulley and clasps, stuffed canvas bag
and charcoal on canvas
Each panel 72 x 34¼ in. (183 x 86.5 cm)
Sold 10.11.82 in New York for $385,000 (£240,625)
Record auction price for a work by the artist
From the collection of Dr and Mrs Joseph A. Gosman of New York

151

FRANK STELLA: *Itata*
1964
Metallic powder in polymer emulsion on canvas
77½ x 133¾ in. (197 x 340 cm)
Sold 10.5.83 in New York for $286,000 (£183,333)
From the collection of Philip Johnson

FRANZ KLINE: *Mars Black and White*
1959
Signed on reverse
Oil on canvas
82 x 55 in. (208.5 x 139.5 cm)
Sold 10.5.83 in New York for
$264,000 (£169,230)
From the collection of
Harriet Mnuchin Weiner

Opposite

MARK ROTHKO: *Untitled*
Signed and dated 1957 on the reverse
Oil on canvas
56¼ x 54¼ in. (143 x 138 cm)
Sold 27.6.83 in London for £259,200 ($404,352)
Record auction price for a work by the artist
From the collection of Mr and Mrs Armand P. Bartos of
New York

WILLEM DE KOONING: *Two Women*
Signed and inscribed with title and dated 1955 on the
stretcher
Oil and charcoal on canvas
40 x 50 in. (101.5 x 127 cm)
Sold 10.5.83 in New York for $1,210,000 (£775,641)
Record auction price for an Abstract Expressionist picture
From the collection of Harriet Mnuchin Weiner,
of New York

155

SAM FRANCIS: *Middle Blue III*
1959
Oil on canvas
72 x 96 in. (183 x 244 cm)
Sold 10.5.83 in New York for $242,000 (£155,128)
Record auction price for a work by the artist
From the collection of Harriet Mnuchin Weiner

Opposite

RICHARD LINDNER: *L'As de Trèfle*
Signed and dated 1973
Oil on canvas
78¾ x 71 in. (200 x 180.5 cm)
Sold 10.5.83 in New York for $330,000 (£211,538)

RICHARD DIEBENKORN: *Seated Nude – Black Background*
Signed with initials and
dated 61
Oil on canvas
84 x 54 in. (213.5 x 137.5 cm)
Sold 10.11.82 in New York for $198,000
(£123,750)
Record auction price for a work by the
artist
From the collection of
Dr and Mrs Joseph A. Gosman
of New York

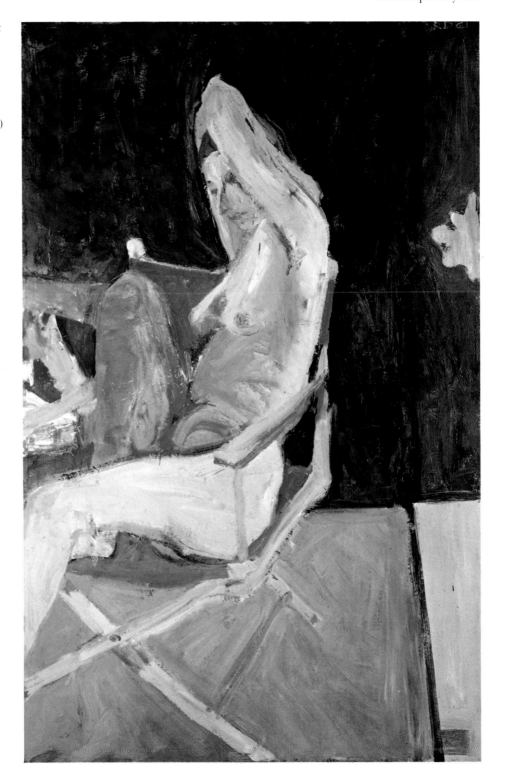

Opposite

YVES KLEIN: *Monochrome Blue*
Signed, inscribed and dated 1959 on
the reverse
Oil on muslin on plywood
36¼ x 28¼ in. (92 x 72 cm)
Sold 30.11.82 in London for
£34,560 ($55,296)

CY TWOMBLY: *Untitled*
1969
Oil on canvas
79 x 103¼ in. (201 x 262.2 cm)
Sold 10.5.83 in New York for $132,000 (£84,615)
From the collection of Philip Johnson

DAVID HOCKNEY: *Boy about to take a Shower*
1964
Acrylic on canvas
36 x 36 in. (91 x 91 cm)
Sold 28.6.83 in London for £66,690 ($104,036)
Record auction price for a work by the artist

SIR ALFRED MUNNINGS, P.R.A.: *Under Starter's Orders, Newmarket*
Signed
Oil on board
17½ x 24 in. (44.5 x 61 cm)
Sold 10.6.83 in New York for $253,000 (£158,125)
From the collection of Mrs C. Oliver Iselin 111

ROBERT BEVAN: *Showing the Paces, Aldridge's*
c. 1914
With studio stamp
Watercolour and soft pencil
12 x 11½ in. (30.5 x 29.2 cm)
Sold 10.6.83 in London for £6,480 ($9,720)

EDWARD SEAGO: *Pin Mill*
Signed
Oil on board
26 x 36 in. (68.8 x 91.4 cm)
Sold 10.6.83 in London for £16,200 ($24,300)

WALTER RICHARD SICKERT, A.R.A.: *Santa Maria della Salute*
c. 1901
Signed
Oil on canvas
23½ x 19 in. (59.7 x 48.2 cm)
Sold 4.3.83 in London for £28,080 ($42,401)

AUGUSTUS JOHN, O.M., R.A.:
Portrait of Gwen John
c. 1897
Pencil
9 x 6½ in. (22.9 x 16.5 cm)
Sold 4.3.83 in London for
£8,100 ($12,231)
From the collection of
Mrs E.M. Salaman

Opposite

HAROLD GILMAN: *Ruth Doggett*
1914 or 1915
Signed
Oil on canvas
30 x 25¼ in. (76.2 x 63 cm)
Sold 12.11.82 in London for
£41,040 ($68,126)
Record auction price for a
work by the artist
Ruth Doggett was a pupil of
both Sickert and Gilman. She
exhibited at the Brighton
exhibition *English Post-
Impressionists, Cubists and Others*,
in 1913 and also with the
Allied Artists' Association and
the London Group (1920)

EDWARD BURRA: *The Dockside Café*
Signed and dated 1929
Tempera on canvas
24 x 19½ in. (61 x 49.5 cm)
Sold 12.11.82 in London for £14,580 ($24,203)
Record auction price for a work by the artist

BOOKS AND MANUSCRIPTS

Psalter, use of the Sainte-Chapelle, Paris
*c.*1285-97
Illuminated manuscript on vellum
7½ x 5 in. (19.1 x 12.8 cm)
Sold 20.5.83 in New York for $66,000 (£42,580)
Probably made for a Queen of France, either for Marie de
Brabant, widow of Philippe III, or for Jeanne de Champagne,
wife of Philippe IV

The Library of John A. Saks

STEPHEN MASSEY

It is unusual that a particular American private library of early printed books, fine bindings, medieval manuscripts, 18th-century illustrated Venetian books and the finest example of the English private presses, formed between 1935 and 1975 and worth today between $2,000,000 and $3,000,000, should not have been more widely known in the rare book world until its dispersal through 10 sales at Christie's New York (one in London) from 1977 to 1983. However, to those among us who were fortunate enough to have known John Saks of Greenwich, Connecticut, we were soon made aware of his own modesty about his indisputable stature when ranked beside the achievements of Perry, Bishop, Kreisler, Hogan and Wilmerding, all of whom had named single-owner auction catalogues of their libraries. Although a few substantial gifts were made to the Pierpont Morgan Library, unlike others of his contemporaries he preferred to return his collection to the market place for competition amongst a new generation. Throughout those 10 sales, and including one sale by private treaty in 1980, 614 lots were sold by Christie's for a total of $2,564,255 (£1,095,702).

John Andrew Saks was born on July 10, 1913, and worked in the department store of the same name. His interest in book-collecting began in December 1935, when he made his first purchases, as Christmas presents, from the Chaucer Head Book Shop, in New York, which was owned by a friend of his, William Liebmann. He started, as many young collectors have done, by buying private press books and these became the heart of his collection. He secured all the Kelmscott, Ashendene and Doves Press books, a fairly notable achievement by itself, except that he set his sights very high indeed by determining to buy the specially limited numbers of each of their publications on vellum. With the one exception of the impossible Doves Press Bible (three copies known) he succeeded. Cresset, Nonesuch, Essex House, Shakespeare Head, Grabhorn followed. He even wired his young wife Arden from the Aleutian Islands, where he was posted by the U.S. Army in 1942, to buy the master binder George Fisher's own set of all of the Gregynog books in special bindings. This collection constituted the private treaty sale by Christie's in 1980, for $140,000 (£59,829).

Marriage, a family, school fees, all brought with them certain changes of direction in Saks' self-confessed *bibliomania* through the years. On December 10th and 17th, 1963, about 500 books and manuscripts were sold at Parke-Bernet (in 168 lots) for a total of $13,035 (£4,655). This was mainly a clearance sale of minor press books, and he wisely decided not to include vellum copies in the sale, knowing that they would add lustre to future sales of his better books. By 1965, nearly all of his expensive purchases had been made but Saks still felt the urge to keep on collecting. A continuing interest in illustrated books brought him into a new area of specialisation – 19th-century Venetian illustrated books.

The first Christie's sale in which John was a consignor was in November 1977. The first of two books was an imperfect copy of Gregorius IX, *Decretales*, Mainz 1473, which all but doubled

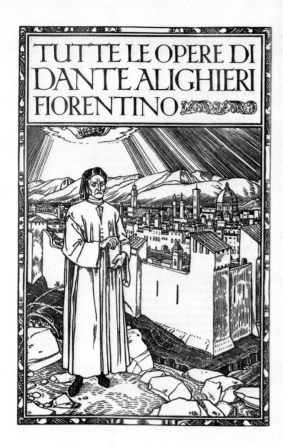

ASHENDENE PRESS:
Dante, Opere
1909
One of six copies on
vellum
Sold 9.11.82 in New
York for $55,000
(£34,375)

the estimate, selling for $15,400 (£9,059), to Zeitlin. The next was the Chatsworth copy of Theodoretus, *Episcopi*, Paris 1519, printed on vellum, and this almost trebled the estimate at $5,060 (£2,976) to Colin Franklin. April 7, 1978 was Gutenberg Bible day and in the accompanying sale, four Saks lots were sold for $15,180 (£8,433). Almost exactly a year later, on April 20, 1979, an otherwise thin sale was enriched by some of his vellum press books held back in 1963. The Cresset Press Bacon and Bunyan realized $4,400 (£2,095) and $5,720 (£2,724); here as well we caught a glimpse of his interest in fine bindings. The tally for 23 lots, a respectable $34,353 (£16,359).

171

William Morris; a Cicero, *De Finibus*, Florence 1410; the Missal of Cardinal Bernardo da Carvajal, Spain *c.* 1515; and the Tongerloo Missal, Praemonstratensian use, Flanders 1552, all for an approximate value of $150,000. At Christie's we failed to sell a pretty Parisian Book of Hours in April, but our sale in October 1980 more than made up for this mutual mistake. The General Theological Seminary had consigned to us a million dollars worth of 15th-century books and a few manuscripts. Most of the books were Latin Bibles and apart from a few of the finest examples they would by themselves have constituted a monotonous sale. To this group, John added 45 15th and 16th-century books and one manuscript Antiphonal (Dutch, Gelderland 1517) representing the entire Saks collection of books from these centuries. The sale was changed from a good one to a great one. This catalogue is the first in which his name appears consistently in the provenance. His first lot, no. 77, was a printed Book of Hours, Antwerp 1570, one of two known copies on vellum. Estimated at $10,000-$15,000 it fetched $28,600 (£13,059). The next lot was William Morris's copy of the fourth German Bible, Augsburg [G. Zainer 1475-76]. John had paid $1,450 for it in 1936. Against an estimate of $15,000-$20,000, it fetched $66,000 (£30,137) to The University of Texas. The Dutch Antiphonal was so large and unwieldy that John had insisted it be offered without reserve with an estimate of $4,000-$5,000. This brought $26,400 (£12,055); but the wildest price of all was the $27,500 (£12,557) paid for the vellum leaf from the Gutenberg Bible. This had cost $400 in the 40s. His total for this sale was $365,993 (£167,120). Thirty-eight further lots, mainly minor press books, were sold in a second book sale in the afternoon for $25,102 (£11,462).

There were now six main sections left of John's library: the three private presses, Kelmscott, Ashendene and Doves (in descending order of value), fine bindings, illuminated manuscripts and the Venetian books. The Doves Press books and bindings were chosen for the sale on May 22, 1981, because so many of his 37 books from the press were clad in decorative morocco by the Doves Bindery and would complement the other bindings. To any collector of English bindings, the name of Thomas James Cobden-Sanderson is of the highest importance. According to his own *Journals*, he personally bound only 122 books between 1884 and 1893 before the foundation of the Doves Bindery, when he gave up binding except in an advisory and a design capacity. Few collectors own any Cobden-Sandersons; Saks had six. His finest was on a copy of William Morris's *Love is Enough*, London 1873, bound for Morris's friend and editor, F.S. Ellis, with each page magnificently illuminated with succulent fruit and flowers by Beatrice Pagden. This example was given to the Morgan Library, and Christie's sale of Saks's property opened with the remaining five. Maggs overcame determined opposition from Breslauer, buying all for a total of $83,600 (£36,991). Lot 361 was a copy of the Bruce Rogers Bible, Oxford 1935, splendidly bound by Douglas Cockerell & Son, and executed in 1939 for exhibition at the British Pavilion of the New York World's Fair in 1940. Bill Liebmann was commissioned to buy it at the fair's close, and John had paid $266, beating Duschnes's hot pursuit by a day or two. Maggs paid $16,500 (£7,301) for this. A binding by Charles Meunier commissioned by Henry Walters with ceramic emblems of Jean Grolier found its way to the Grolier Club via Bart Auerbach at $4,180 (£1,849). There was a tinge of *déjà vu* over the Doves Press books on vellum, since many other examples had been sold at Von Hirsch's sale at Sotheby's (Hodgson's Rooms) in June 1978, but the total was over the top estimate, a respectable $126,990 (£56,190). To end the sale, the Golden Cockerel Press Chaucer, *Canterbury Tales* ($26,400 (£11,681) Harper), two Grolier Club publications bound by Lotic and Riviere ($3,850 (£1,703) and $8,250 (£3,650) Maggs) and the Shakespeare Head Press *Froissarts Cronycles* ($12,100 (£5,354) Fleming), all on vellum, swelled the total sold to $313,291 (£138,624). John's only modern calligraphic manuscript was the final lot, Edward Johnston's ink and gold version of Cobden-Sanderson's, *The Ideal Book or Book Beautiful* ($10,450 (£4,624) Maggs).

The sudden death of Arden Saks in 1980 and John's own ill-health had prompted a move to a smaller house. As a result, he decided to sell his collection of Venetian books. This was the single London sale, the first of its kind, held on 10 June, 1981. The total was £65,703 ($127,463) against an expenditure of approximately $75,000.

There were no Saks sales during the 1981/82 traditional auction season, but by July 1982, in poor health again, he asked us to take delivery of his entire Ashendene Press collection and to catalogue it and await his instructions. The

CHRONIQUE: *Histoire Ancienne*
Paris, *c*.1380
Illuminated manuscript on vellum
Elaborately illustrated, including 76
miniatures within the text.
In the style of an artist who worked
in a *Mirouer Historial* once owned by
Jean de Berry
15½ x 13⅞ in.
(39.7 x 28.3 cm)
Sold 20.5.83 in New York for
$264,000 (£169,092)

Ashendene Press (1895-1936) was founded by a partner of W.H. Smith & Sons, Charles Harry St. John Hornby (1867-1946), and its books, in style and appearance, charted a middle course between the elaborate ornament of Kelmscott and the stark typographical simplicity of Doves. John's collection was certainly the finest ever to have been offered for sale by auction and the only one approaching completeness to have been put together on a book-by-book basis. All of the subscription books were present, on vellum, and only two minor pieces (the Bayford Hockey Club items) were missing. The New York auctions of Cortlandt F. Bishop (1938), John Gribbel (1940), Charles C. Kalbfleisch (1944) and, to a lesser extent, the J.R. Abbey sale in London (1965) provided most of the acquisitions although a few came by subscription and from Chaucer Head and Duschnes. John's and Christie's wish was to attempt to sell the 71 lots as a collection, and we agreed a reserve price of $300,000 (£180,700) (exclusive). There was no bidding past the opening price of $150,000 (£90,000) and the lots were sold singly for a total of $331,705 (£206,541). The choicest prize of the press is the folio Dante on vellum, one of six copies. This was the only copy to have appeared at auction in England or the U.S.A. Another rarity is Malory's *Le Morte Darthur*, one of eight on vellum. These went to Maggs at $55,000 (£34,240) and $35,200 (£21,900) respectively. Indeed, Maggs cornered most of the sale, but the most surprising price by far was the $24,200 (£15,060) paid against them by the Bromers for the Queen Mary's Dolls House Miniature Horace. Duschnes had bought it at the Abbey sale for John in 1965 for £240 and had refused an offer from another bookseller of $2,400 before the sale ended!

Neither his family nor close friends knew that his end was so close, but his decision to sell together the two last remaining groups, Kelmscott and the six medieval manuscripts, should, perhaps have given us some indication. It had always been my understanding that they would be treated separately, and it was with some surprise that I received all that was left on December 16, 1982. May 20, 1983 was the date of his last and greatest sale and he lived just long enough, until May 30, to enjoy the overwhelming response to it. Ironically, Kelmscott Press books on vellum had been among his very first auction purchases, at the Marsden J. Perry sale in 1936, and this cornerstone of his library was the last to go. This 'typographical adventure' founded in 1891 by William Morris, is always ranked first in importance of the three principle English private presses by book collectors and booksellers. Morris was a Renaissance man of the 19th century, having attained, at the age of 57, an already illustrious reputation as writer and designer, as well as accomplished calligraphic artist. All of his successors in the movement were guided by what Beatrice Warde so aptly called "the Divine Fire which glowed in the Kelmscott Press books." According to Sydney Cockerell, the press's secretary, writing in 1898: "There are three complete vellum sets in existence, and the extreme difficulty of completing a set after the copies are scattered makes it unlikely that there will ever be a fourth." The three sets were owned by Morris, Emery Walker and Charles Fairfax Murray. Marsden J. Perry completed a set, mostly from the Morris set, and his 1936 sale contained the only complete vellum group to have appeared at auction. The books had been offered singly and 23 year-old John bought heavily then as well as in the years 1938, 1944, and 1956 at Bishop's, Kalbfleisch's and Cockerell's sales respectively. Here then, at Christie's, 85 years after Cockerell's challenge, was the elusive fourth vellum set. Undeterred by the failure to sell the Ashendenes as one lot in November, we agreed to try the vellum copies (49 items) as one lot with a reserve of $500,000 (exclusive) and to sell the remaining publications on paper, ephemera (almost complete), 19 special bindings, illustrations and association material (a further 59 lots) one by one. Maggs bid on the vellums up to $550,000, but was pushed by Kraus to $660,000 (£425,806). The rest of Kelmscott fetched $113,657 (£73,327). Earlier, the five western medieval illuminated manuscripts had realised $413,050 (£226,484). The two finest examples of these were a Psalter, Paris c. 1285-1297, $660,000 (£42,580) Kraus against Fleming, (now owned by the Morgan Library) and the *Histoire Ancienne*, Paris c. 1380, elaborately illustrated with 79 miniatures. Kraus outbid the Bibliothèque Nationale for this at $264,000 (£169,092).

John Saks was an old-fashioned book collector. He never personally attended an auction sale, as a buyer or a seller, preferring to pay his chosen dealer to act for him. True, he visited the auction house to view books before a sale and he was a frequent social visitor to Christie's. Having worked in a "service business", as he liked to refer to Saks Fifth Avenue, he could be occasionally critical of unanswered telephones or over-ornamental and under-efficient reception staff. It was all well meant. When the time came to sell he was a generous consignor; estimates and reserves were always to be reasonable. "They'll bring what they'll bring," he used to say before a sale – this is another cautionary tale for nowadays! I even offered him a telephone link to his last sale. "No, Gentlemen don't attend book sales!" Especially not by telephone.

NICOLAUS DE LYRA: *Postilla*
England, possibly
London, *c*.1430
Illuminated manuscript
on vellum
19⅝ x 13⅞ in.
(50.5 x 35.5 cm)
Sold 8.12.82 in London for
£27,000 ($43,200)
This was evidently once
part of a set of 10 or 12
volumes and is apparently
unique for the scheme of
decorations in an English
manuscript.

GEORGE BROOKSHAW: *Pomona Britannica; or a collection of the most esteemed fruits at present cultivated in this country, selected principally from the Royal Gardens at Hampton Court*
1812
First edition
90 coloured aquatint plates
Large folio
Sold 20.4.83 in London for £28,080 ($42,120)
Record auction price for a first edition of this book

Opposite

LOUISE O'FERRALL: *An Album containing 58 original drawings of plants mainly native to the West Indies*
Watermarked 1833-35
Quarto
Sold 22.6.83 in London for £25,920 ($39,917)
From the collection of Kammerherre
C.C. Scavenius

Chinese Rose
Rosa Sinensis

CRISPIN VAN DER PAS: *Hortus Floridus*
Utrecht and Arnheim, 1614-16
First edition, all plates in contemporary colouring
Oblong quarto
Sold 20.4.83 in London for £10,800 ($16,200)
The most famous early engraved flower book, extremely rare in this condition

EDWARD LEAR: *Illustrations of the Family of Psittacidae or Parrots*
1832
42 hand-coloured plates
Folio
Sold 20.4.83 in London for £23,760
($35,640)
Very rare subscriber's copy of
Lear's first book in its original state
Record auction price

MACROCERCUS ARARAUNA.
Blue & Yellow Macaw
¼ Nat Size

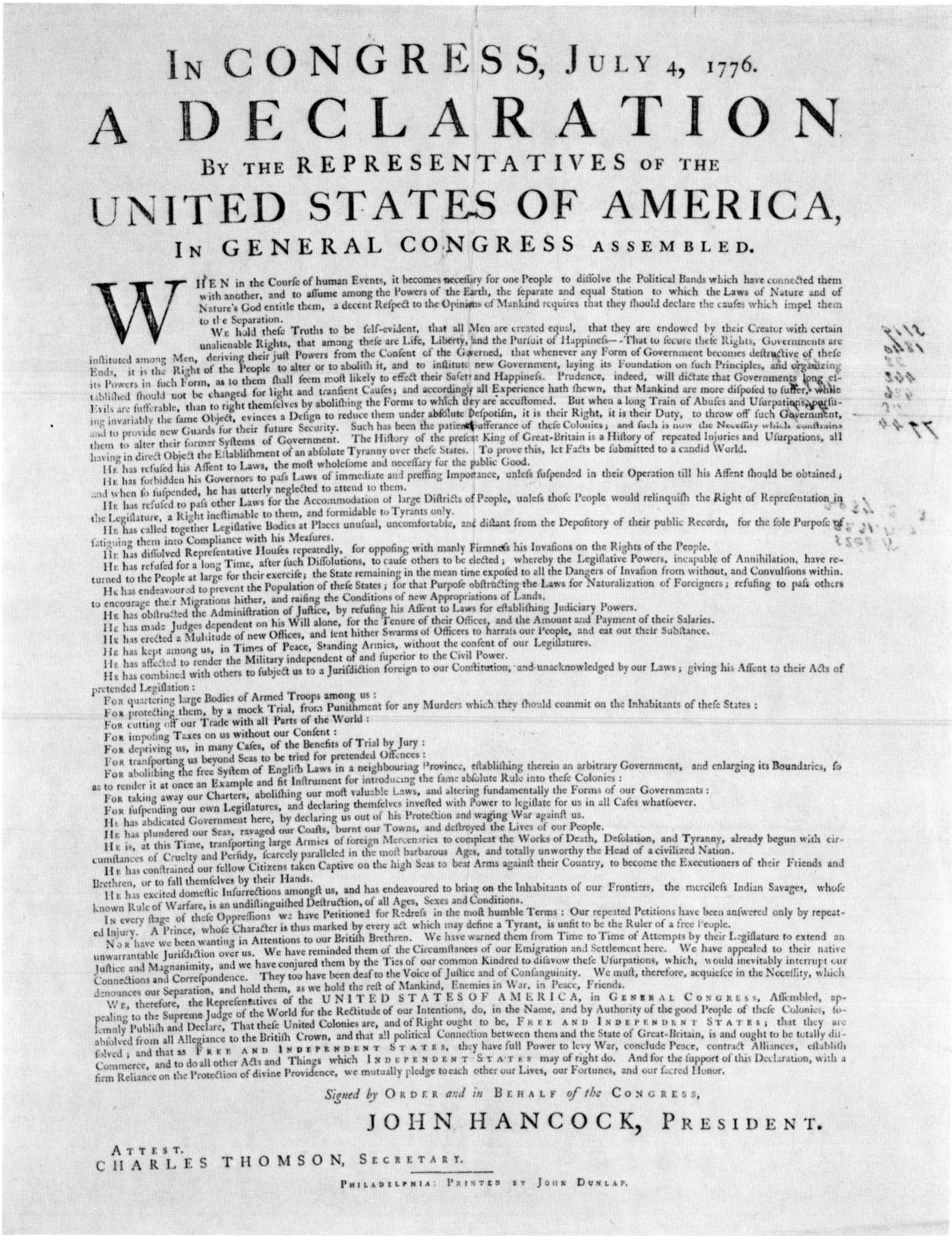

IN CONGRESS, JULY 4, 1776.

A DECLARATION BY THE REPRESENTATIVES OF THE UNITED STATES OF AMERICA, IN GENERAL CONGRESS ASSEMBLED.

WHEN in the Course of human Events, it becomes necessary for one People to dissolve the Political Bands which have connected them with another, and to assume among the Powers of the Earth, the separate and equal Station to which the Laws of Nature and of Nature's God entitle them, a decent Respect to the Opinions of Mankind requires that they should declare the causes which impel them to the Separation.

WE hold these Truths to be self-evident, that all Men are created equal, that they are endowed by their Creator with certain unalienable Rights, that among these are Life, Liberty, and the Pursuit of Happiness—That to secure these Rights, Governments are instituted among Men, deriving their just Powers from the Consent of the Governed, that whenever any Form of Government becomes destructive of these Ends, it is the Right of the People to alter or to abolish it, and to institute new Government, laying its Foundation on such Principles, and organizing its Powers in such Form, as to them shall seem most likely to effect their Safety and Happiness. Prudence, indeed, will dictate that Governments long established should not be changed for light and transient Causes; and accordingly all Experience hath shewn, that Mankind are more disposed to suffer, while Evils are sufferable, than to right themselves by abolishing the Forms to which they are accustomed. But when a long Train of Abuses and Usurpations, pursuing invariably the same Object, evinces a Design to reduce them under absolute Despotism, it is their Right, it is their Duty, to throw off such Government, and to provide new Guards for their future Security. Such has been the patient Sufferance of these Colonies; and such is now the Necessity which constrains them to alter their former Systems of Government. The History of the present King of Great-Britain is a History of repeated Injuries and Usurpations, all having in direct Object the Establishment of an absolute Tyranny over these States. To prove this, let Facts be submitted to a candid World.

HE has refused his Assent to Laws, the most wholesome and necessary for the public Good.

HE has forbidden his Governors to pass Laws of immediate and pressing Importance, unless suspended in their Operation till his Assent should be obtained; and when so suspended, he has utterly neglected to attend to them.

HE has refused to pass other Laws for the Accommodation of large Districts of People, unless those People would relinquish the Right of Representation in the Legislature, a Right inestimable to them, and formidable to Tyrants only.

HE has called together Legislative Bodies at Places unusual, uncomfortable, and distant from the Depository of their public Records, for the sole Purpose of fatiguing them into Compliance with his Measures.

HE has dissolved Representative Houses repeatedly, for opposing with manly Firmness his Invasions on the Rights of the People.

HE has refused for a long Time, after such Dissolutions, to cause others to be elected; whereby the Legislative Powers, incapable of Annihilation, have returned to the People at large for their exercise; the State remaining in the mean time exposed to all the Dangers of Invasion from without, and Convulsions within.

HE has endeavoured to prevent the Population of these States; for that Purpose obstructing the Laws for Naturalization of Foreigners; refusing to pass others to encourage their Migrations hither, and raising the Conditions of new Appropriations of Lands.

HE has obstructed the Administration of Justice, by refusing his Assent to Laws for establishing Judiciary Powers.

HE has made Judges dependent on his Will alone, for the Tenure of their Offices, and the Amount and Payment of their Salaries.

HE has erected a Multitude of new Offices, and sent hither Swarms of Officers to harrass our People, and eat out their Substance.

HE has kept among us, in Times of Peace, Standing Armies, without the consent of our Legislatures.

HE has affected to render the Military independent of and superior to the Civil Power.

HE has combined with others to subject us to a Jurisdiction foreign to our Constitution, and unacknowledged by our Laws; giving his Assent to their Acts of pretended Legislation:

FOR quartering large Bodies of Armed Troops among us:

FOR protecting them, by a mock Trial, from Punishment for any Murders which they should commit on the Inhabitants of these States:

FOR cutting off our Trade with all Parts of the World:

FOR imposing Taxes on us without our Consent:

FOR depriving us, in many Cases, of the Benefits of Trial by Jury:

FOR transporting us beyond Seas to be tried for pretended Offences:

FOR abolishing the free System of English Laws in a neighbouring Province, establishing therein an arbitrary Government, and enlarging its Boundaries, so as to render it at once an Example and fit Instrument for introducing the same absolute Rule into these Colonies:

FOR taking away our Charters, abolishing our most valuable Laws, and altering fundamentally the Forms of our Governments:

FOR suspending our own Legislatures, and declaring themselves invested with Power to legislate for us in all Cases whatsoever.

HE has abdicated Government here, by declaring us out of his Protection and waging War against us.

HE has plundered our Seas, ravaged our Coasts, burnt our Towns, and destroyed the Lives of our People.

HE is, at this Time, transporting large Armies of foreign Mercenaries to compleat the Works of Death, Desolation, and Tyranny, already begun with circumstances of Cruelty and Perfidy, scarcely paralleled in the most barbarous Ages, and totally unworthy the Head of a civilized Nation.

HE has constrained our fellow Citizens taken Captive on the high Seas to bear Arms against their Country, to become the Executioners of their Friends and Brethren, or to fall themselves by their Hands.

HE has excited domestic Insurrections amongst us, and has endeavoured to bring on the Inhabitants of our Frontiers, the merciless Indian Savages, whose known Rule of Warfare, is an undistinguished Destruction, of all Ages, Sexes and Conditions.

IN every stage of these Oppressions we have Petitioned for Redress in the most humble Terms: Our repeated Petitions have been answered only by repeated Injury. A Prince, whose Character is thus marked by every act which may define a Tyrant, is unfit to be the Ruler of a free People.

NOR have we been wanting in Attentions to our British Brethren. We have warned them from Time to Time of Attempts by their Legislature to extend an unwarrantable Jurisdiction over us. We have reminded them of the Circumstances of our Emigration and Settlement here. We have appealed to their native Justice and Magnanimity, and we have conjured them by the Ties of our common Kindred to disavow these Usurpations, which, would inevitably interrupt our Connections and Correspondence. They too have been deaf to the Voice of Justice and of Consanguinity. We must, therefore, acquiesce in the Necessity, which denounces our Separation, and hold them, as we hold the rest of Mankind, Enemies in War, in Peace, Friends.

WE, therefore, the Representatives of the UNITED STATES OF AMERICA, in GENERAL CONGRESS, Assembled, appealing to the Supreme Judge of the World for the Rectitude of our Intentions, do, in the Name, and by Authority of the good People of these Colonies, solemnly Publish and Declare, That these United Colonies are, and of Right ought to be, FREE AND INDEPENDENT STATES; that they are absolved from all Allegiance to the British Crown, and that all political Connection between them and the State of Great-Britain, is and ought to be totally dissolved; and that as FREE AND INDEPENDENT STATES, they have full Power to levy War, conclude Peace, contract Alliances, establish Commerce, and to do all other Acts and Things which INDEPENDENT STATES may of right do. And for the support of this Declaration, with a firm Reliance on the Protection of divine Providence, we mutually pledge to each other our Lives, our Fortunes, and our sacred Honor.

Signed by ORDER *and in* BEHALF *of the* CONGRESS,

JOHN HANCOCK, PRESIDENT.

ATTEST.
CHARLES THOMSON, SECRETARY.

PHILADELPHIA: PRINTED BY JOHN DUNLAP.

The Declaration of Independence
Printed by John Dunlap
Philadelphia, 1776
Association copy of the first printing, first state
Endorsed by Joseph Hewes (1730-79), of North Carolina, and signer of the Declaration
Folio broadside, 18⅝ x 15⅛ in. (47.4 x 38.2 cm)
Sold 22.4.83 in New York for $412,500 (£264,423)
Record auction price for a Declaration of Independence
From the collection of John Gilliam Wood

GEORGE CATLIN: *Souvenir of the North American Indians, as they were in the middle of the 19th century*
215 original crayon portraits copied by Catlin from his original paintings for the Duke of Portland
London 1852-9
Folio 14 x 10½ in.
(35 x 26 cm)
Sold 27.10.82 in London for £194,400
($311,040)

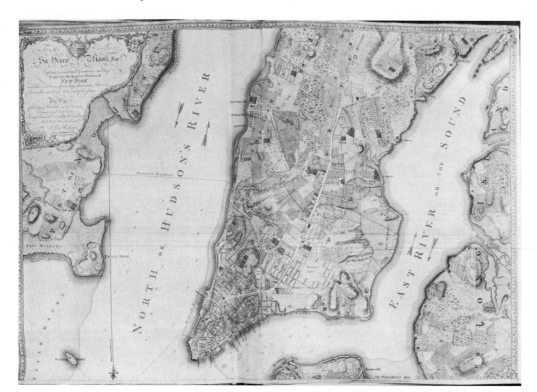

COMPOSITE ATLAS OF AMERICA
A collection of 56 engraved maps
1752-80
Large folio
Sold 20.4.83 in London for
£34,500 ($51,750)
Left is the plan of the City of
New York, 1776, by B. Ratzer

THE HUDSON RIVER PORTFOLIO
By William Guy Wall, John Hill
and John Rubens Smith
New York, *c.*1828
A fine and complete copy of the
later Carvill issue containing 20
coloured aquatint views
Large oblong folio
Sold 22.4.83 in New York for
$88,000 (£56,410)

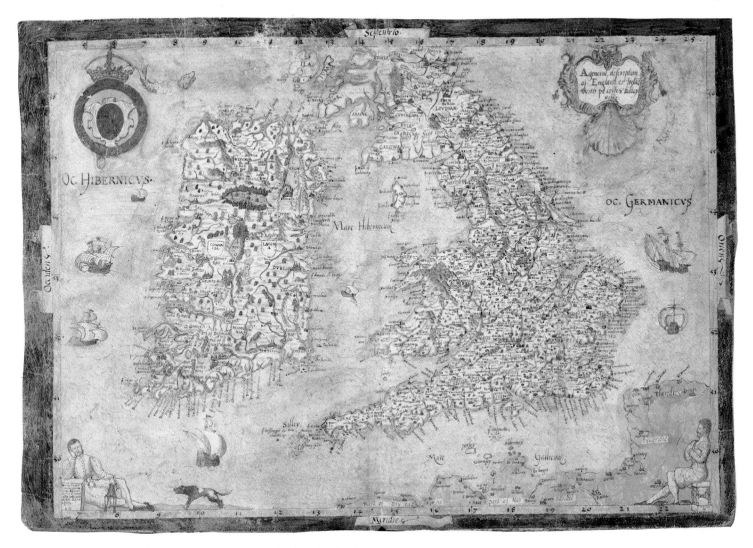

LAURENCE NOWELL: *A general description of England and Ireland*
c.1564
Manuscript map on vellum for William Cecil, Lord Burghley
9¼ x 13½ in. (23.5 x 34 cm)
Sold 8.12.82 in London for £56,160 ($89,856)
From the collection of the Earl of Shelburne.
Regarded as a landmark in Tudor map making. Although probably compiled from literary sources and maps available in
London and at Hatfield House, rather than from fieldwork, the precision and detail are remarkable in Tudor map making, and
it has been postulated that Nowell's maps may have served as the original compilation and source for Mercator's map of 1564.
Now in The British Library.

CAROLI LINNÆI, *SVECI,*

DOCTORIS MEDICINÆ,

SYSTEMA NATURÆ,

S I V E

REGNA TRIA NATURÆ

SYSTEMATICE PROPOSITA

P E R

CLASSES, ORDINES,

GENERA, & SPECIES.

O JEHOVA! Quam ampla sunt opera Tua !
Quam ea omnia sapienter fecisti !
Quam plena est terra possessione tua !

Psalm. CIV. 24.

L U G D U N I B A T A V O R U M,

Apud THEODORUM HAAK, MDCCXXXV.

EX TYPOGRAPHIA

JOANNIS WILHELMI DE GROOT.

CAROLUS LINNAEUS: *Systema Naturae*
Leiden, 1735
First edition
12 leaves, single sheets, on one side only, uncut and unbound as issued
Folio 22 x 17 in. (55.8 x 43 cm)
Sold 2.3.83 in London for £41,040 ($61,560)
A unique copy of the first edition of one of the most fundamental books in the history of science. Linnaeus's original intention was to produce his works as a *mappa naturae*, made up from sheets printed on one side of the paper only, and mounted in the form of a wall chart

GIOVANNI BOCCACCIO: *De Claris Mulieribus*
Ulm, Johann Zainer, 1473
First edition
Folio
Sold 8.12.82 in London for £38,880 ($62,208)
From the collection of Sir William Gladstone, Bt.

Right

JONATHAN SWIFT: *A Catalogue of Books*
Dublin, 1745
Octavo
Sold 29.9.82 in London for £9,720
($16,524)

Far right

ROBERT BOYLE: *The Sceptical Chymist*
1680
First complete edition
Octavo
Sold 2.3.83 in London for £3,456
($5,184)

Right

WILLIAM GILBERT: *De Magnete*
1600
First edition
Folio
Sold 2.3.83 in London for £9,504
($14,256)
The first major English scientific
treatise based on experimental
methods of research

Far right

JEAN LEGOYS: *Abecedaire*
1606
Manuscript bound for presentation
to The Dauphin
Small quarto
Sold 8.12.82 in London for £15,120
($24,192)

185

WOLFGANG AMADEUS MOZART: *Autographed manuscript of the closing bars of the finale of the string quartet in G minor, K.516, scored for two violas and one violoncello*
Vienna, 16 May 1787
9 x 12½ in. (22.9 x 31.6 cm)
Sold 23.2.83 in London for £12,420 ($18,630)
From the collection of the late Sir Clifford Curzon, C.B.E.

JANE AUSTEN: *Autograph poetical manuscript*
c.1811
Four four-line stanzas
5 x 4 in. (12.5 x 10.2 cm)
Sold 20.7.83 in London for £6,480 ($10,044)
From the Godmersham Park Collection
A fine example of Jane Austen's extempore versifying

WILLIAM BUTLER YEATS: *Series of 123 letters to Dorothy (Lady Gerald) Wellesley 1935-38*
Many of the letters containing substantial passages of verse
Sold 20.7.83 in London for £18,360 ($28,458)

DOUGLAS HYDE: *Archive of the private papers of Douglas Hyde, first President of the Irish Republic and gaelic scholar, including a series of letters to Hyde from most of the major figures of the Irish literary revival*
Sold 20.7.83 in London for £15,120 ($23,436)
The photograph shows Hyde sitting for the sculptor Seamus Murphy

KARL MARX: *Autograph letter*
Manchester, 23 May 1873
Acknowledging receipt of 2s. 6d. as membership fee for the International Federation of Workingmen, and promising a complimentary copy of the new book edition of *Kapital*
One page, octavo
Sold 20.7.83 in London for £5,508 ($8,537)

GODMERSHAM PARK

Godmersham Park

GERALDINE NORMAN

Godmersham Park started life in the early 18th century with pretentions to be something more than a manor house. Grand Palladian plasterwork embellishes the interior while a well proportioned brick exterior smiles out across the meandering river Stour and its watermeadows.

In the early years of the 19th century it walked into the sidelines of history when it belonged to Edward Austen Knight who entertained Jane Austen, his novelist sister, there. She is reputed to have based *Mansfield Park* on it. And in the 1930s it gained a new lease of life when it was bought and furnished by Robert and Elsie Tritton.

In June Christie's made Godmersham the talking point of the art-loving jet set with a week long auction of the contents that was more like a garden party. The guests descended from all over the United States, from Paris, Germany and Italy and they were so delighted with what they saw that they may have paid far more than they originally meant to, but that always happens at house sales. The contents of the house sold for £4 million where it was only expected to reach £2½ million.

The Godmersham that charmed bidders was essentially the creation of Mrs. Elsie Tritton who died at the age of 96 in February 1983. Born Elsie Richter of New York, she first married Sir Louis Baron, heir to the Carreras fortune. After his death she married Robert Tritton, one of the first Old Etonian interior decorators. Her first husband's taste was reflected at Godmersham by superb needlework, her second husband's by fine French furniture.

The Trittons bought Godmersham in 1936 and remodelled the house and garden, returning it as far as possible to its 18th century identity. By 1983 it seemed like a time capsule, the epitome of how the rich lived in the 1930s. The gardens were all perfectly dug, pruned, cropped and tended while, inside the house, the nobly proportioned rooms were furnished with superb antique treasures but still conveyed a sense of intimate comfort. The furnishings were a celebration of the typically 1930s delight in the 18th century, from the scrolling ormolu clocks and vases to the modern wastepaper baskets carved in Chippendale style – selling at around £1,800 ($2,844) each, believe it or not.

The bidders of 1983 were in search of the exceptional and bid through the roof for it. The fine needlework with which the house was so well supplied brought some of the most astonishing bids. A pair of George I *petit point* cushion covers worked in bright colours with flowers, fruit, a parrot and butterflies sold for £15,126 ($23,899). Mrs. Tritton had bought them at Christie's in 1932 for 300 gns.

This was the highest auction price ever secured by a cushion, while bright fresh needlework was also responsible for securing the highest ever bid for an English chair at £81,000 ($127,980). It is a George I walnut wing armchair upholstered in magnificent silk and wool *petit point* floral needlework.

The Library

The top price in the sale was £140,400 ($221,832) for a late 15th century Flemish tapestry romantically depicting a betrothal in a garden and there were also ravishing 18th century Soho tapestries, one at £21,600 ($34,128)and a pair at £41,040 ($64,843). The carpets were especially unusual in that nearly all were European, or if Oriental unusually close to European carpets in style. A Queen Anne needlework carpet worked in a dense design of *gros point* scrolling flowers and foliage made £20,520 ($32,422), a mid-18th century English carpet woven with flower sprays £16,200 ($25,596) and a fine Savonnerie carpet of around 1825, £59,400 ($93,852). The set of 13 Chippendale mahogany dining-chairs that had stood on it secured £97,200 ($153,576), a price reflecting their unusual and very successful design.

The more unusual French furniture also made bidders cast caution to the wind. The loveliest French chair stood in Mrs. Tritton's bedroom, a Louis XV giltwood fauteuil dating from the very beginning of Neo-Classical taste. The disciplined classical carving is relieved by scrolling explosions of foliage and flowers, echoing the rococo era. The price was £70,200 ($110,916).

A very fine Louis XVI giltwood library chair, attributed to Georges Jacob, sold for £34,560 ($54,605), while the marquetry commode by Leonard Boudin from the master bedroom

secured £59,400 ($93,852). When Hugh Roberts had moved it out into the room to catalogue he had found the Fontainebleau inventory mark, partly obliterated. He traced its origin to the refurnishing of the Comte de Provence's appartments at Fontainebleau at the time of his marriage in 1771.

The magic appeal of Godmersham was also reflected in the library sale where Jane Austen first editions, bought by the Trittons not left by the Knights, soared to unheard of prices. They are not rare and the estimates reflected normal market prices, but *Pride and Prejudice* sold for £1,944 ($3,071) against an estimate of £300-£400 and *Sense and Sensibility* for £1,404 ($2,218).

Finally came the contents of the linen cupboard and the attic, reflecting just how grand you could be about the minor accessories of life with a large fortune in the 1930s. The sheets and towels were embellished with embroidery and drawn-thread work and worked either with the special monogram designed by Rex Whistler for Elsie Tritton or the initials E.R.T. The jet set went mad about them. A pair of white linen double sheets reached £230 ($363) and a quantity of huckaback hand towels £170 ($269).

Three car cushions from Aspreys, each contained in a tooled leather bag bearing Elsie Tritton's initials in gold, sold for £259.20 ($409.53).

FURNITURE AND WORKS OF ART

One of a pair of George I gilt-gesso pier-glasses
Attributed to John Belchier
88 x 34½ in. (224 x 88 cm)
Sold 7.4.83 in London for £64,800 ($97,200)

Regency satinwood sofa table
64½ in. (164 cm) wide
Sold 6.6.83 at Godmersham Park for £25,920 ($40,953)

Opposite

Queen Anne walnut small bureau on stand
c. 1715
25½ in. (65 cm) wide
Sold 12.3.83 in New York for $50,600 (£33,959)

One of a pair of
George II giltwood
library armchairs
Probably by John
Gordon
c. 1755-1760
40 in. (102 cm) high
Sold 23.10.82 in
New York for
$61,600 (£36,325)

One of a pair of
George II mahogany
library armchairs
31 in. (79 cm) wide
Sold 18.11.82 in
London for £36,720
($58,752)
These two armchairs
are part of a large
group. Other
examples are in
various private
collections and
museums.

Two from a set of 13 George III mahogany dining-chairs
Sold 6.6.83 at Godmersham Park for £97,200 ($153,576)

Two from a set of four George III mahogany open armchairs
Sold 6.6.83 at Godmersham Park for £59,400 ($93,852)

George I green and gold
lacquered bureau-cabinet
40¾ in. (103.5 cm) wide
Sold 6.6.83
at Godmersham Park for
£81,000 ($127,980)

One of a pair of George I giltwood stools
25¼ in. (47 cm) wide
Sold 6.6.83 at Godmersham Park for £38,880 ($61,430)

Japanese lacquer coffer
17th century
54 in. (137 cm) wide
On George II stand, in the manner of John Vardy
Sold 23.6.83 in London for £45,360 ($70,762)
By Order of the Trustees of the Chatsworth Settlement

Queen Anne black and gold lacquer centre table
36 in. (91.5 cm) wide
Sold 6.6.83 at Godmersham Park for £48,600 ($76,788)

George III mahogany
library armchair
28½ in. (72.5 cm)
wide
Sold 6.6.83 at
Godmersham Park for
£48,600 ($76,788)
Previously sold at
Christie's 25.5.33 for
£262

George I walnut wing
armchair
34¼ in.
(87.5 cm) wide
Sold 6.6.83 at
Godmersham Park for
£81,000 ($127,980)
Record auction price
for a chair

One of a pair of George III
painted and gilded secretaire-
cabinets
48 in. (122 cm) wide
Sold 7.4.83 in London for
£194,400 ($291,600)

The Philosophy Cabinet
By William Burges
1879
Long lower drawer inscribed
WILLIAM BURGES A:D: MDCCCLXXIX
94½ in. (240 cm) high
Sold 7.4.83 in London for
£48,600 ($72,900)
From the Collection of
Auberon Waugh, Esq.

One of a pair of George II
giltwood mirrors
Plate 76 x 38½ in.
(193 x 38 cm)
Sold 6.6.83 at Godmersham Park
for £45,360 ($71,668)
Previously sold at
Christie's 12.3.47 for £262

George I giltwood chandelier
31 in. (79 cm) high, 38 in. (96.5 cm) span
Sold 6.6.83 at Godmersham Park for £43,200 ($68,256)

Louis XVI parquetry
and Sèvres porcelain
petite table
By Adam Weisweiler
Stamped A.WEISWEILER
The porcelain with a
date letter for 1776
31 in. (79 cm) high
Sold 9.12.82 in
London for £129,600
($207,360)

Pair of Louis XV marquetry tables à ouvrage
By J.P. Latz
Stamped I.P. Latz
14¼ in. (36.2 cm) and 13¾ (35 cm) wide
Sold 9.12.82 in London for £102,600 ($164,160)
Previously sold at Christie's 29.11.73 for £35,700

Royal transitional
commode
By Léonard Boudin
1771
Stamped L. Boudin
twice and J.M.E.
three times
44 in. (112 cm) wide
Sold 6.6.83 at
Godmersham Park for
£59,400 ($93,852)
This commode was
newly discovered at
Godmersham. It was
originally ordered for
the Cabinet de
Retraite of the Comte
de Provence at
Fontainbleau in 1771
and formed part of the
elaborate furnishings
of the Comte's
appartments at the
château following his
marriage on May 14,
1771 to Marie-Josèphe
de Savoie.

Louis XVI tulipwood,
amaranth and vernis
martin secretaire à
abattant
Late 18th century
23 in. (57.5 cm) wide
Sold 3.5.83 in
New York for $88,000
(£55,696)

One of a pair of Empire mahogany fauteuils
In the manner of G. Jacob
Stencilled R.D. 1063
Sold 19.5.83 in London for £19,440 ($30,326)

Louis XVI giltwood fauteuil de bureau
Attributed to Georges Jacob
23½ in. (59.5 cm) wide
Sold 6.6.83 at Godmersham Park for £34,560 ($54,604)

Louis XV amaranth commode in the manner of Charles Cressent
64¾ in. (164.5 cm) wide
Sold 9.12.82 in London for £91,000 ($146,880)

Louis XV tulipwood, amaranth and marquetry bombé commode
By A. Delorme
Stamped Delorme JME and with an AF monogram
58 in. (147 cm) wide
Sold 19.5.83 in London for £86,400 ($134,784)

Regence giltwood side table
52 in. (132 cm) wide
Sold 6.6.83 at Godmersham Park for £91,800 ($145,044)

Opposite

Louis XV giltwood fauteuil
Attributed to Louis Delanois
28¾ in. (72.5 cm) wide
Sold 6.6.83 at Godmersham Park for £70,200 ($110,916)

Louis XV giltwood canapé à oreilles
By N. Heurtaut
Stamped N. Heurtaut
56¾ in. (144 cm) wide
Sold 19.5.83 in London for £32,400 ($50,544)

Louis XVI black
lacquer secretaire à
abattant
By Martin Carlin
Stamped M. CARLIN
35 in. (89 cm) wide
Sold 9.12.82 in
London for £626,400
($1,002,240)

Opposite

Louis XVI black
lacquer and ebony
bureau plat and
cartonnier
By Martin Carlin
Stamped M. CARLIN
Clock movement
signed *Robin horloger
De Mgneur le Duc de
Chartres*
The bureau 64 in.
(163 cm) wide
The cartonnier 56 in.
(142 cm) high
Sold 9.12.82 in
London for £453,600
($725,760)

One from a set of eight
Louis XV giltwood
fauteuils
By J-B Lebas
Four stamped
I. Lebas
Sold 19.5.83 in
London for £86,400
($134,784)

Louis XIV ebony and boulle side table
After a design by André Charles Boulle
47 in. (120 cm) wide
Sold 14.4.83 in London for £162,000 ($243,000)

Louis XVI ormolu-mounted boulle marquetry and ebony bibliotheque basse
Stamped E*LEVASSEUR, JME
Late 18th century
78¾ in. (199 cm) wide
Sold 20.11.82 in New York for $209,000 (£130,625)

Pair of Louis XVI ormolu-mounted Chinese porcelain vases
The porcelain late Qianlong
18¾ in. (47.5 cm) high
Sold 19.5.83 in London for £59,400 ($92,664)
Previously sold at Christie's 1.7.65 for £2,940

William III tapestry
panel
Signed in the selvedge
I.L.C. and with
Brussels town mark
108½ x 89 in.
(276 x 226 cm)
Sold 13.12.82 at Hill
Court, Ross-on-Wye
for £20,520 ($32,832)
Now at the Palace of
Het Loo

Flemish tapestry
Late 15th century
84 x 85 in. (213 x 216 cm)
Sold 6.6.83 at Godmersham Park for £140,400 ($221,832)

The Artois Clock
Louis XVI ormolu
and Carrara marble
mantel clock
21¾ in. (65 cm) wide
Sold 19.5.83 in
London for £129,600
($202,176)

Chippendale
mahogany kneehole
bureau
Townsend or
Goddard Shop,
Newport, Rhode
Island
1760-1785
38¼ in.
(97.7 cm) wide
Sold 2.6.83 in
New York for
$627,000 (£396,835)

Chippendale mahogany chest on
chest
Philadelphia
1765-1780
44¾ in. (113.6 cm) wide
Sold 22.1.83 in New York for
$99,000 (£66,000)
From the Contents of
The Lindens

Right

One from a set of six Chippendale walnut side chairs
Philadelphia, 1760-1775
40⅛ in. (101.9 cm) high
Sold 22.1.83 in New York for $71,500 (£47,666)
From the Contents of The Lindens

Far right

One of a pair of walnut side chairs
Philadelphia, 1740-1760
20 in. (50.8 cm) wide
Sold·2.6.83 in New York for $66,000 (£41,772)

Right

Oak and pine chest with drawer
Wethersfield, Connecticut, 1685-1700
47½ in. (120 cm) wide
Sold 2.6.83 in New York for $88,000 (£55,696)

Chippendale mahogany sofa
Philadelphia, 1765-1785
94½ in. (240 cm) wide
Sold 22.1.83 in New York for $264,000 (£176,000)
Record auction price for an American sofa
From the Contents of The Lindens

Two from a set of 12 mahogany dining chairs
New York, 1765-1785
25 in. (63.5 cm) wide
Sold 22.1.83 in New York for $308,000 (£205,333)
Record auction price for a set of American chairs
These chairs descended from Matthew Clarkson, a Revolutionary officer who became a major-general in the New York State Militia and a member of the Society of Cincinnati. After the war he served as New York State senator and president of the Bank of New York.
From the Contents of The Lindens

One of a pair of Florentine
rosewood and pietra dura table
cabinets
The stand North European,
probably German
The cabinet mid-17th century,
the stand *c.* 1700
The cabinet 33 in. (84 cm)
wide; the stand 38½ in.
(98 cm) wide
Sold 2.12.82 in London for
£59,400 ($95,040)

Dutch or Flemish bronze of
Hercules and Cacus
Early 17th century
11¾ in. (30 cm) high
Sold 20.6.83 in London for
£17,280 ($26,957)

Tuscan gilt bronze
fountain figure of a
winged putto
Late 15th or early
16th century
24¼ in.
(61.5 cm) high
Sold 20.6.83 in
London for £194,400
($303,264)
From the collection of
Mrs Patrick Gordon-
Duff-Pennington

English marble statue of Venus
By John Gibson
Mid-19th century
Carved with tortoise and inscribed
I. GIBSON FECIT ROMAE
46½ in. (118 cm) high
Sold 15.12.82 in London for £20,520
($33,653)

American marble statue of Cleopatra
By William Wetmore Story
Inscribed with a monogram for
W. Story and ROMA 1878
Statue 54½ x 49¾ x 27½ in.
(138.5 x 126 x 69 cm)
Sold 4.11.82 in London for £81,000
($136,890)
From the collection of The
Worshipful Company of Goldsmiths

American marble statue of Medea
By William Wetmore Story
Inscribed with a monogram of w's
and s's and ROMA 1866
Statue 77 x 27¼ x 26 in.
(195 x 69 x 66 cm)
Sold 4.11.82 in London for £30,240
($51,106)
From the collection of The
Worshipful Company of Goldsmiths

French terracotta
statuette of *La Comedie*
By Louis-Claude
Vassé
Signed Ludovicus
Vassé ft. 1765
22 in. (56 cm) high
Sold 15.12.82 in
London for £8,640
($14,170)

German fruitwood
group, probably
Adam and Eve
Attributed to
Leonhard Kern
17th century
12¾ in.
(32.5 cm) high
Sold 15.12.82 in
London for £15,120
($24,797)

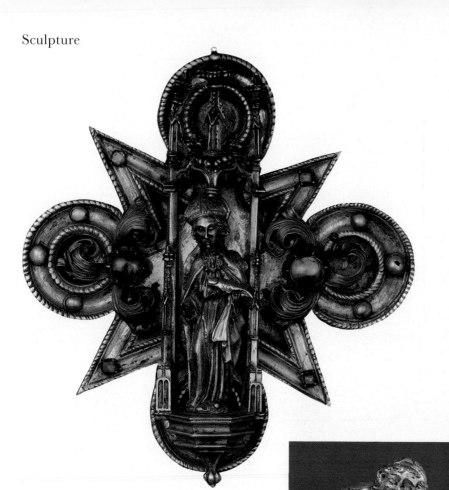

Above

German parcel gilt silver morse of St. Ulrich
Late 15th century or early 16th century
4½ x 4¼ in. (11.5 x 11 cm)
Sold for £24,840 ($40,246)

Above

Rhenish gilt bronze Corpus Christi
Second quarter 12th century
2⅝ x 2¼ in. (6.5 x 6 cm)
Sold for £14,040 ($23,026)

French gilt bronze statuette
Late 15th century
2¾ in. (7 cm) high
Sold for £7,020 ($11,513)

All sold 15.12.82 in London

French plaster bust of
Robert Fulton
By Jean-Antoine
Houdon
Signed *houdon f*
c. 1804
27 in. (68.5 cm) high,
including socle
Sold 20.11.82 in
New York for
$242,000 (£151,250)

A collection of mother-of-pearl
17th century, probably German
Sold 6.6.83 at Godmersham Park for a total of £41,148 ($65,013)

CLOCKS AND WATCHES

Swiss gold minute repeating split-second chronograph with perpetual calendar and moon phases
Signed *Patek Philipp and Co., Geneva, no.112413*
1902
2$^{1}/_{16}$ in. (53 mm) in diameter
Sold 28.6.83 in New York for $49,500 (£31,935)

JOHN KNIBB: Silver
mounted ebony
bracket clock
Signed *John Knibb
Oxon*
c. 1675-80
11¾ in.
(29.5 cm) high
Sold 10.3.83 in
London for £19,440
($29,354)

THOMAS TOMPION, "No.483": Ebonised sidereal and mean time regulator longcase clock of month duration
Signed *Tho: Tompion* on plaque obscuring joint signature *Tho: Tompion: Edw. Banger London*
c. 1709-11
7ft 5in. (226 cm) high
Sold 24.12.82 in London for £34,000 ($55,080)
The earliest recorded example of a sidereal and mean time regulator. The assumption that the deadbeat escapement of this clock is not original may now have to be revised after close examination of the plates and spectroscopic analysis of the wheels

JOSEPH KNIBB:
Charles II walnut
Dutch-striking table
clock
Signed *Joseph Knibb
Londini fecit*
c. 1672-73
20 in. (51 cm) high
Sold 7.10.82 in
London for £17,280
($29,303)

Far right

THOMAS TOMPION:
Charles II walnut longcase clock, not numbered
Signed *Tho: Tompion Londini Fecit*
6ft 10in.
(208.3 cm) high
Sold 20.7.83 in
London for £20,520
($31,806)

Right

THOMAS TOMPION:
Charles II walnut longcase clock, not numbered
Signed *Tho: Tompion Londini Fecit*
6ft 6in. (198 cm) high
Sold 10.3.83 in
London for £21,600
($32,616)

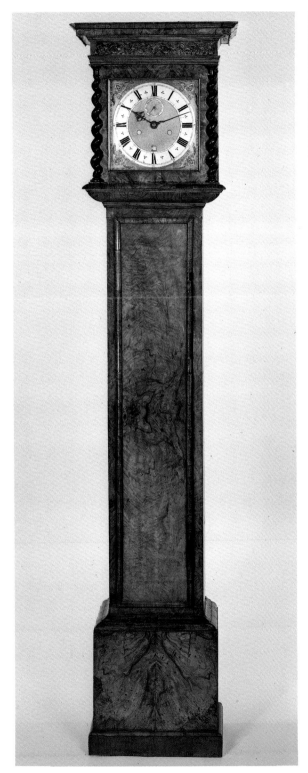

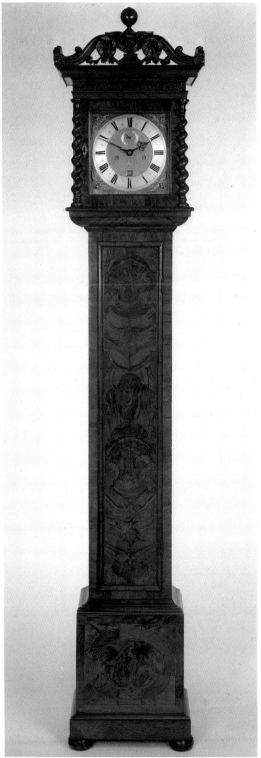

DAN. QUARE, STE. HORSEMAN:
George I ebonised bracket clock
Signed *Dan. Quare Ste: Horseman*
London 246
12½ in. (31.8 cm) high
Sold for £15,120 ($24,494)

R. BOCKET: Late Stuart tortoiseshell
bracket clock
Signed *R. Bocket London*
16 in. (40.5 cm) high
Sold for £5,940 ($9,623)

JOSEPH KNIBB: Ebonised Dutch-
striking bracket clock
Signed *Joseph Knibb Londini Fecit*
c. 1685
12¼ in. (31 cm) high
Sold for £15,120 ($24,494)
From the collection of Mrs Gilbert
Edgar

All sold 16.12.82 in London

Augsburg silver 'Madonna'
automaton clock
Movement by
David Haisermann
c. 1620
12⅛ in. (29.5 cm)
Sold 1.12.82 in Geneva for
Sw.fr.88,000 (£25,360)

Swiss vari-coloured gold hunter-cased minute-repeating chronograph
Signed *Jules Jurgensen, Copenhagen, no.14062*
2⅛ in. (55 mm) in diameter
Sold 28.6.83 in New York for $22,000 (£14,193)
From the collection of the Episcopal Church Home for Children, York, South Carolina

Swiss gold and enamel 'kitchen' automaton watch
Attributed to Simon Gounoulhou
c. 1810
2⅛ in. (60 mm) in diameter
Sold 29.11.82 in Geneva for Sw.fr.62,000 (£17,919)

Late Huaud enamel watch
Interior signed *Freres Huaut*
Movement signed *Louijs Gautier*
1⁵/₁₆ in. (40 mm) in diameter
Sold 16.12.82 in London for £12,960 ($20,995)

Swiss gold and enamel automaton watch
c. 1797
Inscribed *Hommage au General Bonapart Comd. en Chef l'Armée de'Italie, Genev 20 Novembre 1797*
2⅛ in. (60 mm) in diameter
Sold 29.11.82 in Geneva for Sw.fr.88,000 (£25,434)

Gold, enamel and pearl-set watch for the Chinese market
Signed *Barrauds, Cornhill, London No.9531*
1818
2⅛ in. (60 mm) in diameter
Sold for Sw.fr.50,600 (£16,323)

Gold, enamel and diamond-set lever watch for the Near East market
Movement by Audemars
Early 20th century
2⅛ in. (55 mm) in diameter
Sold for Sw.fr.143,000 (£46,129)

One of a 'mirrored' pair of gold and enamel duplex watches for the Chinese market
Signed *Vaucher Fleurier*
2¹/₁₆ in. (52 mm) in diameter
Sold 10.3.83 in London for £18,360 ($27,724)

Gold, enamel and pearl-set watch for the Chinese market
Signed *Charman, London No.9079*
c. 1800
2⅛ in. (62 mm) in diameter
Sold for Sw.fr.48,400 (£15,613)

All sold 10.5.83 in Geneva

Pair of gold-mounted
agate chatelaines with
watch and etui
The watch by Cabrier,
London 7180
c. 1755
7⅞ in. (20 cm)
greatest length
Sold 29.11.82 in
Geneva for
Sw.fr.126,500
(£36,561)

Opposite

Swiss gold and enamel
automaton cylinder
watch
Inscribed *Ilbery London*
2⅜ in. (5.9 cm)
diameter
Sold for £14,040
($21,621)

Swiss vari-coloured
gold musical watch
Stamped M & P
4⁵/16 in. (10.9 cm)
long
Sold for £10,800
($16,632)

Swiss gold and enamel
quarter-repeating
cylinder watch
2⅛ in. (5.6 cm)
diameter
Sold for £31,320
($48,232)

All sold 20.7.83 in
London

Italian viola
1765
By Joannes Baptista Guadagnini
Length of back 15⅛ in. (38.4 cm)
Sold 21.6.83 in London for £18,360 ($28,458)

JEWELLERY

Diamond, chalcedony and pearl choker
Signed by Lalique
Sold 12.5.83 in Geneva for Sw.fr.121,000
(£39,032)

Pair of graduated
diamond collet
pendant earrings
Sold for £23,760
($36,828)

Antique necklace of 46
graduated diamond
collets
Sold for £51,840
($80,352)

All sold 22.6.83 in
London

Navette-diamond
single-stone ring
Weight 3.95 carats
D colour, internally
flawless
Sold for £48,600
($75,330)

Antique necklace of 34
graduated diamond
collets
Sold for £118,800
($184,140)

Both sold 22.6.83 in
London

Diamond choker of 33 graduated circular-cut diamonds
Total weight of 33 round diamonds approximately 125.42 carats
Sold 7.6.83 in New York for $297,000 (£186,792)

Diamond necklace of
173 pear-shaped,
circular and
marquise-cut
diamonds, on
baguette-cut stems
Sold 13.10.82 in
New York for
$264,000 (£155,294)

Diamond pendant set with an octagon-cut
diamond weighing approximately
51.68 carats
Sold 12.4.83 in New York for $159,500
(£104,248)

 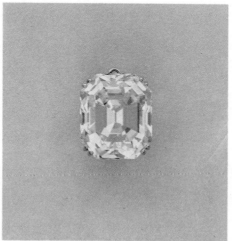 

Diamond ring set with a marquise-
cut diamond weighing
approximately 21.86 carats
Sold 13.10.82 in New York for
$264,00 (£155,294)

Oval-cut diamond weighing
approximately 30.28 carats
With a gemological certificate stating that
the diamond is D colour
Sold 12.4.83 in New York for $638,000
(£416,993)

Diamond ring set with a pear-shaped
diamond weighing approximately
9.55 carats
Signed by Winston
With a gemological certificate stating that
the diamond is D colour, internally
flawless
Sold 14.12.82 in New York for $198,000
(£123,750)

Diamond ring set with an oval-cut
diamond weighing approximately
20.28 carats
With a gemological certificate stating that
the diamond is D colour and VS$_1$
Sold 7.6.83 in New York for $291,500
(£183,333)

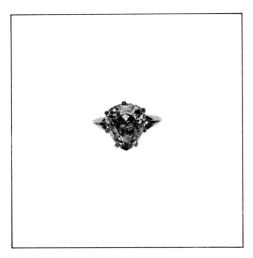

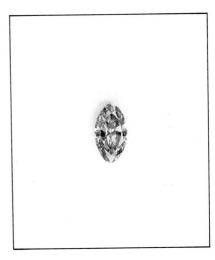

The Marie-Antoinette Blue Diamond
Diamond ring set with a greyish-blue
diamond weighing 5.46 carats
An expertise by Gübelin states that the
colour of the diamond is natural
Sold 12.5.83 in Geneva for
Sw.fr.440,000 (£141,935)

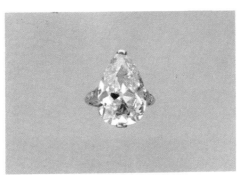

Diamond ring set with a pear-shaped
diamond weighing approximately
12.31 carats
With gemological certificate stating that
the diamond is E colour and potentially
flawless
Sold 13.10.82 in New York for $231,000
(£144,375)

Blue diamond ring set with a
navette-cut diamond weighing
4.61 carats
Signed by Bulgari
With a certificate from the
Gemological Institute of America
stating that the diamond is of fancy
blue natural colour, clarity VVS2
Sold 12.5.83 in Geneva for
Sw.fr.605,000 (£195,161)

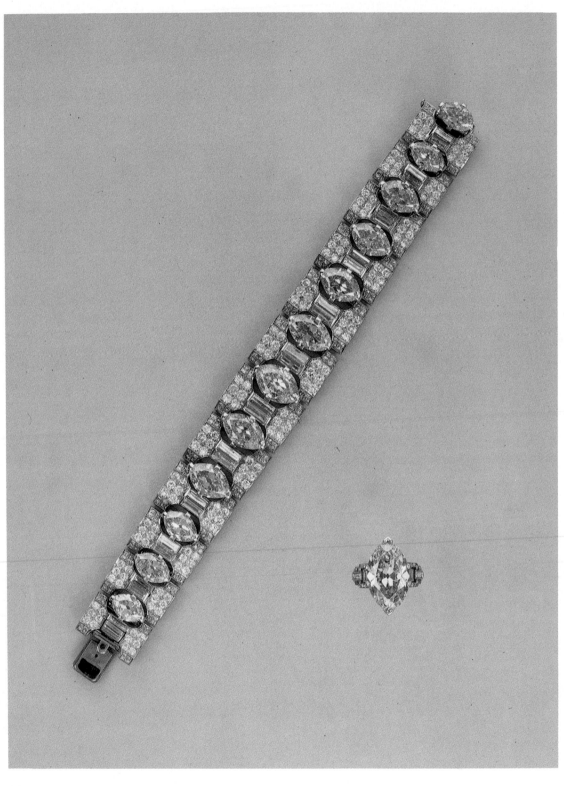

Diamond bracelet set
with 12 graduated
oval and marquise-
cut fancy intense
yellow diamonds
Signed by Cartier,
number 3817859
Sold for $715,000
(£467,320)

Diamond ring set with
an oval-cut fancy
yellow diamond
weighing
approximately
9.69 carats
With gemological
certificate stating that
the diamond is of
fancy intense yellow
natural colour and
VS$_1$
Sold for $297,000
(£194,118)

Both sold 12.4.83 in
New York

Antique emerald, diamond and pearl brooch pendant set with a cut-cornered rectangular emerald weighing 8.35 carats The pendant pearl is detachable
Sold 20.10.82 in London for £41,040 ($69,768)

Antique diamond quatrefoil brooch set with four pear-shaped diamonds
By Freidrich-Theodor Koëchli, St. Petersburg
Sold 12.4.83 in New York for $110,000 (£71,895)

Antique cluster brooch set with cushion-shaped sapphire and diamond collet
Sold 4.5.83 in London for £24,840 ($39,744)

Victorian sapphire, diamond and pearl brooch pendant set with an inverted pear-shaped sapphire weighing 25.62 carats
Sold 22.6.83 in London for £56,160 ($87,048)

A Superb Kashmir Sapphire

MARY M. MURPHY, F.G.A.

For several decades, the most costly gems sold at auction have been large diamonds. However, this year, the highest price for a gemstone at auction was the $770,000 (£484,276) paid for a 37.78 ct. sapphire.

Mounted as a ring, this superb sapphire was the highlight of a fine collection consigned by the Estate of Irene Martin. Mrs. Martin was the widow of Townsend Martin, a New Yorker well-known to the sports world as a thoroughbred breeder and former owner of the New York Jets football team. Townsend Martin was a true connoisseur of rare gems, and it was he who selected most of the jewellery worn by his wife.

In addition to its superb quality, Mrs. Martin's sapphire was particularly desirable because of its mineralogical origin. The colour and gemological characteristics of the gem showed that it was mined in Kashmir, the classic locality for the world's finest sapphires.

The colour and lustre of a fine Kashmir sapphire distinguishes it from sapphires of any other locality. While perfect transparency is demanded in any other variety of fine sapphire, the Kashmir sapphire has a hazy, misty appearance. This haze throughout the stone arises from the presence of minute crystals of another mineral, called rutile, which occurs as inclusions within the sapphire crystal during growth. This slight milkiness imparts a softness to the general appearance of the stone and enriches the beauty of the gem. Kashmir sapphires are also distinguished by their intensity of colour. A fine Kashmir stone is a saturated blue without traces of green, violet or purple. In contrast, sapphires from Sri Lanka tend to be pale in colour, those from Burma are often slightly purplish, while sapphires from Thailand and Australia tend to be inky or greenish in colour.

The Kashmir mines are situated in a remote valley at an elevation of 15,000 feet above sea level. The valley is within the Zanskar Range of the North West Himalaya Mountains, several days journey south-east of the town of Scrinagar. Being near to the limits of perpetual snow, the valley is accessible only by horseback and only for a few months a year.

The sapphire deposits came to general notice in 1881 when a hunter came upon a rockslide which exposed a cliff studded with sapphire crystals. The sparce local population had known of the source for untold ages, but they regarded the stones as mere curiosities of little value. Because of the wild, inhospitable nature of the terrain and the extremely harsh climate, mining activity is still very limited 100 years after the discovery of the deposit.

Because of the romance associated with the Kashmir mining locality, and because the mine is associated with the finest quality sapphires, collectors place great importance on the mine origin of Kashmir sapphires as part of the gem's provenance. The same is true for rubies from Burma, diamonds from Golconda in southern India and emeralds from Muzo or Chivor,

Sapphire and diamond ring
Sold 7.6.83 in New York for
$770,000 (£484,276)

Colombia. Over the past four decades, considerable research has been performed by Dr. Edourd Gübelin of Geneva, Switzerland in determining mine origins for coloured stones through their gemological characteristics. The rise in the study of mine origin has intensified demand for gems whose origins can be pinpointed by the nature of their quality and inclusions. Not all gems can be documented, particularly stones which are virtually flawless. However, a gem which has a telltale inclusion which proves it originated in a classic mine will command a premium price, which allows it to be compared to a fine painting with a clear artist's signature. Mrs. Martin's 37.78 ct. sapphire was accompanied by a gemological certificate from Gemological Laboratory Gübelin and there is no question that the documentation added to the desirability of the gem.

Above

Antique sapphire and diamond brooch set with a domed cabochon sapphire weighing 24.66 carats With an expertise by Gübelin stating that the sapphire is from Kashmir
Sold 2.12.82 in Geneva for Sw.fr.242,000 (£69,540)

Above

Pair of cabochon sapphire and diamond ear pendants, each set with a pear-shaped sapphire weighing approximately 24.29 and 26.21 carats The sapphire drops detach to be worn as brooches
Sold 7.6.83 in New York for $176,000 (£110,691)

Invisibly-set sapphire and diamond flower brooch
Signed by Van Cleef and Arpels
Sold 12.5.83 in Geneva for Sw.fr.115,500 (£37,258)

Sapphire ring set with a cut-cornered rectangular sapphire weighing 22.32 carats
Sold 2.12.82 in Geneva for Sw.fr.330,000 (£94,827)

Pair of bouton pearl and square-cut diamond ear-studs
The pearls have been tested at The Gem Laboratory
Sold for £21,600 ($33,480)

Necklace of 41 graduated pearls with navette-diamond single-stone snap
By Cartier
The pearls have been tested by sample X-ray at The Gem Laboratory
Sold for £54,000 ($83,700)

Necklace of 43 graduated pearls with navette-diamond single-stone snap
The pearls have been tested by sample X-ray at The Gem Laboratory
Sold for £59,400 ($92,070)

All sold 22.6.83 in London
From the Godmersham Park Collection

The Necklace of the Duchesse d'Angoulême

DIANA SCARISBRICK

This ruby and diamond necklace is remarkable not only for its beauty but also for its provenance, being one of the Crown Jewels of France. The great treasury, founded by Francois I in 1530, was plundered by thieves in 1792, and subsequent attempts to reassemble it were intensified by Napoleon after his coronation as Emperor in 1804. Aware of the pyschological value of pomp and magnificence as a means of commanding respect he determined to align his regime with the old hereditary monarchy and return to the spirit of Versailles under Louis XIV. He commissioned marvellous jewels for himself and Josephine, and after the marriage in 1810 with Marie Louise, Archduchess of Austria, ordered his court jeweller, Francois Regnault Nitot to create a series of parures–matching suites of diamonds, pearls, and coloured stones – of a quality unrivalled anywhere in Europe. Each parure consisted of a crown topped by an eagle, massive diadem, comb, necklace, earrings, girdle or clasp for the waist, and a pair of bracelets. The firm of Chaumet, Nitot's successors, have preserved his light and decorative design for the ruby and diamond jewellery made for the Empress in 1810, and the Imperial Inventory records delivery of a parure of oriental rubies and brilliants on January 16th, 1811. This entry does not correspond in all respects with Nitot's model, which could have been altered in the intervening months, such remountings being frequent — and in November 1811 the ruby and diamond crown was remodelled once again. The Crown Jewels passed to the Bourbons in 1814, and they, like Napoleon, felt the need for the brilliance of large and frequent receptions to reinforce their authority. Louis XVIII was a widower, and in the absence of a queen, Marie Therese de Bourbon, his courageous and tragic niece, wife of the future heir to the throne, the Duc d'Angoulême, wore the jewels remodelled by Paul Nicolas Menière, son of the jeweller of her parents, Louis XVI and Marie Antoinette. In collaboration with his son-in-law Everard Bapst, Menière kept the essential elements of Nitot's parure but organised them into a more robust and simple composition, characteristic of the Restoration style. The plaques of large gold mounted oval rubies framed in small round brilliants set in silver were arranged with matching pendants hanging from smaller rubies crowned with diamond palmettes between plain diamond collets. The red velvet fire of the rubies is enriched by the white light radiating from the brilliants, resulting in a jewel of majestic simplicity. This design, dating from 1816, was so successful that it survived all changes of fashion throughout the 19th century and was worn by the elegant Empress Eugenie. Alfred Bapst, her jeweller cased the parure in red leather boxes stamped with the insignia of Napoleon III. After the fall of the Second Empire the Republic decided to dispose of these powerful symbols of royalty, and the French Crown jewels were therefore sold by auction in Paris in 1887, Tiffanys of New York being a major purchaser. Some of the ornaments from the ruby and diamond parure were bought by the American financier Bradley Martin, for his daughter Cornelia, wife of the Earl of Craven, and the pair of bracelets sold after her death in 1961 are now displayed in the Galerie d'Apollon in the Louvre. Like them, the necklace illustrates the taste and skill which the Parisian jewellers, Nitot and Menière, brought to the service of the Bourbon and Napoleonic dynasties.

Ruby and diamond
ring
Mounted with a
cushion-shaped ruby
weighing 11.94 carats
With an expertise by
Gübelin stating that
the ruby is from
Burma
Sold for Sw.fr.495,000
(£142,241)

Antique ruby and
diamond necklace
Sold for Sw.fr.990,000
(£284,483)

All sold 2.12.82 in
Geneva

Antique emerald and diamond
pendant brooch set with a 19.97
carat emerald and an emerald
drop of 5.87 carats
Sold 12.5.83 in Geneva for
Sw.fr.242,000 (£78,064)

Emerald and diamond brooch pendant
set with an oval cabochon emerald
weighing 59.95 carats and two drop-
shaped cabochon emeralds
Sold 12.5.83 in Geneva for Sw.fr.143,000
(£46,129)
By family tradition, the brooch was
given by Napoleon to the Empress
Marie-Louis who in turn bequeathed it to
Archduke Leopold (1823-1898), Viceroy
of Milan (cf. the will of Empress Marie-
Louis, Archivo di Stato of Parma). When
Archduke Leopold died the 24th May
1898, the brooch was inherited by his
brother, Archduke Rainier (1827-1913),
whose wife, Marie-Caroline, wears the
brooch in a portrait painted by Carl
Blaas (in a private collection), engraved
by Freidrich Leybold.

Emerald and diamond ring set
with a rectangular emerald of
15.92 carats
Sold 2.12.82 in Geneva for
Sw.fr.187,000 (£53,736)

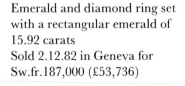

Emerald and diamond ring set
with a rectangular-cut emerald
weighing 14.09 carats
Signed by Boucheron, Paris
Sold 2.12.82 in Geneva for
Sw.fr.242,000 (£69,540)

Emerald and diamond ring set
with a cut-cornered rectangular
emerald of 5.02 carats between
two circular-cut diamonds
weighing 4.35 and 4.31 carats
Sold 2.12.82 in Geneva for
Sw.fr.187,000 (£53,736)

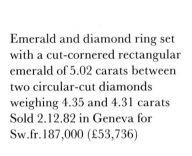

Emerald and diamond ring set with a
rectangular-cut emerald weighing
approximately 10.13 carats
Signed by Winston
Sold 7.6.83 in New York for $198,000
(£124,528)

Antique emerald circular cluster brooch pendant set with a hexagonal emerald weighing 10.02 carats and 12 cushion-shaped smaller emeralds
Sold for £129,600 ($200,880)

Antique emerald necklace of 32 graduated collets
Sold for £97,200 ($150,660)

Both sold 22.6.83 in London

Emerald and diamond
brooch set with six
circular cut emeralds
weighing
approximately 16.98
carats
Signed by
Tiffany & Co.,
Paris
Sold 12.4.83 in
New York for
$110,000 (£71,895)

Antique emerald and diamond collet
pendant cross
Sold 22.6.83 in London for £16,200
($25,110)

Antique emerald and
diamond padlock
heart locket
Sold 22.6.83 in
London for £7,020
($10,881)
From the
Godmersham Park
Collection

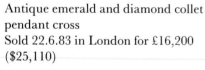

Emerald ring set with
an emerald weighing
3.34 carats
Sold 30.3.83 in
London for £45,360
($66,226)

Antique rectangular
precious topaz brooch
Sold for £3,888
($6,221)

Emerald and diamond
pendant
Signed Fic. Boucheron
Sold for £16,200
($25,920)

Antique diamond
necklace of 54
graduated collets
suspending a
detachable pearl and
diamond circular
pendant brooch
Sold for £54,000
($86,400)

Emerald and diamond
ring set with an
emerald weighing
approximately
3.11 carats
Sold for £3,780
($6,048)

All sold 24.11.82 in
London

Antique alexandrite clasp
set with a cushion-shaped
alexandrite weighing
approximately 10.00 carats
Sold for £34,560 ($53,568)

Pearl and diamond sautoir
Sold for £4,860 ($7,533)

Pearl and diamond bracelet
Sold for £5,940 ($9,207)

Aquamarine two-stone
pendant
Sold for £7,560 ($11,718)

Ruby and diamond ring set
with a cushion-shaped ruby
Sold for £23,760 ($36,828)

Emerald ring set with
hexagonal emerald
Sold for £10,800 ($16,740)

All sold 22.6.83 in London

ART NOUVEAU
AND ART DECO

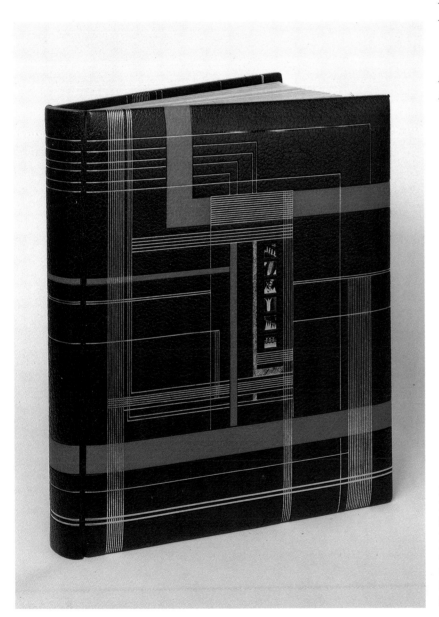

FRANCOIS-LOUIS SCHMIED: *Ruth et Booz*
Paris, 1930
Signed
Edited, illustrated and bound by Schmied
Number 5 of 7 volumes of a limited
edition of 162
Sold 28.11.82 in Geneva for
Sw.fr.24,400 (£7,113)

Pony apple blossom leaded glass and bronze lamp
By Tiffany Studios, New York
17½ in. (44.5 cm) high
Sold 28.11.82 in Geneva for Sw.fr.55,000 (£16,034)

Opposite

Squash leaded glass, favrile glass and
bronze table lamp
By Tiffany Studios, New York
31½ in. (80 cm) high
Sold 11.12.82 in New York for $198,000
(£121,472)

Detail of a floral skylight leaded glass window
By Tiffany Studios, New York
182½ x 88 in. (463.5 x 224 cm)
Sold 11.12.82 in New York for $99,000 (£64,285)

Leaded glass 'Tree of Life' door
Designed by Frank Lloyd Wright, executed by Linden Glass Co. for
the Darwin D. Martin House, Buffalo, 1903-05
65¼ x 25¾ in. (165.5 x 66 cm)
Sold 26.5.83 in New York for $110,000 (£68,750)
Record auction price for a Frank Lloyd Wright window and record
auction price for an American stained glass window.
Sold by order of the Estate of Mrs Darwin R. Martin

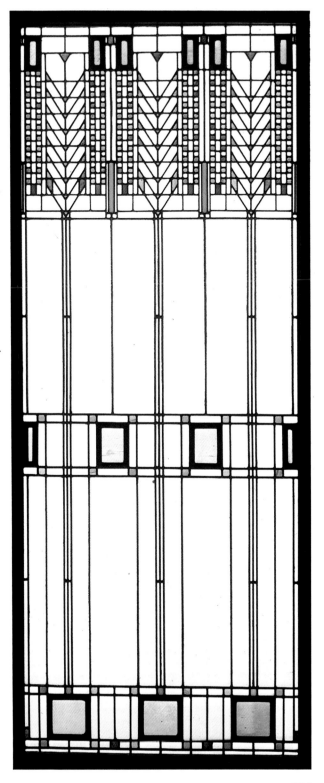

The greatest single influence on Frank Lloyd Wright's designs was the
art of Japan. The inspiration for the window design known as the 'Tree
of Life' is likely to have come from the well-known Kabuki theme of
Sogo No Goro in the arrow-sharpening scene of the play *Koizume Sumida
Gawa*, where the stage scenery features oversized arrows. This theme is
found repeatedly in Japanese theatre prints of the 18th and 19th
century, and Wright was known to have had examples in his large
collection that he collected passionately and viewed daily.

Many unfamiliar with this market were startled by the $110,000
(£68,750) price paid for the 'Tree of Life' door and four other windows
and doors from the same house. In fact, the price is not surprising
considering Wright's world-wide prominence and influence, and if one
were to associate Wright with a single image it would be the 'Tree of
Life' window. The international recognition and interest in Wright's
work was reflected in the diversity of buyers for these five lots, including
private collectors and American, English and French Museums.

Inlaid and carved bureau de dame in the 'umbel' pattern
By Emile Gallé
Signed Gallé in marquetry
38 in. (96.5 cm) wide
Sold 8.5.83 in Geneva for Sw.fr.27,500 (£8,461)

Ormolu-mounted and marquetry vitrine 'aux nenuphares'
By Louis Majorelle
67 in. (170 cm) high
Sold 28.11.82 in Geneva for Sw.fr.66,000 (£19,241)

Above and far right

Pair of inlaid mahogany, ebony and leather side chairs
c. 1907
43½ in. (110.5 cm) high
Sold separately for
$28,600 (£17,546) and
$28,500 (£17,208)
Record auction price for an American 20th century chair

Centre

Honduras mahogany, ebony and glass vitrine
c. 1907
66 in.
(167.6 cm) wide
Sold for $39,600
(£24,294)

All sold 11.12.82 in New York

Left

The '1919 Armchair'
By Gerrit Rietveld
Blue painted and stained panga panga wood
35¾ in. (91 cm) high
Sold 29.7.83 in London
for £7,560 ($11,642)

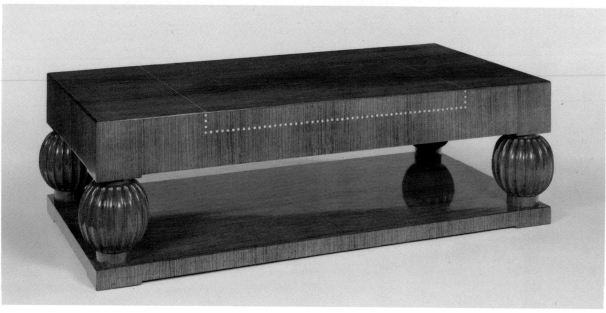

Lacquered wood and chrome screen,
'Lysistrata'
By Donald Deskey
c. 1930
53¾ x 83¾ in. (135 x 213 cm)
Sold 9.10.82 in New York for $26,400
(£16,500)
Record auction price for a Deskey screen
Donald Deskey created this screen for
Gilbert Seldes, a noted drama critic of the
time, who was writing an adaptation of
Aristophanes' play *Lysistrata*

Opposite above

Stoneware stemmed vase
By Hans Coper
20¾ in. (52 cm) diameter
Sold 29.6.83 in London for £3,780
($5,821)

Opposite below

Rosewood and mother-of-pearl
coffee-table
By Emile-Jacques Ruhlmann
Branded Ruhlmann and with the 'A'
atelier mark
57¼ in. (144.8 cm) wide
Sold 11.12.82 in New York for
$33,000 (£20,625)

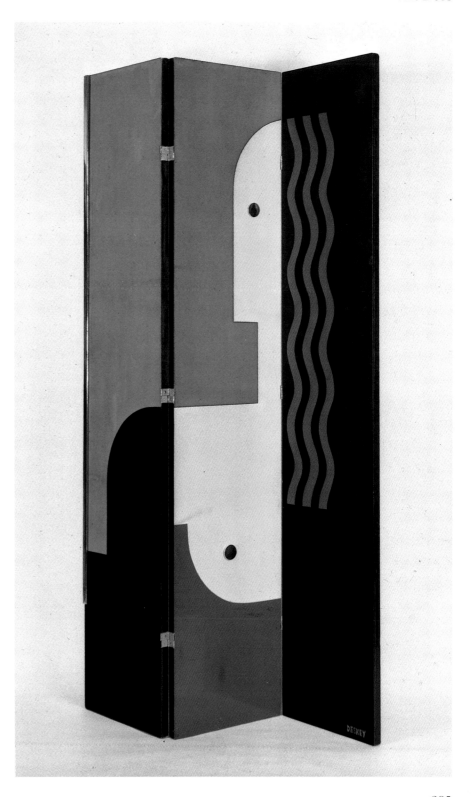

Opposite

TAMARA DE LEMPICKA: *Nu aux Buildings*
1930
Signed
Oil on canvas
28¼ x 35½ in. (72 x 90 cm)
Sold 26.5.83 in New York for $209,000
(£130,630)
Record auction price for a work by the
artist

Etched and engraved glass sculpture
By Aristide-Michel Colotte
Signed
25¾ in. (65½ cm) high
Sold 8.5.83 in Geneva for Sw.fr.46,400 (£14,275)

287

French gilt and cold-painted bronze and ivory figure of 'Thais'
By Demêtre Chiparus
Signed
22⅛ in. (56.2 cm) high
Sold 26.5.83 in New York for $55,000 (£34,380)
Thais, a courtesan in Christian Alexandria, is the subject of an opera written in 1894 by Jules Massenet. Based on a story by
Anatole France, and one of the composer's most popular works, the opera was performed in Paris almost annually until after
World War II

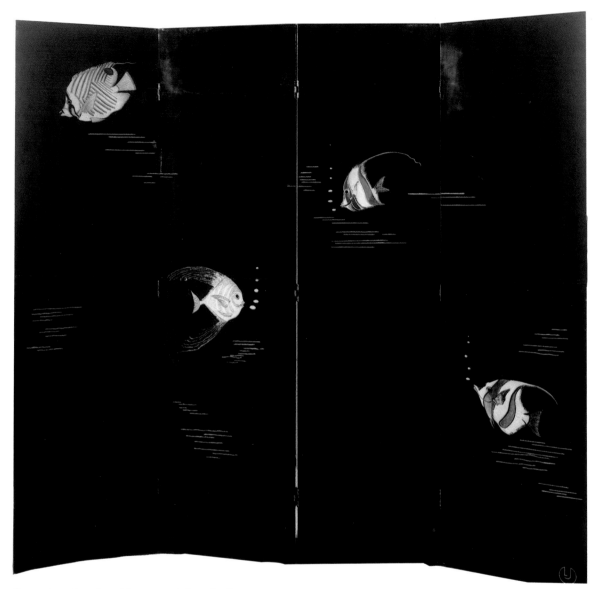

Carved, painted and lacquered four-leaf screen
By Leon Jallot
With intaglio monogram
82 x 73¼ in. (208 x 186 cm)
Sold 29.6.83 in London for £9,720 ($14,969)

A selection of
Bizarre pottery
By Clarice Cliff
Sold 29.6.83 in
London for a total
of £6,489 ($9,993)

SILVER

Parcel-gilt vase and plinth
By J.S. Hunt
London, 1846
Stamped on plinth: 'Hunt & Roskell late
Storr Mortimer & Hunt'
39 in. (99.5 cm) high
Sold 12.5.83 in Geneva for Sw. fr. 264,000 (£85,161)
The Emperor's Plate was established at Ascot in 1844 by Tsar
Nicholas I after his state visit to Windsor as the guest of
Queen Victoria. A new cup was presented every year until the
outbreak of the Crimean War in 1854. This vase was
described in the Illustrated London News of 5 June 1847.
The panels on the vase depict scenes from the life of Peter the
Great and those on the plinth depict Russian Imperial residences.
The Imperial arms are applied to each angle.

Queen Anne chocolate-pot
By William Denny, 1705
10 in. (25.4 cm) high
Sold for £15,660 ($24,430)

Queen Anne coffee-pot
By Simon Pantin, 1709
9¾ in. (24.7 cm) high
Sold for £28,080 ($43,080)
Previously sold at Christie's
28.3.62 for £2,800 and
26.3.69 for £11,500

William III chocolate-pot
By William Lukin I, 1701
8½ (21.6 cm) high
Sold for £32,400 ($50,544)

All sold 12.7.83 in London

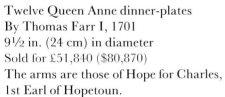

Twelve Queen Anne dinner-plates
By Thomas Farr I, 1701
9½ in. (24 cm) in diameter
Sold for £51,840 ($80,870)
The arms are those of Hope for Charles,
1st Earl of Hopetoun.

Sold 12.7.83 in London

Octagonal basket
By George Lewis
Late 17th century
12⅝ in. (32.3 cm) wide
Sold 15.6.83 in London for £28,080 ($43,805)
From the collection of the Whitaker Family

Pair of Regency silver-gilt wine-coolers
By Robert Garrard, 1816
10¾ in. (27.3 cm) high
Sold 15.6.83 in London for £33,480 ($52,229)
Applied Royal arms and the badge of the
Order of the Bath
From the collection of the Whitaker Family

Opposite

George II gold two-handled cup and cover
By David Willaume II, 1739
12½ in. (37.1 cm) high
Sold 15.6.83 in London for £237,600 ($370,656)
From the collection of The Lord Walpole, T.D.
The cover is surmounted by the Walpole crest and the cup engraved on
one side with the arms of the Netherlands and on the other with the arms
of the Seven Provinces of the Netherlands.

The Morgan Collection of English and Continental Silver

D.W. WRIGHT, Registrar and Archivist, *The Pierpont Morgan Library*

New York's October 26 sale of silver by the descendants of the American financier Pierpont Morgan (1837-1913) brought to light a notable group of English and Continental pieces, many of historical importance. This cache, containing many of the last remaining pieces of silver from the distinguished collection Morgan assembled between 1890 and 1913, provided a glimpse of taste during the Edwardian Age and the discernment of a pre-eminent collector of that period.

Among the rediscovered pieces, the Renaissance silver-gilt tazza with a finial of the Roman Emperor Vespasian and finely chased bowl with scenes derived from Suetonius's *The Twelve Caesars* embodied the taste of the *fin de siècle* collector. It originally formed part of a set of tazzas, each surmounted by one of the 12 Caesars, which was associated with Ippolito Aldobrandini (Pope Clement VIII) and Prince Giovanni Battista Pamphili. The set subsequently passed into the hands of the English retailer Kensington Lewis and was recorded in his stock in 1826. Later the tazzas belonged to Charles Scarisbrick from whose estate they were sold by Christie's in 1861 for £1,200. By 1891, six of them, including the Vespasian tazza, belonged to the Parisian dealer Frederic Spitzer who replaced the bases with "grander" Spanish mounts. The late John Hayward described the set as "the most impressive single monument of Italian and perhaps European goldsmiths' work of the 16th century." American collectors and museums agreed; the Morgan tazza remained in private hands at $231,000 (£135,882).

An unusual event in scholarship and collecting was afforded by the sale of the Morgan Charles II silver-gilt toilet set, and this opportunity was recognised when the service fetched $418,000 (£245,882), a record for English silver at auction in North America. Each of the 12 pieces was clearly marked and the set bore a striking resemblance to another by the same maker, the famous Calverley service now in the Victoria and Albert Museum.

A favorite Morgan piece was the small Henry VIII beaker, an extremely rare example of English silver from the period ending about 1525. Only two other earlier hall-marked English beakers are known to exist. This circular bowl with its broad band of flat-chased lobes appealed to modern tastes as well and made $187,000 (£110,000), thereby establishing a value for pieces of this early period which so rarely reach the auction room.

Four finely preserved George II candlesticks by Paul de Lamerie achieved $209,000 (£122,941), the highest price ever paid for Lamerie's work at auction. The beauty of their rococo forms was supplemented by their association through an engraved crest and coronet with one of Lamerie's leading patrons, Algernon Coote, 6th Earl of Mountrath and Bradford. Lamerie was also represented in the sale by a set of three condiment urns. These only extant examples of this shape by the famous maker brought $77,000 (£45,294).

An Indian jewelled and enamelled gold garniture, made in Benares or Lucknow in the late 18th century, might also be said to epitomize the taste of the Belle Epoque. Its green enamel

Opposite

The Aldobrandini Vespasian tazza Renaissance silver-gilt tazza 1570-85 Probably Italian, the Spanish foot and stem of the period but associated, unmarked except for later 19th century French import mark 16 in. (40.6 cm) high Sold for $231,000 (£135,882)

ground enriched with native-cut diamonds and a multi-colored enamelled parrot finial held a special appeal: Edward VII himself seems to have admired these vessels when he visited Morgan's London house in 1906. The four pieces made $60,500 (£35,588).

An elaborately chased and repoussé salver of the Charles II period which fetched $55,000 (£32,353) contained a tantalizing clue to its maker's identity. The mark, PB in monogram, may well be related to the name and date inscribed on the base, "Paul Beuren Ao 1663." The quality and richness of the salver, along with the possible identification of a maker, lent further historical and scholarly interest to the sale.

Other notable lots included a German parcel-gilt nef by Tobias Wolff, $26,400 (£15,530); four fine Henry VIII apostle spoons in two lots, $12,100 and $11,000 (£7,117 and £6,470); a Rhenish tiger-ware jug with parcel-gilt mount from 1557, one of the few remaining pieces made during the reign of Mary I, sold for $35,200 (£20,705); a William and Mary parcel-gilt Monteith, $31,900 (£18,764); and a Storr covered vegetable dish $28,600 (£16,823).

The emphasis in many of the lots was clearly on history, association, and quality. Bidders registered for the sale from nine states and the District of Columbia, and from Canada, West Germany, England, and Switzerland; the sold total for the 68 lots was $1,598,520 (£940,306). The prices achieved might not have surprised Morgan who was always willing to pay for unique works of art, but he undoubtedly would have been pleased that many of the pieces remained in private hands. The sale gave modern collectors a chance to emulate Morgan, a man who enjoyed the chase and acquisition of beautiful objects with a passion rarely equalled in this century.

Opposite

Charles II silver-gilt toilet-service
London, 1683
Maker's mark WF
Sold for $418,000 (£245,882)

Henry VIII beaker
London, 1525
Maker's mark (?) SC
4 in. (10.2 cm) diameter
Sold for $187,000 (£110,000)

Elizabeth I silver-gilt
mounted tigerware jug
Norwich, 1568
Maker's mark a five-
petalled rose
9 in. (22.8 cm) high
Sold 23.11.82 in
London for £18,360
($29,192)

Pair of George II
silver-gilt waiters
By Francis Nelme, 1728
6 in. (15.3 cm)
diameter
Sold for £7,344
($11,530)

George II silver-gilt
cream-jug
By Peter Archambo,
1733
Sold for £7,020
($11,021)

George II silver-gilt
cream-jug
Unmarked, *c.* 1730
Sold for £3,888 ($6,104)

All sold 27.4.83 in
London

Pair of George II
tea-caddies
By Paul de Lamerie
1742
Sold 12.7.83 in
London for £28,080
($44,535)

George IV silver-gilt
centrepiece
By Paul Storr, 1821
19⅞ in. (50.5 cm) high
Sold 27.4.83 in London for
£25,920 ($40,694)

The Ismay Testimonial
By Hunt and Roskell, 1881, 1884
Parcel-gilt service
Sold 33.11.82 in London for £64,800 ($109,512)
The centrepiece is engraved 'The service of Plate is presented to THOMAS HENRY ISMAY, Esq., by the Shareholders of the WHITE STAR LINE in token of the esteem in which he is held by them, and in recognition of the fact that to the sound judgement, untiring energy, and singleness of purpose he had displayed in the management of their affairs for the past 15 years, the prosperity of the Company is mainly due. Liverpool, 1884'
The service was designed and modelled by G.A. Carter of the Hunt and Roskell design department
From the collection of a member of the Ismay Family

Caster
By John Coney
Boston, 1710-1720
5⅞ in. (14.9 cm) high
Sold 22.1.83 in
New York for $55,000
(£35,483)

Parcel-gilt mounted coconut tankard
Rapperswil, first half of 17th century
Struck twice on base with town mark
6¼ in. (15.5 cm) high
Sold 1.12.82 in Geneva for Sw.fr.30,800 (£8,876)

Louis XVI two-handled soup-tureen, cover, and stand
By Joseph-Robert Auguste
Paris, 1784
Tureen 11 in. (28 cm) diameter
Sold 1.12.82 in Geneva for Sw. fr.198,000 (£57,061)
The pair to this tureen stands in the Museé Nissim de Camondo, Paris

Parcel-gilt model of an owl
Maker's mark S, a triangle above
Augsburg, *c.* 1630
8¼ in. (21 cm) high
Sold 12.5.83 in Geneva for Sw. fr.52,800
(£17,032)

Opposite

Silver-gilt hanukah lamp
Maker's mark a pineapple
Probably Polish, *c.* 1810
20½ in. (51.4 cm) high
Sold 25.10.82 in New York for $42,900
(£25,235)

Silver-gilt
toilet- service
By Johann
Pepfenhauser,
Abraham IV
Drentwett, Johann
Gelb, Abraham IV
Warnberger, Johann
V Beckert and others
Augsburg, 1745-1747
and 1747-1749
Sold 12.5.83 in
Geneva for
Sw. fr.286,000
(£92,158)

OBJECTS OF ART
AND VERTU

Gold-mounted, enamelled and jewelled
jasper egg-shaped bonbonnière
By Fabergé
Workmaster Michael Perchin
St. Petersburg, 1886-1903
2¾ in. (7 cm) long
Sold 17.12.82 in London for £22,680
($36,741)

Jewelled badge of the Imperial Order of St. Andrew
Late 18th, early 19th century
Inscribed on the reverse in Russian
The Empress Marie Feodorovna agreed to wear this Badge on November 26th, 1890
5⅛ in. (13 cm) high
Sold 11.5.83 in Geneva for Sw.fr.330,000 (£106,451)

Diamond-set badges of this type were only worn by the Emperor, the Tsarina and the Tsarevich. They always had to be returned to the Treasury of the Crown Jewels. The Grand Duchess Catherine Pavlovna, however, was the preferred sister and *confidante* of Tsar Alexander I. The Grand Duchess married Duke George of Oldenburg who received the Order of St. Andrew and the title *Imperial Highness* on his marriage in 1809. He died in 1812, leaving a son, Duke Peter of Oldenburg, by whom the order was inherited.

A member of the Oldenburg family gave the present badge to Empress Maria Feodorovna, the wife of Emperor Alexander III, on the occasion of St. George's Day in 1890 as stated on the engraved inscription. Later, a great grandson of Grand Duchess Catherine, Duke Peter of Oldenburg, married Grand Duchess Olga Alexandrova, sister of Tsar Nicholas II in 1901.

Right

Parcel-gilt and niello
plate
Late 17th century
9⅜ in. (23.8 cm)
diameter
Sold for Sw.fr.14,300
(£4,145)

Centre

Silver-gilt and nielloed
beaker
Late 17th century
16⅞ in. (17.3 cm)
high
Sold for Sw.fr.27,560
(£7,925)

Above right

Parcel-gilt and niello
plate
*c.*1680
Stamped with double-
headed eagle mark,
Moscow
9¼ in. (23.5 cm)
diameter
Sold for Sw.fr.16,500
(£4,783)

All sold 30.11.82 in
Geneva

Enamelled gold
Imperial presentation
cigarette-case
Interior engraved
Ludvig Castenskiold
By Fabergé
Workmaster August
Holmström
St. Petersburg,
late 19th century
3¾ in. (9.5 cm) long
Sold for Sw.fr.24,200
(£7,014)

Jewelled and
gold-mounted
bowenite desk-clock
By Fabergé
Workmaster Michael
Perchin
St. Petersburg,
late 19th century
3⅞ in. (9.7 cm) high
Sold for Sw.fr.37,400
($10,778)

Enamelled gold
cigarette-case
Interior engraved
*From Baron Maurice de
Rothschild 1913*
By Fabergé
Workmaster August
Holmström
St. Petersburg,
late 19th century
Sold for Sw.fr.20,900
(£6,058)

Silver-gilt and agate revolving
frame
By Fabergé
Workmaster Victor Arne
St. Petersburg, late 19th century
9⅛ in. (23 cm) high
Sold 30.11.82 in Geneva for
Sw.fr.50,600 (£14,582)

Silver-gilt and enamel
combined table clock
and photograph frame
By Fabergé
Workmaster Michael
Perchin
St. Petersburg,
1899-1908
9⅞ (24 cm) long
Sold 11.5.83 in
Geneva for
Sw.fr.63,800 (£20,580)

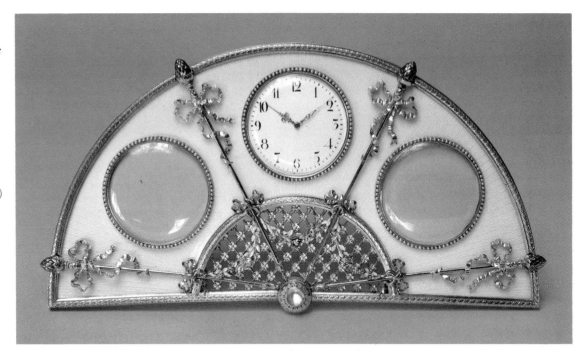

Pair of two-colour
gold-mounted
jewelled, enamelled
and cut-glass perfume
bottles
By Fabergé
Moscow, late 19th
century
Retailed by Tiffany,
London
5 in. (12.6 cm) high
Sold 23.3.83 in
New York for $15,500
(£22,940)
From the collection of
the late Elizabeth
Arden

Silver-mounted
bowenite desk-set
By Fabergé
Workmaster Julius
Rappoport
St. Petersburg, 1893
The candlesticks
6⅝ in. (17 cm) high
Sold 11.5.83 in
Geneva for
Sw.fr.74,800 (£24,129)

Enamelled parcel-gilt
Imperial presentation
photograph frame
By Fabergé
Workmaster, Hjalmar
Armfeldt, assaymaster
A. Richter
St. Petersburg,
1899-1908
13 in. (33 cm) high
Sold 23.3.83 in
New York for $17,600
(£11,871)
The frame encloses an
original photograph,
signed and dated, of
Nicholas II by the
Boisonnas et Eggler
Studio, St. Petersburg

Silver-gilt and shaded
cloisonné enamel kovsh
By Fabergé
Engraved on base *5. Marz 1908*
Signed with initials of Fedor
Rückert
Moscow, 1899-1908
11⅜ in. (29 cm) long
Sold 11.5.83 in Geneva for
Sw.fr.33,000 (£10,645)

Silver-gilt and cloisonné
enamel Imperial presentation
vodka set
Inscribed *Presented to the
Marquess of Lansdowne, Viceroy of
India, by H.I.H. The Czarevich of
Russia, Calcutta 1891*
Signed with Imperial Warrant
mark of P. Ovchinnokov
Moscow, 1891
The tray 24 in. (61 cm) long
Sold 30.11.82 in Geneva for
Sw.fr.60,500 (£17,435)

The Archangels Michael
and Gabriel
Greek
Dated 1716
47⅞ in. (121.5 cm) high
Sold 29.4.83 in London for £8,640
($13,478)

JOHN SMART: *John Sutton*
Signed with initials and dated
1791
2³⁄₈ in. (6 cm) high
Sold for £3,780 ($6,426)

JOHN BARRY: *An Infantry Officer*
2⁵⁄₈ in. (6.5 cm) high
Sold for £1,944 ($3,305)

NATHANIEL PLIMER: *A Lady*
Signed with initials and dated
1787
1³⁄₄ in. (4.5 cm) high
Sold for £2,808 ($4,774)

JOHN BOGLE: *Commodore George Johnstone*
Signed
3⁷⁄₈ in. (9.9 cm) high
Sold for £21,600 ($36,720)
Previously sold at Christie's
24.6.35 for 85 gns. , 16.2.49 for
92 gns. and 9.2.60 for 170 gns.

All sold 12.10.82 in London
All from the collection of
Edward Grosvenor Paine

GEORGE ENGLEHEART: *Anne Chetwode*
Dated 1787
1⁷⁄₈ in. (4.8 cm) high
Sold for £5,400 ($9,180)

Right

FRAGONARD: *A Boy*
1½ in. (4 cm) high
Sold for £4,140
($6,748)

Far right

FRAGONARD: *A Boy*
1½ in. (4 cm) high
Sold for £6,480
($10,562)

Centre

FRAGONARD: *A Boy*
2⅝ in. (6.8 cm) high
Sold for £15,120
($24,646)

Right

FRAGONARD: *A Girl*
2⅝ in. (6.8 cm) high
Sold for £4,140
($6,748)

Far right

SCHOOL OF HALL:
A Child
2½ in. (6.4 cm) high
Sold for £5,400
($8,802)

All sold 8.12.82 in
London
From the collection of
Mrs Elizabeth Parke
Firestone

Both Jean Honoré Fragonard and his wife, Anne-Marie Gérard, are known to have painted miniature portraits, but as they did not sign, no certain criterion has been found of deciding which of the two artists painted the group of miniatures sold under the name of Fragonard.

FERDINANDO QUAGLIA: *Julie-Lucine d'Angennes*
Signed and dated 1819
3 in. (7.7 cm) high
Sold 10.5.83 in Geneva for Sw.fr.31,900 (£10,290)

DANIEL SAINT: *A Lady, possibly Hortense de Beauharnais*
Signed
12½ in. (32 cm) high
Sold 27.4.83 in London for £5,940 ($9,266)

Right

RICHARD COSWAY: *Madame de Montolieu, Baroness St. Hippolite*
2¾ in. (7 cm) high
Sold 13.7.83 in London for £6,480
($10,044)

Below right

JOHN SMART: *Robert Home*
Signed with initials and dated 1791
2¾ in. (7 cm) high
Sold 27.4.83 in London for £6,480
($10,109)

Below left

HENRY EDRIDGE: *General Sir Ralph Darling, G.C.H.*
2½ in. (6.3 cm) high
Sold 13.7.83 in London for £5,184
($8,035)

JOHN SMART: *A Lady*
Signed with initials and dated 1767
1⅜ in. (3.6 cm) high
Sold 13.7.83 in London for £6,480
($10,044)

JOHN SMART: *A Young Boy*
Signed with initials and dated 1776
1½ in. (3.8 cm) high
Sold 13.7.83 in London for £8,100
($12,555)

Left

ANDREW PLIMER: *Hugh Hammersley (1774-1840)*
3 in. (7.5 cm) high
Sold 13.7.83 in London for £2,376
($3,682)

Gold signet ring with crystal
bezel
*c.*1570
Sold for £3,240 ($5,054)

Gold and enamel locket
*c.*1620
1¼ in. (3.2 cm) high
Sold for £3,672 ($5,728)

Long gold chain
Late 16th or early 17th century
6ft 4in. (193 cm) long
Sold for £8,640 ($13,478)

All sold 28.4.83 in London

Gem-set gold pendant: St. George
slaying the Dragon
Attributed to Abraham Lotter
*c.*1580
South German
2¼ in. (5.7 cm) long
Sold 10.5.83 in Geneva for
Sw.fr.33,000 (£10,645)

Sardonyx cameo of the
Emperor Shah Jahan
The cameo possibly Mughal,
*c.*1660; the mount Golconda/
Hyderabad late 17th or early 18th
century
1¼ in. (3.2 cm) diameter
Sold 7.12.82 in London for £6,480
($10,368)

Louis XV gold and enamel presentation set comprising:

Snuff-box by Jean Formey, Paris, 1760
2¾ in. (7 cm) wide

Bonbonnière with rock-crystal body
By François Tiron, Paris, 1760
2⅝ in. (6.8 cm) wide

Chatelaine with rock-crystal scent-bottle between bonbonnière and thimble case
By Jean Marc Antoine Ecosse, Paris, 1762
8 in. (25 cm) long

Chatelaine with pendant watch, calendar key and fob-seal
By Jean Marc Antoine Ecosse, Paris, 1760
7 in. (18 cm) long

Sealing-wax case
Paris, 1760
4¾ in. (12.5 cm) long

All sold 28.4.83 in London for a total of £140,000 ($219,024)

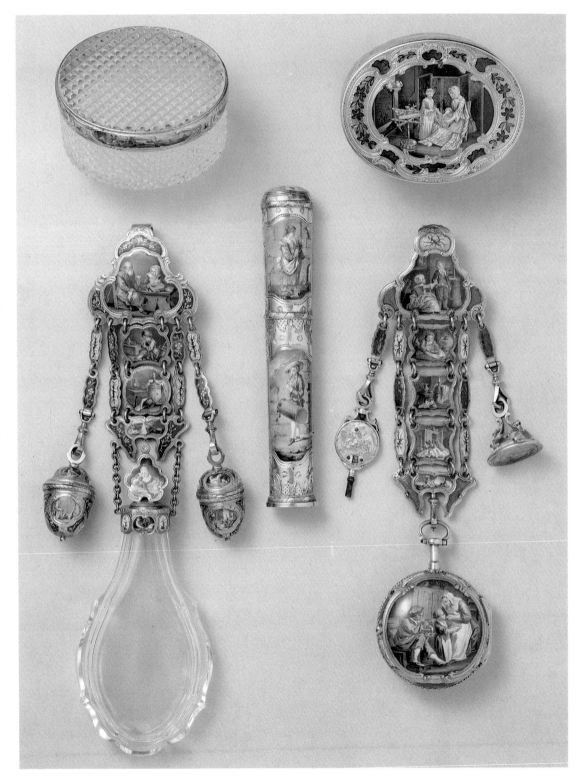

Collection of scent-bottles
*c.*1760
Sold individually 8.12.82 in
London for a total of £13,068
($20,909)
From the collection of the late
Sir Hugh Dawson, Bt.

THE KORFF BOX
Russian gold and enamel box
Attributed to Jean-Pierre Ador
*c.*1765, unmarked
3⅛ in. (8 cm) long
Sold 10.5.83 in Geneva for
Sw.fr.385,000 (£124,193)
The cover of the box is enamelled with
the Russian Order of St. Andrew, the
front with the Prussian Order of the
Black Eagle, the reverse with the Polish
Order of the White Eagle, the sides
with the Orders of St. Anne and St.
Alexander Nevsky and the base with
the coat-of-arms of the Korff family

Typical for mid-18th century Russian snuff-boxes, this box is umarked. By comparison of technical and stylistic details, it can safely be attributed to Jean-Pierre Ador. Ador, a Swiss who was active in Geneva until 1759, settled in St. Petersburg at the beginning of the 1760s and became goldsmith to the Court of Catherine the Great. Based on the biography of Baron Korff, this snuff-box can be dated between 1762 and 1766, that is the year he received the Order of St. Andrew and the year of his death.

Baron Nicolaus von Korff, 1710-1766, was one of the German Balts who made a career in Russia where he joined the army at the age of fourteen. He married in 1740 Catherine, the daughter of Count Carl Skavronski. She was the cousin of Grand Duchess Elizabeth, daughter of Peter the Great and his wife Catherine I, née Skavronska. With the accession to the throne of Elizabeth Petrovna on November 24th, 1741, Korff was promoted to the Imperial Guard and given a mission to accompany the designated heir to the Russian throne, Duke Carl Peter of Holstein, (later Tzar Peter III) from Kiel to St. Petersburg. He received in 1742 the Order of St. Anne of Holstein.

In connection with the Treaty of Abo and a mission to Stockholm, Korff was decorated in 1744 with the Order of St. Alexander Nevsky. During the Seven Years' War he received, in 1758, as the Russian Governor of parts of Prussia with residence in Köngberg, the Polish Order of the White Eagle. While the head of the Police of St. Petersburg from 1760 onwards, he was decorated by Peter III on January 10, 1762, with the Order of St Andrew.

The same year Frederick the Great awarded him the Prussian Order of the Black Eagle and Catherine the Great made him a member of the State Council. Korff died in St. Petersburg on April 24th, 1766.

The Geneva Snuff-box and its Hallmarks

GEZA VON HABSBURG

A PRELIMINARY INVESTIGATION

Swiss-made snuff-boxes have always set something of a problem for specialists. Only a few decades ago no Swiss 18th century gold snuff-box had been identified with certainty. All objects bearing anything resembling French hallmarks were unfailingly given a French origin. Today collectors have realized, often to their dismay, that Switzerland was one of Europe's main centres in the production of objects of vertu and that large numbers of snuff-boxes previously called French were in fact the produce of Geneva. We have also learned that apart from Geneva no other city in Switzerland made gold snuff-boxes in the 18th century.

The Genevese gold boxes closely follow examples made in Paris, often copying them quite literally, which accounts for many previous errors of attribution. They were doubtlessly produced for exportation to France in competition with the far more expensive French originals. To the layman a French original and a Swiss contemporary copy look very much alike. Specialists, however, denote a certain lack of quality in detail and a touch of gaudiness in the choice of enamel colours on which to base their attribution to Geneva. Many a Swiss 18th century box defies localization without a close-up look at the hallmarks.

It is only after the loss of their rich French clients following the Revolution that the Genevese craftsmen ceased to imitate their favourite prototypes. With the annexation of the City of Geneva by Napoleon in 1797, a new type of snuff-box makes its appearance. Of flat rectangular shape, it is applied with polychrome enamel plaques decorated mainly with mythological subjects. This type of box, unmistakably Swiss, is becoming increasingly popular with collectors today.

THE PROBLEM OF THE GENEVA HALLMARKS

Paris gold boxes of the 18th century usually show three sets of hallmarks – the 'charge' of the *Fermier Général*, the date-letter of the *Maison Commune* and the maker's mark – applied on the interior of the cover, base and side, as well as a minute 'discharge' mark on the lip. *Geneva* box-makers imitate these marks, stamping cover and base (never the sides), and very rarely using a 'discharge'. Moreover, Geneva hallmarks are applied haphazardly, mixing-up the correct dates of the *Fermier* with date-letters which do not correspond. These marks are in most cases recognizable as 'fakes'. Geneva snuff-boxes, as their French counterparts, also bear a type of maker's mark, a set of crowned initials, often recurring on boxes similar in style. These still continue to baffle experts. Although the hallmarking of silver was statutory in Geneva, no gold snuff-box of the 18th century has been found with a Geneva City mark. Apparently there seems to have been no hallmark foreseen to indicate the official standard of 18 carat gold used.

328

Swiss four-colour gold
snuff-box
Geneva, *c*.1780
Maker's mark
crowned PG, bearing
French prestige marks
3¼ in. (8.4 cm) long
Sold 10.5.83 in
Geneva for
Sw.fr.30,000 ($9,677)
This type of box is
modelled on French
Louis XV originals

A careful study of the Geneva City archives shows why such a confusion reigns in the identification of the Genevese snuff-box, and why the long-due monograph on the subject has been so long delayed. A *Livre de Maîtrise des Orfèvres* was begun in 1701, setting out the regulations that govern the Corporation. Candidate master-goldsmiths had to submit a *chef d'oeuvre* (masterpiece). But although the hallmarking of silver is exactly prescribed, no mention is made of any obligation to mark gold objects. The *Livre* lists all gold and silversmiths admitted into the Corporation from 1657 to 1797 (last entry in April). As from 1719 it also mentions the *chef d'oeuvre* submitted. Most candidates were jewellers, only a few were silversmiths or goldsmiths. Although silver snuff-boxes were made as early as 1721, the first gold snuff-box submitted dated from 1733. It should be noted that the 20 goldsmiths who specialised in the production of gold boxes were called *maîtres orfèvres*, not *monteurs de boëtes*. The latter belonged to a separate Corporation and were only allowed to make watch-cases, another major Genevese export article. Only one of the above-mentioned 18th century goldsmiths is known to us through his work, Jean George Remond of Hanau, *maître* in 1783. Unfortunately, none of the initials of any goldsmiths tally with those found on 18th century Geneva snuff-boxes – the most frequently found are crowned, EC, FJ, LFT, MM. One thing is certain: these *poinçons*, be they the initials of individuals or perhaps the mark used by a *fabricant* or retailer are found on boxes consistent in style and obviously made by one goldsmith or an association of such craftsmen working together.

In 1798 (and until 1814) Geneva becomes *Département du Léman*. At that time, 231 gold and silversmiths were still active. On May 1, 1799, their Corporation was disbanded and the proceeds from the sale of its assets shared among them. These included the copper plates on which all craftsmen had entered their *poinçon*, and which were sold as scrap metal for 144 florins. During this period a small control mark 'G' in a cartouche was introduced and used until 1815.

Below

Swiss gold and enamel snuff-box
Geneva, *c*.1790
Maker's mark crowned LFT
Painted in the manner of
Claude Lorrain
2⅞ in. (6 cm) diameter
Sold 10.5.83 in Geneva for
Sw.fr.14,000 (£4,516)

Left

Swiss documentary enamelled
gold snuff-box
Geneva, *c*.1790
Maker's mark crowned R
Inscribed *Ne suis-je pas homme et ton frere*
3¼ in. (8.4 cm) long
Sold 10.5.83 in Geneva for
Sw.fr.22,000 (£7,097)

In 1816 a new register *Insculpation des Poinçons des Fabricans d'ouvrage d'or et d'argent du Départment du Léman* was begun, listing 166 craftsmen still active in 1815 together with drawings of the hallmarks they used up to this date. A number of these occur on early 19th century snuff-boxes and can thus be identified. The best known of these are Jean George Remond, Jean-Baptiste Mercier, François Magnin, Jean-François Bautte et Jacques-Dauphin Moulinié.

This "roll-call" of gold and silversmiths includes only about a dozen survivors from the 18th century *Livre de la Maîtrise*. Lozenge-shaped hallmarks were introduced in 1816, all active craftsmen's punches modified to meet the new requirements, and struck on two copper plates still in existence. *Poinçons* nos. 1-166 are those of the craftsmen who had been active between 1800 and 1815. As from 1816 and until 1863 the *poinçons* and names of further 528 *maîtres orfèvres* were entered (nos.201-729).

After 1816 no city hallmark, no charge, discharge or control mark allows the certain attribution of any gold box to Geneva. This is done today only on the basis of style and the recognition of a *poinçon de maître* if it can be found on the two plates in the Geneva archives.

This is but a brief summary of how far research has advanced up to this day. A monograph on the Geneva snuff-box is in preparation for 1984.

Above

Swiss gold and enamel
musical automaton
box
Geneva, *c*.1800
Maker's mark
crowned M
The miniature by
Jean-Louis Richter
3½ in. (8.8 cm) long
Sold 30.11.82 in
Geneva for
Sw.fr.286,000 (£82,421)

Louis XV enamelled vari-coloured gold snuff-box
By Jean-Marie Tiron
Paris, 1766, with the poinçons of J.J. Prevost and the
countermark of his successor J. Alaterre
3 in. (7.6 cm) long
Sold 19.11.82 in New York for $143,000 (£89,375)
From the collection of Mrs Elizabeth Parke Firestone

Louis XV enamelled gold snuff-box
By Jean-Marie Tiron
Paris, 1759, with the poinçon of E. Brichard
The miniatures attributed to Pierre-Nicolas de Malliée
3½ in. (9 cm) long
Sold 19.11.82 in New York for $88,000 (£55,000)
From the collection of Mrs Elizabeth Parke Firestone

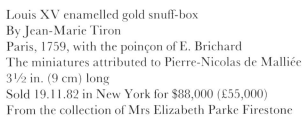

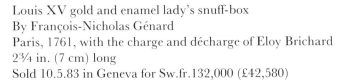

Louis XV gold and enamel lady's snuff-box
By François-Nicholas Génard
Paris, 1761, with the charge and décharge of Eloy Brichard
2¾ in. (7 cm) long
Sold 10.5.83 in Geneva for Sw.fr.132,000 (£42,580)

Louis XV enamelled three-colour gold snuff-box
Probably by J.F. Garand
Paris, 1764, with the charge and décharge of
Jean-Jacques Prevost
3½ in. (9 cm) long
Sold 30.11.82 in Geneva for Sw.fr.66,000 (£19,020)

Louis XV gold-
mounted Japanese
lacquer-box
By François Thomas
Germain
Paris, 1754, with the
poinçons of J. Berthe
3⅜ in. (8.5 cm) long
Sold for $176,000
(£110,000)

Louis XV jewelled
and enamelled gold
presentation snuff-box
By Daniel Govaers
(Gouers)
Paris, 1725, with the
poinçons of C. Cordier
Signed on the flange
Rondet aux Galleries
3¼ in. (8.3 cm) long
Sold for $308,000
(£192,500)
Both sold 19.11.82 in
New York
Both from the
collection of
Mrs Elizabeth Parke
Firestone

Gold freedom box celebrating the
signing of the Treaty of Nanking
By John Linnit
London, 1844
4 in. (10 cm) wide
Sold 28.4.83 in London for £28,080
($43,805)

George III enamelled gold
table-necessaire
By James Cox
London, *c.*1770, unmarked
The watch movement signed *Jas.Cox,*
London 1000
3⅛ in. (8 cm) long
Sold 10.5.83 in Geneva for
Sw.fr.275,000 (£88,709)

Continental enamelled and jewelled gold
snuff-box
Probably Austrian, *c*.1760, unmarked
3¼ in. (8.1 cm) long
Sold 19.11.82 in New York for $55,000 (£34,375)
From the collection of Mrs Elizabeth Parke
Firestone

German gold-mounted hardstone snuff-box
By Johann Christian Neuber
Dresden, *c*.1775, unmarked
Sold 10.5.83 in Geneva for Sw.fr.198,000
(£63,870)

A collection of
Chinese gold coins
1907-1925, sold for a
total of £24,950 ($39,920)

Vatican, Paul
III, 2-Fiorini di
camera, £8,800
($14,000)

Ferrara,
Hercules I
d'Este, Ducat,
£3,000 ($4,800)

Munster,
Friedrich von Wied,
Goldgulden,
£4,400 ($7,000)

Hall-in-
Schwaben under
Francis I,
Ducat, 1746,
£1,000 ($1,600)

Sassanian,
Hormizd II
(A.D. 303-309),
Dinar, £1,600
($2,500)

Fatimid, al-
Mustansir,
Dinar, A.H. 437,
£200 ($320)

Modena, Francis I
d'Este, 8-Scudi
d'or, £8,800
($14,000)

Bishops of Liège,
John of Bavaria,
Griffon d'or, £4000
($6,400)

Australia, George
V, Penny, 1930,
£1,800 ($2,900)

Henry VI, Noble,
London, £560
($900)

U.S.A., Massachusetts,
Pine Tree Shilling,
1652, £1,200 ($1,900)

Cromwell, Crown, 1658, £900 ($1,450)

Austria, Ferdinand III, 10-Ducats, 1683, £5,500
($8,800)

Duke of Marlborough,
Battle of Blenheim, 1704,
£130 ($210)

Willian IV, gold
Coronation medal, 1831,
£440 ($700)

William and Mary, silver
Coronation medal, 1689,
£140 ($220)

George II, gold
Coronation medal, 1727,
£650 ($1,050)

Anne, Battle of Malplaquet, 1709,
£420 ($670)

William III, Londonderry
Relieved, 1689, £360 ($580)

James II, Flight from Ireland,
1690, £280 ($450)

Coins and Medals

RAYMOND SANCROFT-BAKER

At the outset Harold Catchpole's Dickin Medal brought in by our consultant, John Hayward, was regarded with little more than curiosity. Given a provisional value of £250 it was certainly not envisaged as the high flier it was to become. But that was before Alison Beckett, art sales correspondent of *The Daily Telegraph*, and Graham Heathcote of *Associated Press* were to write of Mercury's exploits and capture the imagination of newspaper readers not only in the United Kingdom but throughout the world with stories of the Blue Hen's 480-mile non-stop flight with a secret message from Denmark during the Second World War; a flight which was to culminate in her being awarded the 'Animal V.C.'

The People's Dispensary for Sick Animals at Woking, founded by Maria Elizabeth Dickin, O.B.E., made the award to Mercury in 1946 for the 'most outstanding single performance' of any one pigeon on special service...one of 16,554 missions flown by British pigeons during the war of which only 1,842 were successful. Mercury's heroic flight took place July 30, 1942. The message, believed to be from a Danish resistance group, has never been made public under regulations governing publication of classified information for 50 years.

Pre-sale research and press inquiries were to reveal Mercury as the most famous of 31 pigeons to have been given the Dickin Medal awarded 53 times between 1942 and 1949. Other recipients have included 13 dogs, three horses and the last, posthumously, in 1949 to Simon the cat who was on board *HMS Amethyst* when the frigate made her famous dash down the Yangtse River.

'The Army took two birds from each of 50 fanciers, including my father's, all down the East Coast,' Mr Catchpole of Epsom Drive, Ipswich, recalled in the days leading up to the sale. 'We found out later that the birds were put in baskets and parachuted into Denmark. On this special mission Mercury was the only one that came home with a secret message in a tube on her leg. She was a very special bird...we all loved her.'

Following her heroic flight, Mercury lived out her days in retirement at Mr Catchpole's father's loft in Cemetery Road, Ipswich, where she was born. She died at the age of 10 and was buried in Mr Catchpole's garden.

Interest in Mercury's medal soared as the sale approached, including one enquiry from a former U.S. airman living in Dallas, Texas, who spent the war years parachuting pigeons, as opposed to people, into Europe. His commission bid was to fall far short of the mark, however. Mr Louis Massarella – known to fanciers for his world-famous pigeon stud near Loughborough – was to pay £5,000 ($7,750) for the medal together with Mercury's silver-plated Army Pigeon Service Award of 1944 and her certificates of appreciation from the Secretary of State for Air and the Secretary of State for War. They are for presentation to the Royal Pigeon Racing Association Museum.

Pair of medals to Mercury, Army Pigeon Service, Special Section, The Dickin Medal (1942), and The Army Pigeon Service Award, £5,000 ($7,750)

Seven to Flight Lieutenant
E.P. Roberts, M.C., D.F.C.,
D.C.M., £4,000 ($6,400)

The Most Noble Order of
the Garter, Lesser George,
Badge and Star, *c.* 1815,
£9,000 ($14,400)

CERAMICS AND GLASS

London Delft polychrome royalist
caudle-cup
Dated 1662
2⅞ in. (7.5 cm) high
Sold 13.6.83 in London for £41,040
($61,560)
Record auction price for a piece of
English pottery

Meissen group of the
Dutch or Tyrolean
dancers
Modelled by
J.F. Eberlein
c.1736
6⅛ in. (15.5 cm) high
Sold 4.7.83 in London
for £10,260 ($15,903)

Meissen Kakiemon tankard and cover with
silver-gilt mounts
1725-28
8¼ in. (21 cm) high
Sold 4.7.83 in London for £8,100 ($12,555)

Meissen Kakiemon Hob-in-the-Well plate
c.1725
9⅛ in. (23 cm) diameter
Sold 3.12.82 in Geneva for Sw.fr.33,000 (£9,483)

Meissen chinoiserie arbour figure
Modelled by Johann Gottlieb Kirchner
1730-35
17⅞ in. (45.5 cm) high
Sold 4.7.83 in London for £36,720
($56,916)
Now in the Toledo Museum of Art, Ohio

Ludwigsburg group, *Autumn*, from a set
of the seasons
Modelled by J. Göz with the assistance
of G. Fr. Riedel
1760-62
7¾ in. (19.5 cm) high
Sold 4.7.83 in London for £5,940
($9,147)

Pair of Nymphenburg white figures of the Virgin and St. John
Modelled by Franz Anton Bustelli
*c.*1756
12⅜ in. (31 cm) high
Sold 4.7.83 in London for £15,120 ($23,436)

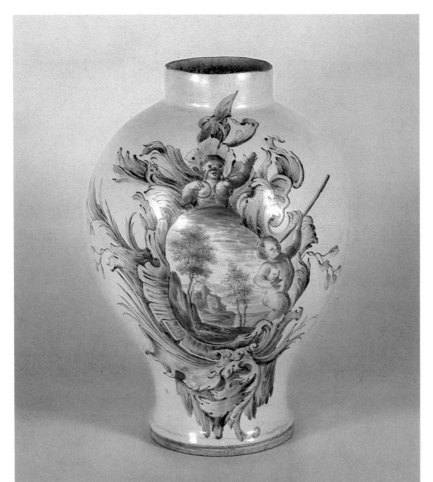

Höchst faience vase
Painted by Ignaz Hess
Painter's mark E.H.
c.1750
9⅞ in. (24 cm) high
Sold 28.3.83 in
London for £5,180
($7,563)

Below left

Strasbourg (Paul
Hannong) figure of a
running dog
Modelled by
J.W. Lanz
c.1750
7½ in. (19 cm) long
Sold for £4,104
($5,991)

Below right

Strasbourg (Paul
Hannong) figure of a
wild boar
Modelled by
J.W. Lanz
c.1750
9⅞ in. (24 cm) long
Sold for £7,560
($11,038)

Both sold 28.3.83 in
London

Opposite

Vincennes figure of a
seated poodle
Inscribed on the collar
Sophie
c.1752
9¼ in. (23.5 cm) high
Sold 28.3.83 in
London for £32,100
($47,304)

Above left

One of a pair of Böttger beakers
*c.*1725
3¼ in. (8.2 cm) high
Sold 3.12.82 in Geneva for Sw.fr.20,000 (£5,831)

Above

Meissen chinoiserie gold-mounted snuff-box
*c.*1735
3 in. (7.5 cm) wide
Sold 3.12.82 in Geneva for Sw.fr.49,500 (£14,224)

Left

Meissen oval snuff-box
*c.*1730
2⅜ in. (6 cm) wide
Sold 9.5.83 in Geneva for Sw.fr.55,000 (£17,081)

Right

Würzburg figure of
Scaramouche from the
Commedia dell'Arte
1775-80
6 in. (13.5 cm) high
Sold 9.5.83 in Geneva
for Sw.fr.28,600
(£8,881)

Far right

Ansbach figure of
Harlequin
*c.*1767
5 in. (12.5 cm) high
Sold 3.12.82 in
Geneva for
Sw.fr.6,600 (£1,896)
Record auction price
for an Ansbach figure

Meissen thimbles
*c.*1740
$^{11}/_{16}$ and $^{13}/_{16}$ in.
(1.7 and 2 cm) high
Sold individually for a
total of Sw.fr.25,300
(£8,162)

All sold 3.12.82 in
Geneva

Eleven Meissen
Commedia dell'Arte
figures from the
series modelled by
J.J. Kändler and
P. Reinicke for the
Duke of Weissenfels
1743-45
The series sold 3.12.82
in Geneva for a total
of Sw.fr.365,200
(£104,942)

Below left
Kloster Veilsdorf
figure of Dr Boloardo
or Polovard
Modelled by Wenzel
Neu
1764-65
5½ in. (14 cm) high
Sold for Sw.fr.24,200
(£6,954)

Below Centre
Kloster Veilsdorf
figure of Harlequin
Modelled by Wenzel
Neu
1764-65
5¾ in. (14.5 cm) high
Sold for Sw.fr.16,500
(£4,741)

Right
Naples figure of
Scaramouche
1790-95
5⅞ in. (15 cm) high
Sold for Sw.fr.41,800
(£12,011)
Record auction price
for a Naples figure
Previously sold at
Christie's, London
1964 for 280 gns.

All sold 3.12.82 in
Geneva

Above

Sèvres rose Pompadour milk-jug
Painter's mark S for Méreaud père
1757
5 in. (12.5 cm) high
Sold 28.3.83 in London for £3.780 ($5,519)

Above right

Pair of Sèvres biscuit busts of Louis XVI and Marie Antoinette
Modelled by Boizot
Late 18th century
15⅜ and 16⅛ in. (39 and 41 cm) high
Sold 4.7.83 in London for £10,260 ($15,903)
Given by Louis XVI to the Ambassadors of Tippoo Sultan in 1786

Right

Casteldurante dish
Dated 1541
7½ in. (19 cm) diameter
Sold 29.11.82 in London for £9,720 ($15,552)

St. Cloud figure of a recumbent cat
*c.*1745
7⅛ in. (18 cm) long
Sold 28.3.83 in London for £9,720 ($14,191)

Two Bristol Delft
polychrome campana
vases
*c.*1760
7⅝ in. (19.5 cm)
Sold for £4,104 ($6,730)

Bristol Delft blue-dash
tulip charger
*c.*1720
13 in. (33 cm) diameter
Sold for £1,296 ($2,125)

Staffordshire saltglaze
Jacobite mug
Inscribed *Our Prince is
Brave, His cause is Just, in
God alone, we put our trust*
*c.*1745
5⅛ in. (13 cm) high
Sold for £4,320 ($7,085)

One of a pair of Bristol
Delft polychrome flower
bricks
*c.*1750
5⅞ in. (15 cm) wide
Sold for £1,836 ($3,011)

English Delft
polychrome mug
*c.*1730
4¾ in. (12 cm) high
Sold for £1,188 ($1,948)

All sold 6.12.82 in
London

English ceramics

London Delft blue and white
two-handled bowl and cover
Dated 1695
6⅛ in. (15.5 cm) wide
Sold 6.12.82 in London for
£4,860 ($7,970)

Bristol Delft powdered-manganese bowl
c.1740
10 in. (25.5 cm) diameter
Sold 6.12.82 in London for £3,024 ($4,959)

Creamware commemorative
mug
c.1797
6⅛ in. (15.5 cm) high
Sold 13.6.83 in London for
£345 ($546)

Bristol Delft blue and white miniature
chamber-pot
c.1715
4¾ in. (12 cm) wide
Sold 13.6.83 in London for £3,456 ($5,184)

Wedgwood creamware punch-pot and cover
c.1800
12⅛ in. (32 cm) wide
Sold 13.6.83 in London for £3,024 ($4,536)

Worcester blue and
white miniature part
tea and coffee-service
1760-65
Sold 13.6.83 in
London for a total of
£4,449 ($6,674)

Staffordshire saltglaze
owl jug and cover
*c.*1720
7½ in. (19 cm) high
Sold 13.6.83 in
London for £15,120
($22,680)

Above

Bow figure of a tabby cat
*c.*1758
3⅛ in. (8 cm) high
Sold 20.12.82 in London for £756
($1,210)
From the collection of the
W.A.H. Harding Trust

Bow cockerel and hen with three
chickens
*c.*1758
The cock 4⅜ in. (11 cm) high
Sold 20.12.82 in London for £3,024
($4,838)
From the collection of the late
Myra, The Hon. Lady Fox

Bow group of the Fortune-Teller
By the Muses Modeller
1750-52
6¾ in. (17 cm) high
Sold 13.6.83 in London for £2,160
($3,240)

Longton Hall cos lettuce tureen, cover and stand
*c.*1755
The tureen 9½ in. (24 cm) long
Sold 20.12.82 in London for £3,240 ($5,184)

Royal Worcester reticulated
ewer
By George Owen
1909
8⅜ in. (20 cm) high
Sold for £1,728 ($2,938)

Royal Worcester reticulated
vase
By George Owen
1909
12½ in. (31.5 cm) high
Sold for £4,968 ($8,446)

Royal Worcester reticulated
vase
By George Owen
1909
8¾ in. (22 cm) high
Sold for £2,700 ($4,590)

All sold 11.10.82 in London

Bow blue and white vase
1755-58
10⅝ in. (27 cm) high
Sold 20.12.82 in London for £2,052 ($3,283)

Kurfursten humpen
Central Germany,
perhaps Franconia
18th century
8¼ in. (21 cm) high
Sold for £5,184
($8,294)

'Reichsadler' humpen
Bohemia
Dated 1605
11¼ in. (30 cm) high
Sold for £4,104
($6,361)

'Jagd' humpen
Franconia
Dated 1713
6⅞ in. (17.5 cm) high
Sold for £4,536
($7,258)

Armorial
'stangenglas'
Bohemia
17th century
13⅝ in.
(34.5 cm) high
Sold for £5,400
($8,640)
It has been suggested
that the date of 1589 is
a later addition

'Heldten' humpen
Franconia
Dated 1711
9½ in. (24 cm) high
Sold for £3,456
($5,530)

All sold 14.6.83 in London
All from the collection of The Los Angeles Museum of Art

English glass

Right

Williamite engraved
decanter
*c.*1750
Inscribed THE IMMORTAL
MEMORY OF THE GLORIOUS
KING WILLIAM
10 in. (25.5 cm)
Sold 5.4.83 in London for
£2,268 ($3,357)

Far right

Cameo vase
By Stevens & Williams
Dated 1885
10½ in. (26.5 cm) high
Sold 2.11.82 in London
for £5,184 ($8,294)

Stipple-engraved
facet-stemmed goblet
By David Wolff
*c.*1795
6⅞ in. (17.5 cm) high
Sold 14.6.83 in London
for £4,320 ($6,523)

Cut-glass part service
*c.*1820
The decanters 11⅝ in. (29.5 cm) high
All sold 5.4.83 in London for a total of £6,069 ($8,982)

Right

Newcastle enamelled goblet
By William Beilby
*c.*1765
7⅛ in. (18 cm) high
Sold 5.4.83 in London for
£6,480 ($9,720)
From the collection of the
late Sir Hugh Dawson, Bt.

Far right

Airtwist landscape goblet
Attributed to
William Beilby
*c.*1765-70
6⅞ in. (17.3 cm) high
Sold 14.6.83 in London for
£4,536 ($7,258)
From the collection of the
late Sir Hugh and
Lady Dawson

Four Beilby wineglasses
from a series of 24
1765-70
The 24 sold individually
14.6.83 in London for a
total of £44,442 ($66,663)
From the collection of the
late Sir Hugh and
Lady Dawson

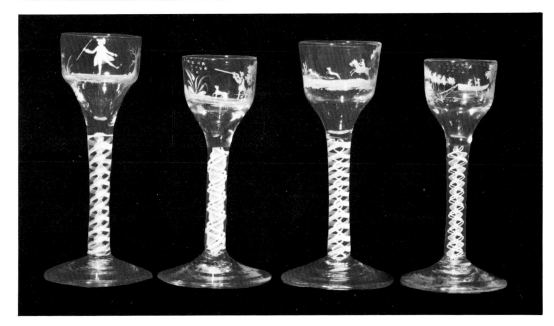

Far left

Clichy faceted flat bouquet
weight
3 in. (7.5 cm) diameter
Sold for £4,104 ($6,566)

Left

St. Louis encased
pink-overlay upright
bouquet weight
3⅛ in. (8 cm) diameter
Sold for £5,940 ($9,504)

Centre

Clichy close concentric
millefiori pedestal weight
3 in. (7.5 cm) diameter
Sold for £4,320 ($6,912)

Far left

St. Louis flat bouquet
weight
3⅛ in. (8 cm) diameter
Sold for £4,104 ($6,566)

Left

Clichy flower weight
3⅜ in. (8.5 cm) diameter
Sold for £3,240 ($5,184)

All sold 14.6.83 in London

ORIENTAL CERAMICS
AND WORKS OF ART

Sancai red pottery pillow
Song Dynasty
9½ in. (24 cm) wide
Sold 13.12.82 in London for
£19,440 ($31,104)

Far left

One of a pair of blue and yellow saucer-dishes
Encircled Yongzheng six-character marks and of the period
8¼ in. (21 cm) diameter
Both sold 13.12.82 in London for £22,680 ($36,288)
From the collection of Mr W.K. Ma of Hong Kong

Left

Famille jaune dish
Kangxi six-character mark and of the period
16 in. (40.5 cm) diameter
Sold 19.4.83 in London for £30,240 ($45,360)

Northern celadon deep conical bowl
Song Dynasty
9¼ in. (23 cm) diameter
Sold 5.7.83 in London for £15,120 ($23,436)

Famille rose 'hundred deer' vase
Qianlong six-character seal mark and of the period
17¾ in. (45 cm) high
Sold 5.7.83 in London for £36,720 ($56,916)

Sancai buff pottery
figure of a Bactrian
camel
Tang Dynasty
31¼ in.
(79.5 cm) high
Sold 19.4.83 in
London for £66,960
($100,440)
Sold by order of the
Trustees of the Mount
Trust

Blue and white
double-gourd vase
Mid/late 14th century
20¼ in. (51 cm) high
Sold 13.12.82 in
London for £226,800
($362,880)

Ming blue and white dish
Xuande six-character mark below
the rim and of the period
11¾ in. (29.5 cm) diameter
Sold 5.7.83 in London for £44,280
($68,634)

Early Ming blue and white deep
dish
Yongle
17½ in. (44.2 cm) diameter
Sold 19.4.83 in London for
£62,640 ($93,960)

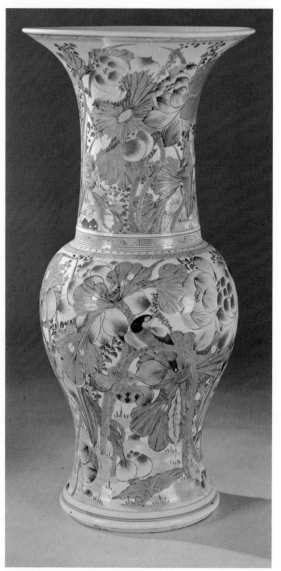

Famille verte yanyan vase
Kangxi
18 in. (46 cm) high
Sold 23.6.83 in New York for $55,000 (£34,483)
Sold by order of the Trustees of the Estate of
Rafi Y. Mottahedeh

Ming Wucai pen-tray
Wanli six-character mark and of the period
12½ x 4½ in. (31 x 11 cm)
Sold 13.12.82 in London for £21,600 ($34,560)

Famille rose dinner service with the arms of Brydges, Duke of Chandos
*c.*1795
Sold 30.3.83 in London for £28,080 ($40,997)
Sold by order of the Trustees of the Doughty House Trust

Group of famille rose porcelain
Yongzheng and Qianlong
Sold individually 30.3.83 in London for a total of £12,636 ($18,436)

Group of armorial porcelain
18th century
Sold individually 30.3.83 in London for a total of £27,000 ($39,393)

Above

YAO SHOU (1422-1495):
*Landscape in
Commemoration of
Retirement to Wu-shan*
Handscroll, ink and
colour on paper
11 x 39 in.
(28 x 98.8 cm)
Sold for $88,000
(£55,000)

Left

CHEN XIAN-ZHANG
(1428-1500): *Cursive
Script Calligraphy*
Handscroll, ink on
paper
Inscribed and dated
*Written by Shi-zhai in
Bao-shing Temple on the
tenth day, second month of
Gui-mao year of the
Chenghua era (1483)*
12¾ x 256 in.
(32 x 640 cm)
Sold for £44,000
(£27,500)

Both sold 2.12.83 in
New York

372

Rock crystal sphere
11⅜ in. (29 cm) diameter
Sold 23.6.83 in New York for $143,000 (£92,258)
The sphere is one of the world's largest known flawless examples, the largest being in the permanent collection of the Smithsonian Institute in Washington, donated by Mrs Worcester S. Warner, the widow of a telescope maker. The Smithsonian example, measuring 12⅞ inches (32.70 cm) in diameter, purportedly was fashioned by Chinese artisans in Shanghai in the 1920s from a half ton block of Burmese rock crystal. The current example may well be Japanese in origin, owing to the quality of the fitted leather case and elaborate silvered gilt metal stand and the whole Japanese late 19th century tradition of fashioning rock crystal into spheres from the material quarried in central Japan. The lustre of the hand polishing, using finely ground iron oxide, is of a quality rarely achieved with modern gem polishing machinery.

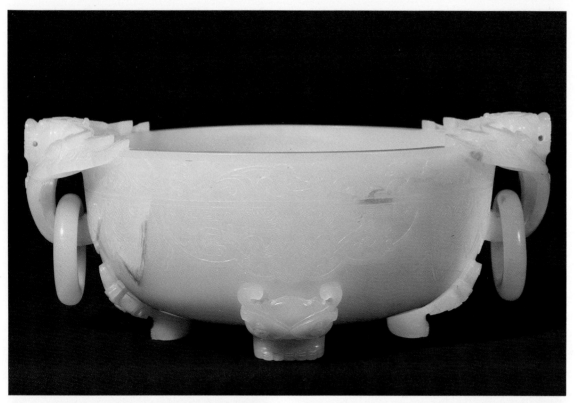

Slightly flecked white
jade tripod bowl
18th century
8¾ in. (22 cm) across
the handles
Sold 10.12.82 in
London for £21,600
($34,560)

Pair of white jade
screens
Late 18th/19th
century
Each plaque
13¾ x 9¾ in.
(35 x 25.5 cm)
Sold 6.7.83 in London
for £27,000 ($41,850)

Right

Mottled pale celadon
and lavender jade vase
and cover
19th century
16¾ in. (43 cm) high
Sold for £18,360
($28,458)

Far right

White jade finger
citrus
18th century
11 in. (28 cm) high
Sold for £11,340
($17,577)

Right

Flecked jade tripod
censer and cover
Late Qing Dynasty
8¼ in. (20.5 cm)
across the handles
Sold for £25,920
($40,176)

Far right

Mottled jade monkey
Late Ming Dynasty
3¾ in. (10.5 cm) high
Sold for £14,040
($21,762)

All sold 6.7.83 in
London
From the collection of
the Whitaker Family

Far left

Archaic bronze food
vessel, *gui*
Shang Dynasty,
*c.*1300 B.C.
10½ in. (27.5 cm)
across the handles
Sold 23.6.83 in
New York for $77,000
(£49,677)

Left

Ming cinnabar
lacquer box and cover
Yongle six-character
mark, 15th century
7¼ in. (18.5 cm)
diameter
Sold 2.12.82 in
New York for $55,000
(£34,375)

Cloisonné and Beijing enamel gold alloy tripod
libation vessel and stand, *jue*
Qianlong four-character mark and of the period
5¾ in. (15 cm) high
Sold 13.12.82 in London for £34,560 ($55,296)

Ming ivory square plaque
14th/15th century
4¼ x 4 in. (11.1 x 10.8 cm)
Sold 19.4.83 in London for £16,200 ($24,300)
From the collection of Mr R.H. Newsholme

Pair of pale huanghuali yokeback
armchairs
17th century
42 in. (107 cm) high
Sold for $63,800 (£41,428)

Pair of huanghuali cupboards
17th century
65½ in. (166.5 cm) high
Sold for $93,000 (£60,322)

All sold 23.6.83 in New York

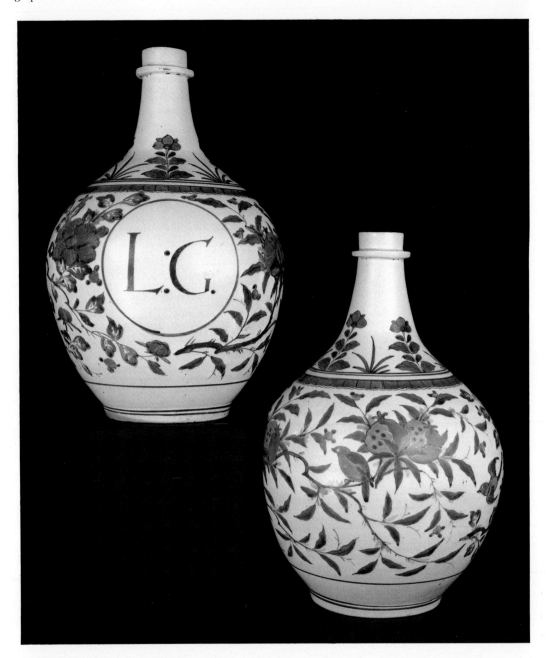

Pair of Arita apothecary bottles
*c.*1670
19⅝ in. (49.8 cm) high
Sold 22.2.83 in London for £8,100 ($12,150)

Pair of Imari baluster jars
Early 18th century
30¾ in. (78.2 cm) high
Sold 22.2.83 in London for £4,860 ($7,290)

Komai dish
Signed on base Nihon koku Kyoto ju Komai sei
19th century
21⅜ in. (54.1 cm) diameter
Sold 26.4.83 in London for £7,560 ($11,340)

Bronze model of a Buddhist figure
Signed Miyao zo
Late 19th century
23 in. (58.5 cm) high
Sold 22.2.83 in London for £4,860 ($7,290)

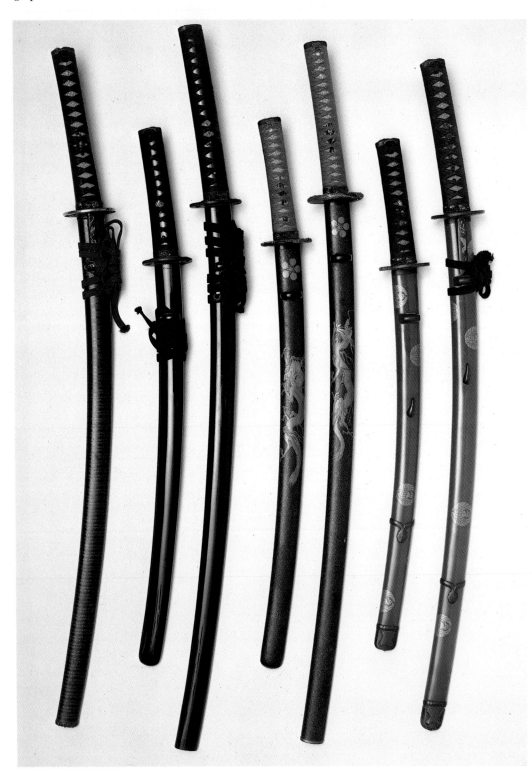

From left to right
Katana, the scabbard inlaid
with powdered shell
The mounting 19th century
The blade signed Yamashiro
Daijo Fujiwara Kunikane
17th century
26⅞ in. (68.2 cm) long
Sold for £3,456 ($5,184)

Daisho, the scabbards black
lacquer and hilts bound with
indigo braid
19th century
The blades 16th century
18 in. (45.5 cm) long
Sold for £4,536 ($6,804)

Daisho, the scabbards inlaid
with powdered shell and
decorated with gold lacquer
dragons
19th century
The long blade 17th century
The short blade
15th/16th century
22¼ in. (56.5 cm) long
Sold for £7,020 ($10,530)

Daisho, the scabbards of red
lacquer with 'dancing crane'
heraldic badges in red lacquer
19th century
The blades 17th century
17⅝ in. (44.7 cm) long
Sold for £2,376 ($3,564)

All sold 26.4.83 in London

Armour
*c.*1800-50
Sold 26.4.83 in London for £3,024
($4,536)

Top

One of a pair of six-leaf screens
Late 17th century/early 18th century
Each leaf approximately 59½ x 23 in.
(151 x 58.5 cm)
Sold 25.4.83 in London for £10,800 ($16,200)

Above

One of a pair of six-leaf screens
17th century
Each leaf approximately 60 x 23½ in.
(152 x 59.5 cm)
Sold 25.4.83 in London for £7,020 ($10,530)

Travelling shrine for the Christian market
Momoyama period
Oil on copper panel
Case 16¼ in. (41.5 cm) high
Sold 2.12.82 in New York for $170,500 (£106,562)

Suzuribako
Early 19th century
10¼ x 9⅝ in.
(26.5 x 24.3 cm)

Document box
(ryoshibako)
Early 19th century
16⅝ x 13⅜ in.
(42.1 x 33.8 cm)

Both sold 22.2.83 for a
total of £6,480
($9,720)

Shibuichi sleeve inro
19th century
Sold for £3,456
($5,184)

Four-case Kinji inro
Signed Kajikawa
19th century
Sold for £2,484
($3,726)

Five-case inro
Signed Sochosai
Late 18th century
Sold for £756 ($1,134)

Four-case Kinji inro
Signed Hojitsu, Edo
school
19th century
Sold for £3,240
($4,860)

All sold 22.2.83 in
London

387

SHARAKU: *Oban tate-e; an okubi-e
portrait of the actor Sakata
Hangoro III*
*c.*1794
Signed Toshusai Sharaku ga
Sold 3.12.82 in New York for
$77,000 (£48,125)

Ivory netsuke of a Dutchman
Late 18th century
Kyoto school
Sold 3.12.82 in New York for
$26,400 (£16,296)

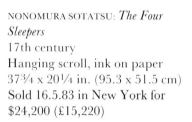

NONOMURA SOTATSU: *The Four Sleepers*
17th century
Hanging scroll, ink on paper
37¾ x 20¼ in. (95.3 x 51.5 cm)
Sold 16.5.83 in New York for
$24,200 (£15,220)

The Godman Collection

OLIVER HOARE

The collection of Frederick Du Cane Godman is an incalculable treasure, and the single most important collection to go to the British Museum this century. The 600 pieces of pottery, as well as numerous fragments, two magnificent Mamluk glass mosque-lamps, and a single silver-inlaid brass pen-box, make up a corpus which is unrivalled by any museum in the world. The Isnik pottery of Ottoman Turkey is even unmatched by the collections of Istanbul, and the Hispano-Moresque lustreware is one of the three outstanding groups in the world. The formation of this collection was one of the main elements which made possible the proper classification and understanding of Islamic pottery. It is also an extraordinary chronicle of collecting in the second half of the 19th and early 20th centuries.

Apart from the brief introduction to his catalogue published in 1901[1], Mr. Godman left no written record of his collection. Fortunately he numbered his pieces according to the sequence of acquisition, and by pegging against this the few known purchase-dates, it is at least possible to gain an interesting insight into the evolution of his collecting. The sources of most of his masterpieces remain a tantalising mystery, and although clues may await discovery in the collection and sales catalogues of the period, it is sad that no traces of the dealers and their trade remain. It must be remembered that at the time that Mr. Godman collected almost nothing was known about Islamic pottery. He had only his own remarkable eye on which to rely, and perhaps the encouragement and advice which came through his friendship with Sir Augustus Wollaston Franks, who acted as the lynch-pin to a pioneering group of collectors. Franks was Keeper of the British Museum and an outstanding collector, and the bequests of those he gathered around him, such as Salting, Slade and Henderson, greatly enriched the collections of both the British Museum and the Victoria and Albert Museum.

Mr. Godman began collecting in 1865. For 10 years he bought nothing but Isnik, amassing an extraordinary group of 144 pieces, including five mosque-lamps. His initial taste for Turkish pottery was probably influenced by a visit he made to Constantinople in 1854 while still an undergraduate. Isnik pottery had certainly long been appreciated in the West, as the jugs with Elizabethan silver mounts testify[2], but it had only ever been sought after as an exotic addition to Western collections, like some rare oriental spice. Mr. Godman's encyclopaedic approach to collecting, and his search for the finest examples of every conceivable type was a complete innovation in the field. Quite early on he made a major discovery in the form of a blue-and-white jug bearing an Armenian inscription: *This mass cruet commemorates the servant of God Abraham of Kutahya. Anno Armen 959* (A.D. 1510). Thus, with a place-name in Turkey and a date, he would have already been able to situate correctly his other magnificent examples of the so-called 'Abraham of Kutahya', group, and must also have been in a position to speculate on the

Two large basins of the 'Abraham of Kutahya' and 'Damascus' groups

close connection between this early group of Isnik and the other later pieces which he possessed. Soon after this he bought a covered bowl with cartouches containing poetic inscriptions in Turkish, which finally convinced Franks of the Turkish origin of Isnik pottery. Being one-eyed in the valley of the blind must, however, have had its frustrations, because everyone else remained convinced that Isnik pottery was made in Persia.

Persia seems to have had an almost mystical appeal to the Western collector, who fervently wished that everything Islamic came from there. The dealers naturally fed this fantasy because their sales depended on it. In 1868, to give one example, Mr. C. Drury Fortnum read a paper to the Society of Antiquaries about one of the Isnik lamps made for the Mosque of Omar in Jerusalem in 1549, which he insisted was 'Persian ware'. That same year saw the publication of the second edition of Fitzgerald's Quatrains of Omar Khayyam which heralded the 'cult of Omar', and further fanned the flames of the Persian obsession. No doubt Sir F. Leighton decided to buy his marvellous 'Abraham of Kutahya' jug in Damascus because the dealer from whom he bought it insisted that it came from Persia[3]. Descriptions of Persian Pottery became increasingly lyrical, going as far as to claim that 'the Persian potter moved on a higher plain'[4]. Even Mr. Salzman who brought back the news that large numbers of Isnik dishes were to be found on Rhodes, (and coined the term 'Lindus ware') still insisted on their Persian origin[5]. It is tempting to speculate that the blinding effect of this obsession was the major cause of delay in accurately classifying Islamic pottery; that it was more misleading than the 'innate mendacity of the Oriental nomad who is mostly the purveyor of these relics', and more of a barrier than the 'violent animosity in the breast of the Turkish official' towards any type of research[6].

In 1876, the South Kensington Museum purchased a group of early Persian lustreware wall-tiles from a certain Monsieur Richard, a French physician who had lived in Tehran for many years. Among the lot was a large *mihrab* tile bearing a date equivalent to 1308 A.D. This acquisition was the cause of great excitement, because it was the very first early lustreware seen

Two Isnik mosque lamps of the 'Abraham of Kutahya' group made for the tomb of Bayazid II (d.1512) The lamp on the right was Mr Godman's first acquisition in 1865 The central lamp dated from c.1530

in this country. Here at last, it was assumed, was the origin of the lustre technique, so much admired in its later developments of Safavid Iran and Arab Spain. That same year the Museum also purchased an outstanding collection of Safavid pottery brought back from Persia by Sir Robert Murdoch Smith, including fine examples of every variety.[7] It seems probable that these events persuaded Mr. Godman to diversify his collection, because they coincide with his first purchases outside the field of Isnik. He bought a group of early lustreware tiles, including a magnificent frieze of four large tiles decorated with plaited Kufic. Characteristically Mr. Godman's acquisition was finer than anything bought by the South Kensington Museum[8]. Monsieur Richard must also have been the source of Mr. Godman's tiles, who therefore must have known of the excavations undertaken by Monsieur Richard between 1871 and 1875 on the site of the ruined city of Rayy, just south of Tehran. These digs produced a number of vases and bowls which predated the destruction of the city by the Mongols in 1220. One of the bowls was sold in Paris in 1873, and one can assume that the impossible rarity of such pieces must have concentrated Mr. Godman's mind in a wonderful way. By 1885, when the Burlington Fine Arts Club put on the first exhibition of Persian ceramics, Mr. Godman owned three of the four early vases shown. One of these came from the sale of Consul Churchill who had brought it from Persia, and subsequently he was to benefit from other consular sources, including Sir William Preece who had been Consul in Isfahan, and Mr. Wrench, vice-Consul in Constantinople.

In 1889, Monsieur Richard appeared again, with 59 pieces of lustreware which he showed at the Paris Exhibition. Mr. Godman bought the lot, and was particularly pleased with the seven early examples among them. Sometime after 1894 he found the first vase bearing a date, equivalent to 1231 A.D. Up until this discovery, lustre vessels had been situated in relation to

The wing-handled vase made for
Cosimo or Lorenzo De Medici
Valencia, *c.*1465
Acquired in the Hollingworth Magniac
Sales, previously belonging to Horace
Walpole of Strawberry Hill

the tiles of which numerous dated examples were known from between 1217 and 1339. Eventually he built up a group of 27 vessels, as well as numerous fragments, and a superb selection of tiles. In addition to the early Persian wares, he also collected a group of 11 early Syrian pieces, including three magnificent albarelli decorated in lustre on dark blue. Two of these were purchased after 1885 from Mr. C. Drury Fortnum, author of the *Catalogue of Maiolica in the South Kensington Museum (1873)*, who had bought them in Milan in 1875. Syrian lustreware was known long before its Persian counterpart, although few artefacts can have had so many origins attributed to it. In 1864, when the South Kensington Museum acquired four examples, it was known as 'Siculo-Arabic', probably as a result of Mr. E. Falkener finding two ovoid jars in Sicily. In 1885, at the time of the Burlington Fine Arts Club exhibition, it was attributed to Persia, although Baron Davillier felt able to prove that it came from Manises. At the turn of the century, Henry Wallis was inclined to attribute it to Cairo because of the large number of lustreware sherds discovered by Mr. Frank Dillon at Fustat. Interestingly the first mention of Rakka as a site comes from a report of the British Consul in Aleppo in 1906, who noted that 'Mr.

Makrides of the Stamboul Museum' carried off a large quantity of samples from there.

If Mr. Godman's achievement in the realm of Persian pottery looks less impressive today, it is because since the 1940s, excavations in Persia, both legal and illegal , have brought to light a huge quantity of early pieces in perfect condition [9]. Nevertheless, his lustreware vases and bowls retain a particular fascination for being among the first examples known in the West. Beyond this, their significance is tremendous because they provided the stepping-stone to the realm of Spanish lustre pottery, which began to interest Mr. Godman in the early 1880's. It was a logical step to pursue the technique of lustre from its origins in the East to its great flowering in the 15th century at the Western limits of the Islamic Empire. He was in close contact with Senor Don G.J. de Osma, founder of the Instituto de Valencia de Don Juan, who shared his interest in early Persian lustreware, and must have been an encouraging influence in the field of Hispano-Moresque. Unlike Isnik and Persian wares, Hispano-Moresque pottery had always been popular in Europe, ever since the noble families of Spain and Italy ordered it in Valencia, often incorporating their coats-of-arms into the design. By 1887, Mr. Godman was already able to make an important contribution to the exhibition of Spanish pottery organised by the Burlington Fine Arts Club[10]. It was at the Hollingworth Magniac sale in 1892 that he bought his most important piece, the wing-handled vase made for either Cosimo or Lorenzo de Medici in about 1465. It had previously been in the collection of Horace Walpole at Strawberry Hill. In the course of the 1890s, Mr. Godman concentrated on collecting examples from the early 15th century, which have a much more marked Islamic character. Outstanding among these is the large dish showing two seated Arab figures, which was bought at the sale of the collection of the Duc de Dino in Paris in May, 1894. By the time of the Spanish Exhibition in 1896, he had developed a classification of 10 different groups of Hispano-Moresque pottery, all fully represented by examples in his own collection.

A visit to the Misses Godman at their home in Horsham was always the ultimate treat in the life of an Islamic art-student. The collection is now available to a far wider public, which is singularly appropriate in view of the resurgence of interest in Islamic Art, both in the West and in the Middle East. Mr. Godman had expressed the wish that his collection should eventually go to the British Museum. It is gratifying that this has now been made possible, 64 years after his death, by the Treasury's acceptance of the collection in lieu of Capital Transfer Tax arising on the death of Miss Eva Godman in 1982. This has prevented the dispersal of a collection of which the value is incomparably greater than any monetary equivalent. It will remain as a testimony to Mr. Godman's extraordinary abilities.

1. The Godman Collection of Oriental and Spanish Pottery and Glass. London, 1901.
2. Mounted tankards, dated 1586 and 1592, were in the collections of the Earl of Dysart and Lord Swaythling.
3. Burlington Fine Arts Club. Illustrated catalogue of an exhibition of Persian and Arab Art, London, 1885.
4. Burlington Fine Arts Club, 1885. The Faience of Persia and the Nearer East, London, 1907.
5. Burlington Fine Arts Club, 1885.
6. Charles Hercules Read's introduction to Burlington Fine Arts Club catalogue, 1907.
7. Henry Wallis. The Godman Collection. Persian Ceramic Art.London, 1894.
8. Henry Wallis. The Thirteenth Century Lustred Wall Tiles in the Collection of Mr. F. Du Cane Godman. London, 1893.
9. Dr. Mehdi Bahrami, Gurgan Faiences. Cairo, 1949.
10. Burlington Fine Arts Club. Exhibition of Spanish Pottery. London, 1887.

Mughal ivory howdah
55 x 35 x 24 in. (140 x 89 x 61 cm)
Sold 13.10.82 in London for £5,616 ($9,547)

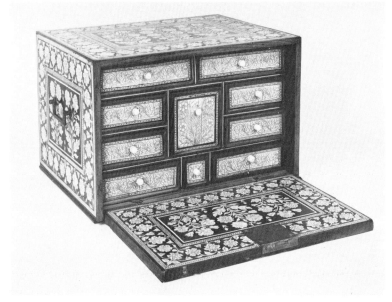

Indian teak chest inlaid with ivory
c.1800
16¾ in. (42.5 cm) wide
Sold 13.6.83 in London for £3,456 ($5,460)

Tibetan ritual bronze and
iron dagger [Phur-pa]
16th century
11¾ in. (30 cm) high
Sold 1.12.82 in New York
for $24,200 (£15,125)
From The Pan Asian
Collection

Nepalese gilt copper figure of Durga
15th century
8¾ in. (22.5 cm) high
Sold 1.12.82 in New York for $71,500 (£44,687)
From The Pan Asian Collection

Tibetan thanka, depicting the arhat
Ajita
One of three similar lots sold 13.6.83 in
London for a total of £4,536 ($7,167)

Silk Koum Kapu rug
6ft 1in. x 4ft 4in. (186 x 132 cm)
Sold 21.4.83 in London for £19,440 ($30,326)

Antique Konya rug
5ft 4in. x 3ft 11in.
(163 x 120 cm)
Sold 13.6.83 in
London for £6,480
($10,238)

Antique Turkish rug
18th century
6ft x 5ft
(183 x 152 cm)
Sold 13.6.83 in
London for £8,100
($12,798)
Previously sold at
Christie's 13.1.75 for
£3,045

Kashan Mochtasham rug
6ft 10in. x 4ft 9in.
(208 x 145 cm)
Sold 14.10.82 in London for
£15,120 ($25,704)

Antique Yomut 'C'-Gul carpet
10ft 1in. x 5ft 11in. (307 x 180 cm)
Sold 13.6.83 in London for £25,920 ($40,954)

Antique Caucasian rug
18th century
9ft 2in. x 3ft 8in. (279 x 112 cm)
Sold 13.6.83 in London for £19,440 ($30,715)

Ghiyas ud-Din ibn Human ud-Din (called
Khwand Amir): Habib us-Siyar
(Juz IV, Vol. III)
Qazwin or Isfahan, *c*.1590-1600
Text and miniatures
11 x 6 in. (28 x 15.2 cm)
Folio 17 x 10½ in. (43.2 x 26.8 cm)
Sold 13.6.83 in London for £70,200
($110,916)

Orange-Headed Ground Thrush
By Zain al-Din
Calcutta, 1778
23½ x 31½ in. (59.5 x 80 cm)
Sold for £7,560 ($11,945)

Red-Whiskered Bulbul
by Zain al-Din
Calcutta, 1777
20¾ x 29⅛ in. (53 x 70 cm)
Sold for £7,560 ($11,945)

Both sold 13.6.83 in London

A Pilgrim
Mughal, *c.*1570
7½ x 5 in. (19 x 12.7 cm)
Sold 13.6.83 in London for £18,360
($29,009)

Illustration to the Baburnama
Mughal, *c*.1590
9 x 5⅛ in. (22.8 x 13 cm)
Folio 13⅝ x 9 in. (34.6 x 22.7 cm)
Sold 13.6.83 in London for £6,480 ($10,238)
From The Pan Asian Collection

ANTIQUITIES AND ETHNOGRAPHICA

Snake-thread glass goblet
2nd-3rd century A.D.
4¼ in. (10.1 cm) high
Sold 13.7.83 in London for £23,760 ($36,828)
From the collection of the Corning Museum of Glass

Black basalt figure of Horus the falcon
Inscribed *Horus, Lord of Mesen-the-divine. the great god,
lord of Dr. t...*
*c.*3rd century B.C.
21¼ in. (54 cm) high
Sold 16.12.82 in London for £32,400 ($52,488)

Marble portrait head of Augustus
Early 1st century A.D.
15½ in. (39.5 cm) high
Sold 13.7.83 in London for £32,400 ($50,220)

Celtic Bronze Age gold 'ribbon' torque
c. 1200-900 B.C.
5 in. (12.8 cm) in diameter
Sold 16.12.82 in London for £7,020 ($11,372)
From the collection of Col. Stewart-Wilson

There is an almost identical figure in the Staatlichen Museum für Völkerkunde, Munich. Most of the Pacific collections in that Museum were acquired from the Wittelsbach family of Bavaria, who bought two major groups of sculpture: one thousand pieces from Lamare Piquot in 1841, and a group from a Dr Wagler, who is alleged to have bought some from Sir Joseph Banks. Lamare Piquot was sailing in the Pacific during the 1830s and amongst his collection is a Rarotonga staff god finial, but the Wagler group includes a Rarotonga fisherman's god (which could not have been bought from Banks as he died in 1820), and an Easter Island emaciated man. It is therefore highly likely that the Easter Island figure was collected by Lamare Piquot, which would date the present example to some time before 1840.

Far left

Easter Island wood
standing male figure,
moai kavakava
17 in. (43 cm) high
Sold 29.6.83 in
London for £30,240
($46,872)

Left

Easter Island wood
'lizard man', *moai moko*
18½ in. (47 cm) long
Sold 29.6.83 in
London for £70,200
($108,810)
These figures were
suspended in pairs
inside the porch-like
doorway of a house to
keep out intruders

Tlingit wood comb
Early 19th century
9¾ in. (25 cm) high
Sold 29.6.83 in London for
£10,800 ($16,740)

Rarotonga wood staff god section
c. 1820
33½ in. (84.5 cm) long
Sold 29.6.83 in London for £37,800 ($58,590)
A description by Williams of these large staff gods is given in his book *A Narrative of Missionary Enterprises in the South Sea Islands* (1837). He also mentions that 'one was sent to England which is now in the Missionary Museum'. This figure is now in the Museum of Mankind, London, and was cut into three sections before being transported. Being cut into sections appears to have been the fate of all the large staff gods which escaped the bonfires, and unfortunately the lowest ends were usually burned, being no doubt considered too rude for the eyes of those at home.

A Maori jade figure neck pendant, *hei tiki*
4 in. (10.5 cm) high
Sold 29.6.83 in London for £23,760 ($36,826)

Opposite

A group of early American Indian quillwork brought back to England by Charles, 1st Marquis, 2nd Earl Cornwallis (1738-1805)
Huron tanned skin pouch
7½ in. (19 cm) high

Eastern Sioux quillwork panel
17¼ in. (44 cm) wide

Iroquois false-embroidered burden strap
Central panel 25 in. (63.5 cm) long

Captive's tie, probably Iroquois
Approximaely 411 in. (10 m 7 cm) long
The tie was probably used by the Iroquois to bind the captive to take home. Men taken in raids would be bound and led back to the captor's village, where they would be adopted by a family who had suffered a loss in war. The captive might be retained by the family, or be tortured to death by fire and other means

All sold 29.6.83 in London for a total of £14,904 ($23,101)
From the collection of the Hon. R.H.C. Neville

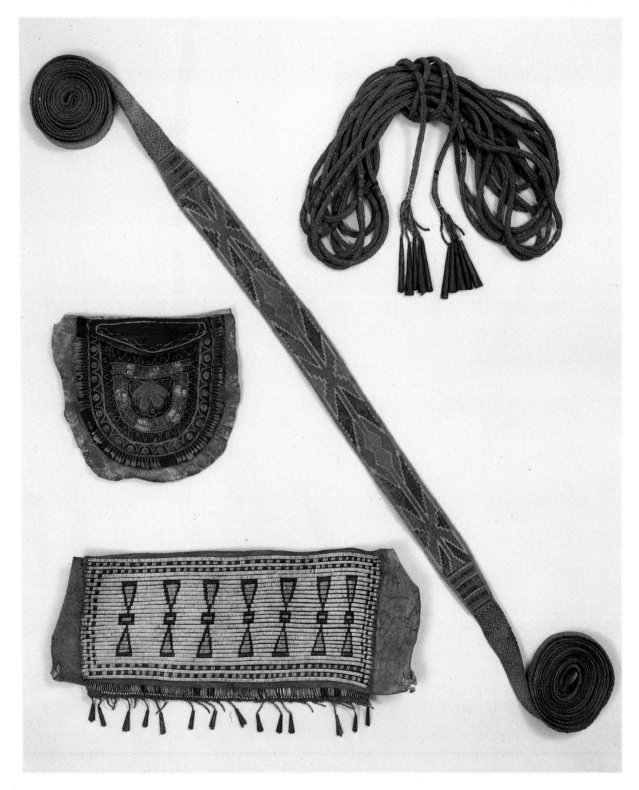

Luba wood ceremonial
spear, *mokuki*
58½ in. (149 cm) long
Sold 1.12.82 in London for
£19,440 ($31,104)

This spear is very rare by comparison with the
relatively common Luba chiefs' staves, in which
the sculptural content is generally somewhat
subordinated to the decorative figure, 10¾ in.
(27.3 cm) high, is virtually free-standing. A similar
spear, but with a less fine figure, is in the National
Museum of Anthropology and Ethnology in
Florence; it was collected in Mulongo village by
E. Brissoni in 1902.

The sculptural mastery of the carver stands out
in every view, and may be further studied in a
magnificent water pipe at Tervuren recently
published by Neyt, which is almost certainly by
the same hand. The female figure squats upon the
water container and is of equal beauty with the
present piece. It was collected on the lower Lukuga
east of the Lualaba (as the Zaire is called in this
region), and the same location is appropriate. This
is further corroborated by Louis de Strycker, who
has seen the spear, and suggests that its origin is
around the chieftaincy of Malamba Nkulu.

ARMS AND ARMOUR AND MODERN SPORTING GUNS

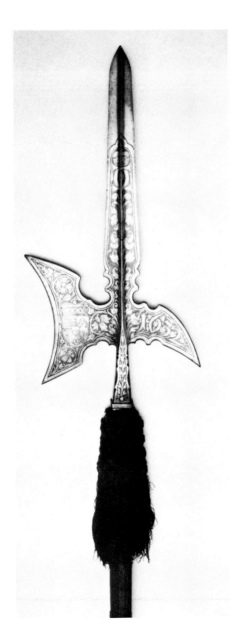

Halberd made for the
guard of Prince Carl
Von Liechtenstein
German/Austrian dated 1632
Head 24½ in. (62.2 cm)
Sold 11.5.83 in London for £10,800 ($16,956)

German flintlock holster pistol
By Christopher Treffler
Augsburg, c. 1660
21½ in. (54.6 cm)
Sold 15.12.82 in London for
£12,960 ($20,736)
From the collection of Mount
Melleray Abbey, Co. Waterford

Medieval sword
Late 14th century
Inscribed in *Naskhi* script *Inalienably
bequeathed to the armouries of the frontier town of
Alexandria the well guarded, from what was
presented during the days of our master, chief of the
emirs, al-Saifi al-Nasiri Aristai*
Saif addin Aristay al-Zahiri was governor of
Alexandria in 1400-1401
Sold 20.10.82 in London for £12,960 ($20,032)

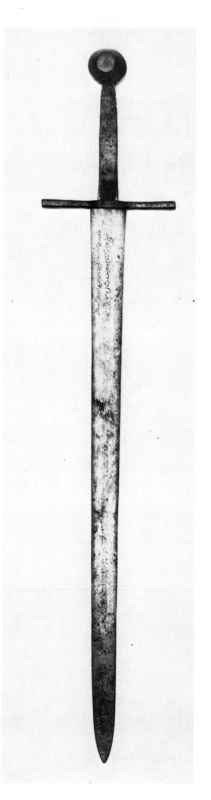

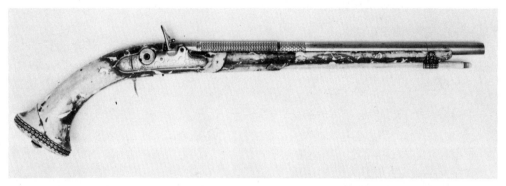

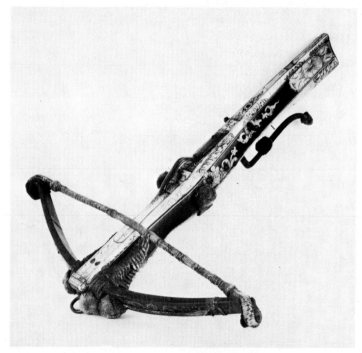

German crossbow
Late 16th century
24 in. (61 cm)
Sold 11.5.83 in London for £9,180 ($14,413)

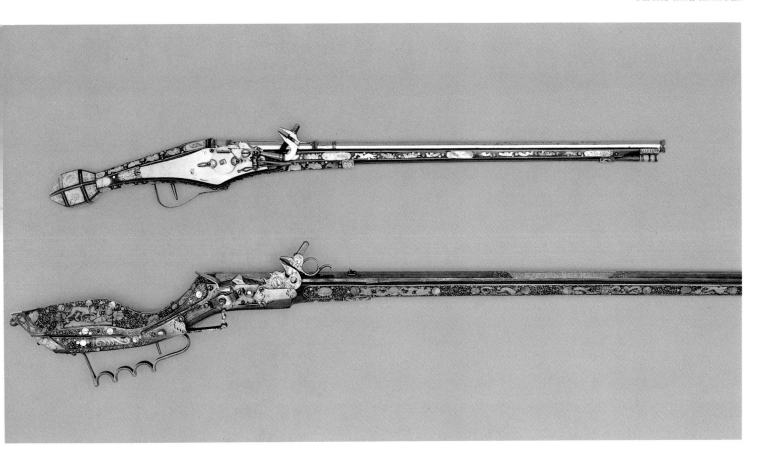

German long wheel-lock holster pistol
Maker's mark GDB, a cinquefoil above
Early 17th century
31¼ in. (79.3 cm)
Sold 15.12.82 in London for £17,280 ($27,648)

Silesian wheel-lock tschinke
Second quarter of the 17th century
34½ in. (87.6 cm) barrel
Sold 15.12.82 in London for £8,640 ($13,824)

Swiss Gothic halberd
Late 15th century
17 in. (43.2 cm) head
Sold 20.7.83 in London for
£8,640 ($13,306)

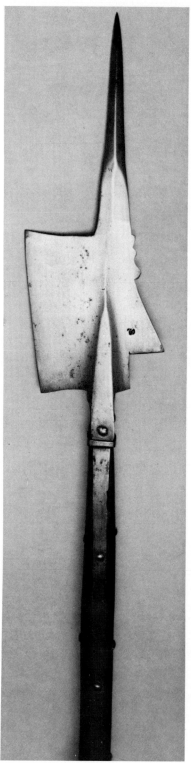

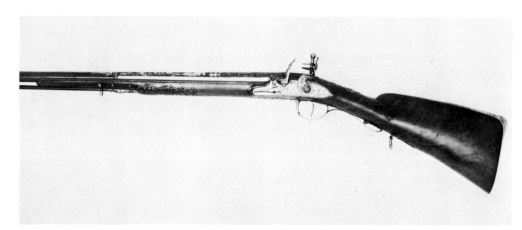

Above

French left-handed lock
flintlock fowling-piece
By Delety à Paris, Rue
Coquillière
c. 1780
41½ in. (105.4 cm) barrel
Sold 15.12.82 in London for
£5,184 ($8,294)

Saxon sporting crossbow
By Johann Gottfried
Hänisch
Dresden *c.* 1730-1740
25½ in. (64.8 cm)
Sold 20.7.83 in London
for £5,940 ($9,147)

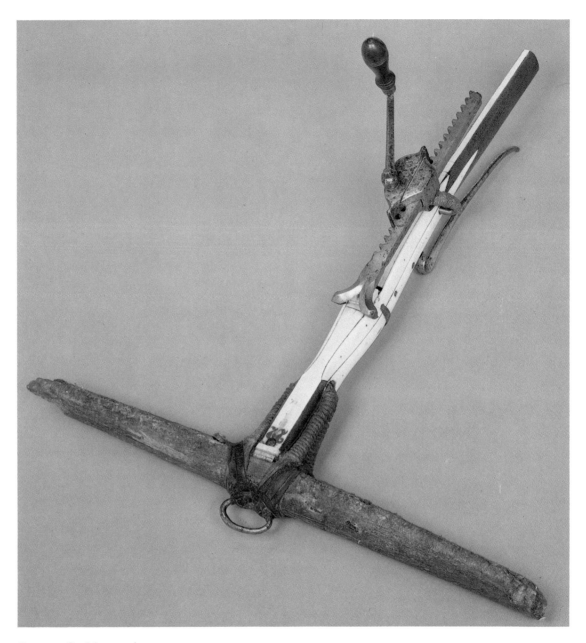

German Gothic crossbow
Late 15th century
30 in. (76.2 cm)
Sold 15.12.82 in London for £18,360 ($29,376)

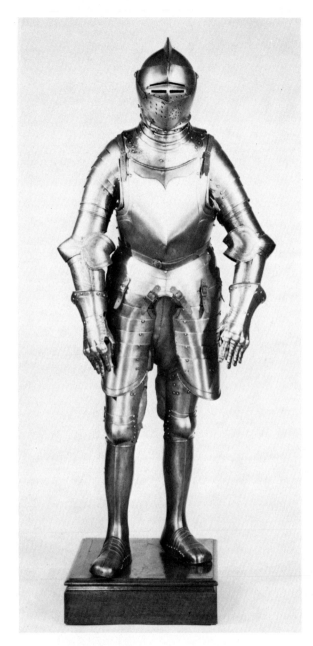

Composite full armour
Mid- to late 16th century, the helmet *c.* 1550
Sold 20.7.83 in London for £7,020 ($10,810)

German composite black and white half-armour
Third quarter of the 16th century
Sold 20.7.83 in London for £4,320 ($6,652)

Pair of single-trigger
sidelock ejector
12-bore d.b. guns
By J. Purdey, London
Built in 1928 and little
used
Sold 15.9.82 for
£18,900 ($32,697)

Pair of lightweight
sidelock ejector
12-bore d.b. guns
By J. Purdey, London
Built in 1936/7
Sold 22.6.83 for
£14,040 ($21,622)

Pair of sidelock ejector
12-bore(2¾in) d.b.
guns
By Boss, London
Built in 1971 and little
used
Sold 22.6.83 for
£14,040 ($21,622)

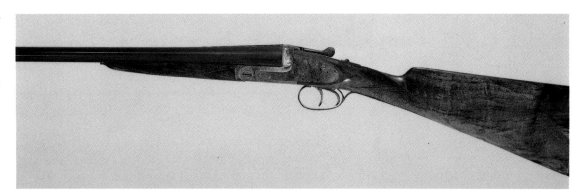

Single-trigger sidelock
ejector 12-bore d.b.
gun
By J. Purdey, London
Built in 1979 and
unused
Sold 22.6.83 for £8,640
($13,306)

All sold in London

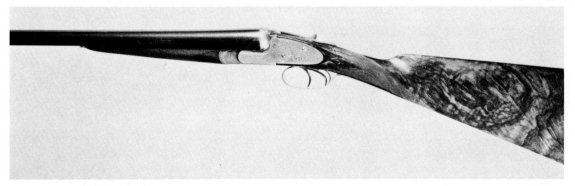

Pair of sidelock ejector
12-bore(2¾in) d.b.
guns
By W. Evans, London
Built in 1898 and
rebarrelled *c.* 1978
Sold 15.9.82 for £4,320
($7,474)

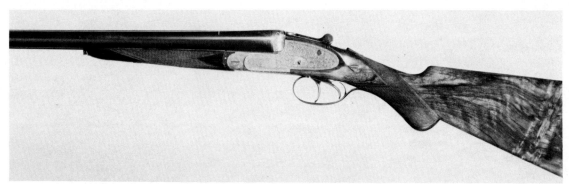

Pair of 'Premier
XXV' sidelock ejector
12-bore d.b. guns
By E.J. Churchill,
London
Built *c.* 1930
Sold 22.6.83 for £8,640
($13,306)

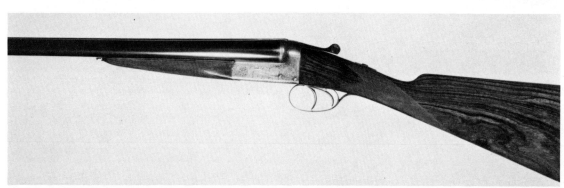

Pair of 'Utility XXV
Easy-Opening'
boxlock ejector 12-
bore d.b. guns
By E.J. Churchill,
London
Built in 1937
Sold 23.3.83 for £4,320
($6,420)

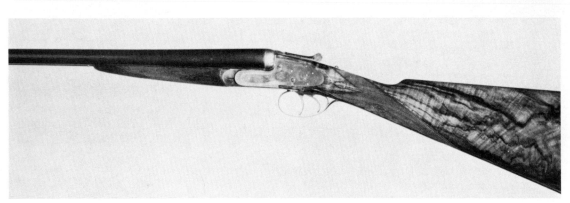

Sidelock ejector
12-bore d.b. gun
By J. Purdey, London
Built in 1897
Sold 22.6.83 for £4,860
($7,484)

All sold in London

Composite pair of
sidelock ejector 12-bore
d.b. guns
By J. Woodward,
London
Built *c.* 1900
Sold 22.6.83 for £5,400
($8,316)

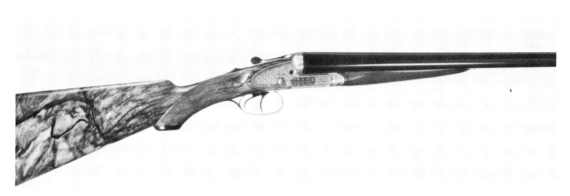

Sidelock ejector 12-bore
d.b. gun
By F. Beesley, London
Built in 1929
Sold 22.6.83 for £4,536
($6,985)

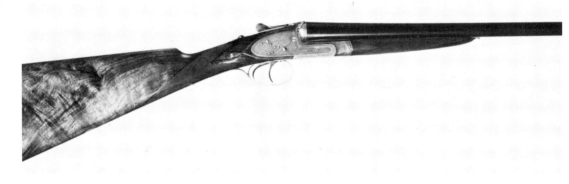

'Spring-Opener' sidelock
ejector 16-bore d.b. gun
By H. Atkin, London
Built in 1937
Sold 23.3.83 for £3,456
($5,136)

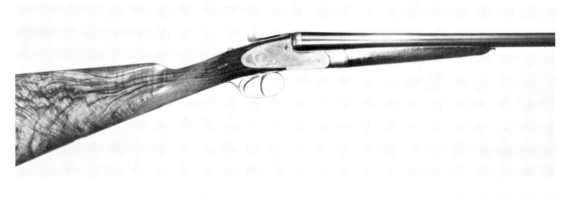

Self-opening over-and-
under sidelock ejector 12-
bore(2¾in) d.b. gun
By Harrison & Hussey,
London
Built *c.* 1927
Sold 22.6.83 for £4,968
($7,651)

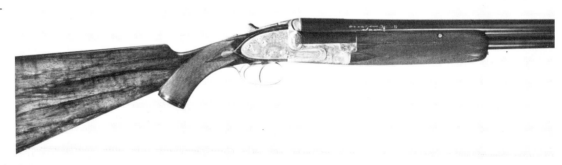

All sold in London

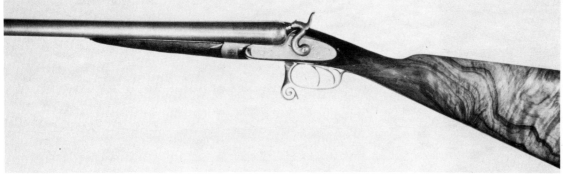

Pair of Purdey 1863
Patent snap-action
underlever bar-in-
wood sidelock
hammer 12-bore d.b.
guns
By J. Purdey, London
Built in 1877
Sold 23.3.83 for £1,944
($2,889)

Jones 1859 Patent
rotary-underlever
backlock hammer
8-bore d.b. shot-and-
ball gun
By J. Purdey, London
Built in 1877
Sold 15.9.82 for £1,944
($3,363)

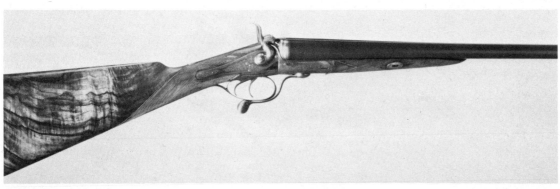

Pair of Jones 1859
Patent rotary-
underlever backlock
hammer 12-bore d.b.
guns
By S. Grant, London
Built in 1867, the year
after Grant opened his
own business
Sold 22.6.83 for £972,
($1,497)

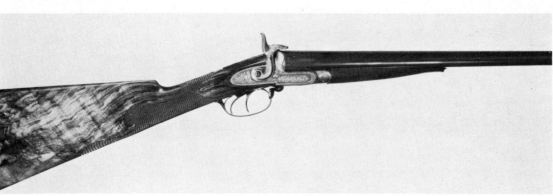

Pape 1866 Patent
snap-action thumb-
underlever sidelock
hammer 16-bore(pin-
fire) d.b. gun
By W.R. Pape,
Newcastle-upon-Tyne
Built c. 1868
Sold 22.6.83 for £810
($1,247)

All sold in London

Pair of 'Superbritte' vertical-hinge side-opening under-and-over ejector 12-bore(2¾in) d.b. guns
By J. Bury, Liège
Built *c.* 1935
Sold 22.6.83 for £4,536 ($6,985)

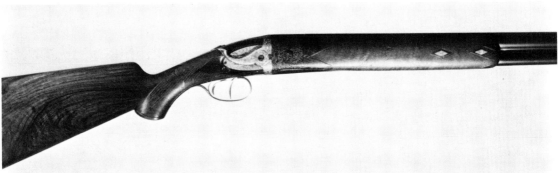

Mauser Model 1896 self-loading 7.63mm carbine-pistol, with leather holster
By Mauser, Oberndorf am Neckar
Retailed by Westley Richards in 1899
A rare variant of the Model 1896, combining a pistol-style frame and a carbine-style barrel-assembly
Sold 15.9.82 for £2,808 ($4,858)

'Welt Patent' 9mm(rim-fire) d.b. gun with barrels of variable inclination
Inscribed 'Scurimobile No.8D', Liège proof
Built *c,* 1895
Neither the patent nor the purpose of this curious weapon has been identified
Sold 8.12.82 for £432 ($707)

All sold in London

'Royal' backlock ejector .458 d.b. big-game rifle, with telescope
By Holland & Holland, London
Completed in 1982 and unused
Sold 8.12.82 for £12,960 ($21,216)

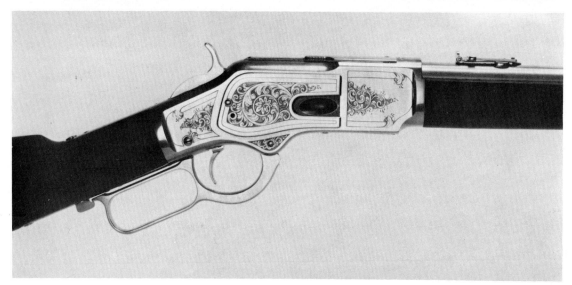

Winchester Model 1873 repeating carbine in .44-40 calibre, factory-engraved and nickel-plated (refinished)
By Winchester Repeating Arms Co., New Haven
Shipped in 1885
Sold 23.3.83 for £2,700 ($4,012)

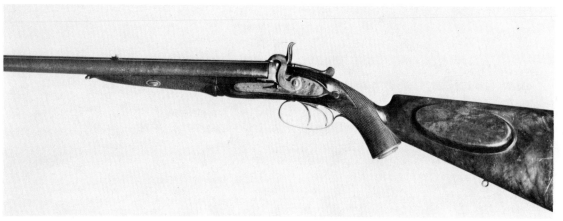

Westley Richards 1859 Patent bar-in-wood sidelock hammer .500(No.2) d.b. rifle
By Westley Richards, Birmingham and London
Built in 1871, incorporating various Westley Richards patents from 1859 to 1871
Sold 8.12.82 for £950 ($1,555)
All sold in London

SALES IN ITALY, THE NETHERLANDS, CHRISTIE'S EAST, NEW YORK AND AT CHRISTIE'S & EDMISTON'S, GLASGOW

ETTORE TITO: *Hanging the Washing*
Signed and dated 1905
Oil on canvas
60¼ x 31 in. (153 x 79 cm)
Sold 3.3.83 in Rome for L.20,520,000 (£9,039)

PETER BRUEGHEL THE YOUNGER: *The wife clothes her husband with a cloak, or in other words he is unaware that he is being deceived*, from a Flemish Proverb
Signed
Oil on panel
5⅞ in. (15 cm) in diameter
Sold for L.74,50,000 (£32,929)

PETER BRUEGHEL THE YOUNGER: *Hay runs after the horse or in other words the world is upside-down*, from a Flemish Proverb
Signed
Oil on panel
5⅞ in. (15 cm) in diameter
Sold for L.69,000,000 (£30,000)

Both sold 10.5.83 in Rome

GIOVANNI BATTISTA
RUOPPOLO: *Still Life*
Oil on canvas
36¼ x 60¾ in.
(92 x 154 cm)
Sold 2.12.82 in Rome
for L.28,500,000
(£12,555)

Right

ALESSANDRO ALLORI: *The*
Infant Jesus Engarlanding
the Virgin Mary
Oil on canvas
53¼ x 35½ in.
(135 x 89 cm)
Sold 2.12.82 in Rome
for L.17,100,000
(£7,533)

Far right

DOMENICO MAGGIOTTO:
The Astronomer
Oil on canvas
52½ x 37¾ in.
(133 x 96 cm)
Sold 10.5.83 in Rome
for L.16,100,000
(£7,092)

ALBERTO SAVIANO: *The Wicked Angel*
Signed and dated 1930
Oil on canvas
23¼ x 28 in. (59 x 71 cm)
Sold 23.11.82 in Rome for L.91,200,000
(£40,176)

CARLO CARRÀ: *Canal*
Signed and dated 1959
Oil on canvas
15¼ x 19¾ in. (38.5 x 50 cm)
Sold 18.5.83 in Rome for L.46,000,000
(£20,264)

Right

Louis XV ormolu Cartel clock
Signed J.B. du Tertre a Paris
35½ in. (90 cm) high
Sold 14.10.82 in Rome for
L.13,680,000 (£6,026)

Far right

Diamond brooch
By Bulgari
Sold 27.5.83 in Rome for
L.11,500,000 (£5,066)

Right

Urbino Istoriato dish
Dated 1543
11 in. (28 cm) diameter

Venetian jug
Late 16th century
From the workshop of Maestro
Domenico
7⅛ in. (18 cm) high

Urbino Istoriato dish
c. 1540
10½ in. (26.8 cm) diameter

All sold 25.5.83 in Rome for a total
of L.506,000,000 (£22,290)

ESAIAS VAN DE VELDE: *Travellers Ambushed on a Country Road*
Signed and dated 1625(?)
Oil on panel
10½ x 15½ in. (26.8 x 39 cm)
Sold 26.4.83 for D.fl.68,000
(£15,350)

LUDOLF BACKHUYZEN: *Dutch Shipping off the Coast*
Signed and dated 1684
Oil on canvas
20½ x 26 in. (52 x 66 cm)
Sold 7.12.82 for D.fl.142,000
(£32,054)

MAURICE DE VLAMINCK: *Route de Village, Hiver*
Signed
*c.*1927
Oil on canvas
22 x 26 in. (56 x 66 cm)
Sold 16.11.82 for D.fl.90,400 (£20,406)

JAN BRUEGHEL THE YOUNGER AND HENDRIK VAN
BALEN: *The Holy Family with the Infant St. John the Baptist*
Oil on panel
40¾ x 28½ in. (104 x 73 cm)
Sold 26.4.83 for D.fl.96,900 (£21,873)

435

ROELANT SAVERY: *The Conversion of St. Paul*
Signed and dated 1617
Oil on vellum laid down on panel
5½ x 7½ in. (14.2 x 19.3 cm)
Sold 7.12.82 for D.fl.39,900 (£9,006)

Set of four silver-gilt candlesticks
By Pieter de Keen
Amsterdam, 1734
8 in. (21 cm) high
Sold 9.12.82 for D.fl.31,920 (£7,205)

Louis XV bread-basket
By Reynier Brandt
Amsterdam, 1753
16¼ in. (41.5 cm) long
Sold 9.9.82 for D.fl.122,800 (£5,146)

Above left

BART ANTONY 'BART' VAN DER LECK:
Bij de Haard
Signed with initials and
dated '13
Casein oil on asbestos
27½ x 14¾ in. (70.5 x 38 cm)
Sold 16.11.82 for D.fl.57,000
(£12,866)

Left

Sitzmachine chair in bentwood
Designed by Josef Hoffman and
executed by J & J Kohn, Vienna
c.1905
43¼ in. (110 cm) high
Sold 3.3.83 for D.fl.36,480
(£8,234)

Above

South German or Austrian
softwood cupboard with
walnut veneer
18th century
87¼ in. (221 cm) high
Sold 10.9.82 for D.fl.75,240
(£16,984)

437

Berlin porcelain tête-à-tête
in leather travelling case
1780-90
Sold 25.11.82 for D.fl.38,760
(£8,749)

Silver-mounted stoneware jug
By Jan Emens
Raeren, 1583
Silver dated 1585
Sold 16.12.82 for D.fl.62,700 (£14,153)

Gilded bronze figure of
Avalokiteshvara
11th-12th century
Li tan Kingdom,
Song Dynasty
11¾ in. (30 cm) high
Sold 16.12.82 for D.fl.62,700 (£14,153)

Louis XVI style ormolu-
mounted, parquetry,
kingwood and satinwood
concert piano
The works by Erard,
Paris
Inscribed GRANDE PRIX
Exposition De Paris, 1889
60 in. (152.3 cm) wide
Sold 1.3.83 for $63,800
(£41,699)
From the Estate of
Arlene Beauclaire

Louis XV ormolu-
mounted and marquetry
commode
In the manner of Charles
Cressent
Signed Sormani, Paris
75 in. (190.4 cm) wide
Sold 1.3.83 for $33,000
(£21,568)
From the Estate of
Arlene Beauclaire

Louis Philippe Sèvres
porcelain-mounted ebony
cabinet
Paris, *c*.1845
50 in. (126.9 cm) wide
Sold 5.10.82 for $50,600
(£29,941)

Laminated rosewood open armchair
By John Henry Belter
c.1850
44 in. (111.76 cm) high
Sold 17.5.83 for $13,750 (£8,702)

Laminated rosewood and marble rococo
revival centre-table
By John Henry Belter
c.1840
30¼ in. (76.4 cm) diameter
Sold 17.5.83 for $35,200 (£22,278)

Viennese enamel vase
*c.*1875
17 in. (43.18 cm) high
Sold 1.3.83 for $15,400
(£10,065)

19th century French bronze
group of huntmaster and hounds
Cast from a model by Pierre-Jules
Mêne
Inscribed *P.J. Mêne, 1869*
26½ in. (67.31 cm) high
Sold 17.5.83 for $19,250 (£12,340)

Pair of gem-set angelfish clips
Sold 17.2.83 for $7,040 (£4,540)
From the Estate of Arlene Beauclaire

Silver centrepiece
By Gorham Co.
1871
11 in. (28 cm) wide
Sold 16.2.83 for $2,970 (£1,916)

Above

RICHARD HAYLEY
LEVER: *Dockside*
Signed
Oil on canvas
40 x 49½ in.
(101 x 125.7 cm)
Sold 26.1.83 for
$13,200 (£8,800)
From the Estate of
Sarah Hunter
Kelly

Yombe maternity group in wood
10 in. (25.4 cm) high
Sold 11.5.83 for $15,400
(£9,871)

Star of Bethlehem pieced and
appliqued quilt
Inscribed *Rachel Trundle,
Mt Auburn, Frederick Co.*
*c.*1860
94 x 96 in. (241.5 x 244 cm)
Sold 9.3.83 for $2,310 (£1,509)

Fortuny gold pleated silk
'Delphos' and a Fortuny gold
velvet jacket
Both sold 16.9.82 for a total
of $3,960 (£2,329)

Regina Sublima Corona No.37 automatic
changer 20½ in. disc music box
c.1900
76 in. (192.9 cm) high
Sold 8.12.82 for $6,600 (£4,125)

Bru bisque-headed bébé
Incised BRU Jner 11
24 in. (61 cm) high
Sold 9.3.83 for $3,850
(£2,516)

Double action pedal harp
By Lyon and Healy
Chicago, 1967
71 in. (180 cm) high
Sold 19.1.83 for $6,600 (£4,125)

443

THOMAS FAED, R.A., H.R.S.A.: *'From Hand to Mouth – he was one of the few who would not beg'*
Oil on canvas
61 x 85 in. (154.8 x 215.8 cm)
Sold 7.7.83 in Glasgow for £26,000 ($40,300)
Record auction price for a work by the artist

SIR JOHN LAVERY, R.A., R.S.A.: *Zächra*
Signed and dated 1914
Oil on canvas
29 x 20 in. (73.66 x 50.8 cm)
Sold 30.11.82 in Glasgow for £15,000 ($24,000)

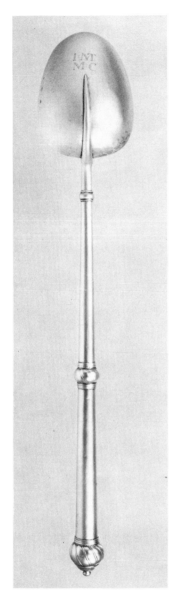

Queen Anne basting spoon
Maker's mark ML
Inverness
19¼ in. (49 cm) long
Sold 29.3.83 in Glasgow for
£5,200 ($8,268)
From the collection of the
Shaw Family

George II monteith
By James Ker
Edinburgh, 1746
The cypher and coronet are for John Hope,
2nd Earl of Hopetoun
Sold 29.3.83 in Glasgow for £23,000 ($36,570)
One of only nine recorded Scottish monteiths

Above

George II cake-basket
By James Ker, 1745;
assay master Hugh
Gordon
13 in. (33 cm) long
Sold 29.3.83 in Glasgow
for £21,000 ($30,660)
The arms are those of
Hope and the cypher and
coronet for John Hope,
2nd Earl of Hopetoun
(1704-1781), who
succeeded his father in
1742. This appears to be
one of the earliest
Scottish cake-baskets
recorded
From the collection of the
Shaw Family

445

Regency mahogany pedestal
partner's desk
60 in. (152.30 cm) wide
Sold 5.7.83 at Raith, Kirkcaldy,
Fife for £52,920 ($82,026)

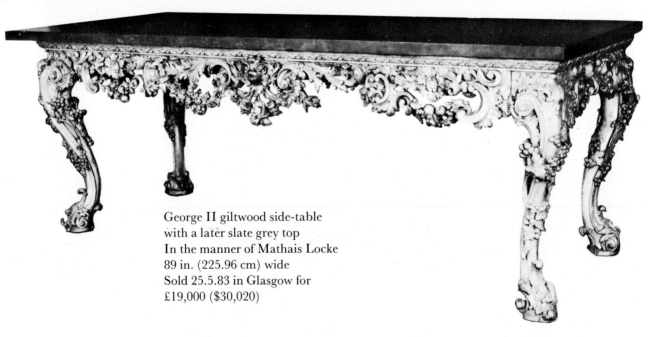

George II giltwood side-table
with a later slate grey top
In the manner of Mathais Locke
89 in. (225.96 cm) wide
Sold 25.5.83 in Glasgow for
£19,000 ($30,020)

PHOTOGRAPHS
CHRISTIE'S SOUTH KENSINGTON
AND CHRISTIE'S EAST, NEW YORK

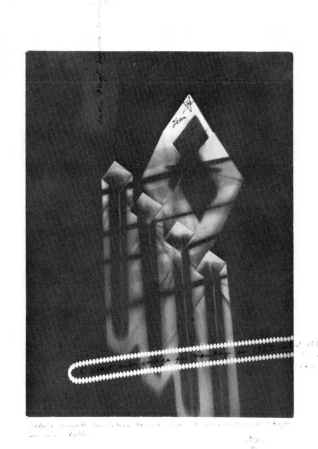

MAN RAY: *Rayograph*
Signed, dated and inscribed on the mount *à Jean Cocteau – Avril 1922*, OUTILS *pour* COLORADO, *Man Ray, Paris*. The image and mount signed and inscribed by Jean Cocteau. The inscription within the configuration of pearls reads *c'était mon image par Man Ray en 1922 – Est elle encore exacte?*.
Sold 9.5.83 in New York for $17,600 (£11,000)
From the Estate of Prince Theodore of Russia

PAUL OUTERBRIDGE, JR.:
Abstraction, 1922
Platinum print, 1922
Signed and dated on
mount
Sold 9.5.83 in New York
for $26,400 (£16,500)
Record auction price for a
work by the artist

ALEXANDER GARDNER: *Abraham Lincoln*
Albumen print, 1863
Sold 9.5.83 in New York for $10,450
(£6,531)
This rare vignetted profile showing the
seldom photographed left side of
Lincoln's face was taken in Washington,
November 8, 1863, 10 days before he
delivered his Gettysburg Address.

PAUL OUTERBRIDGE, JR.: *Ide collar*
Platinum print, 1922
Signed and dated on mount
Sold 8.11.82 in New York for $24,200
(£15,125)
The photograph originally appeared as a
full page advertisement in the November
1922 edition of Vanity Fair.

ALFRED STIEGLITS: *The Hand of Man, 1902*
Gelatin silver print, *c.* 1921
Signed, titled and dated
Sold 8.11.82 in New York for
$24,200 (£15,125)

CONSTANTIN BRANCUSI: *Interior of Brancusi Studio*
Gelatin silver print, *c.* 1928
Sold 8.11.82 in New York for
$7,700 (£4,812)

449

GUSTAVE LE GRAY: *Seascape with Coastline*
Albumen print, early 1850s
Sold 28.10.82 in London for £4,200
($7,098)

EUGENE ATGET: *Le Pont Marie, Paris*
Early 20th century
Sold 24.3.83 in London for £2,300
($3,404)

JOHN DILLWYN LLEWELYN and other photographers:
Eleanor and her Donkey, from an album of 139 photographs
1853
Sold 23.6.83 in London for £19,000 ($29,830)

FELICE BEATO, BARON VON STILLFRIED, KUSAKABE KIMBEI and
other photographers:
Japan
An album of 80 photographs
1860s
Sold 24.3.83 in London for £2,000 ($2,840)

Queen Victoria's Dogs
Two albums of 90 photographs by various photographers
1850-90s
Sold 24.3.83 in London for £1,222 ($1,735)

Great Exhibition of the Works of Industry of All Nations
Descriptive and illustrated catalogues
1851
Sold 24.6.82 in London for £5,000 ($7,700)

CHRISTIE'S SOUTH KENSINGTON AND MODELS AT THE BRITISH ENGINEERIUM

RESURGAM. One-man submarine built by Arthur Johnson and completed in May 1968. Welded throughout in ³/₁₆ in. mild steel plate. The submarine appeared at the request of United Artists at the world premier of the Beatles film *Yellow Submarine* in 1968
Sold 26.4.83 for £1,400 ($2,198)

Christie's South Kensington

WILLIAM BROOKS

The art market at Christie's South Kensington was consistently buoyant throughout the 1982/83 season. It has enabled us to increase our turnover to a new all time high in our ninth year of trading.

Some 55 different categories are now established at South Kensington and with our more selective approach to incoming goods for sale, the result is a considerable increase in the average price per lot, as well as creating and encouraging numerous new vendors and buyers.

Among the many interesting prices achieved this season was the record price of £35,000 ($53,200) paid for a 19th century mahogany extending dining table by the celebrated London cabinet maker Robert Jupe. It aroused keen interest from all over the world with its ingenious mechanism of revolving to incorporate eight extra leaves and thereby extending from 66 in to 98 in diameter. The design had proved extremely popular among collectors.

Christie's South Kensington achieved another record, equalling the world record of £260,000 ($400,500) set by the Hurricane at Strathallan in 1981, for a MKIX Spitfire MH 434, sold along with 50 other historic aircraft at a sale of Historic Aircraft held at the Imperial War Museum, Duxford. The sale, held on April 14th was a huge success attended by over 2,000 people.

There have been several innovations to the South Kensington salerooms, the most noticeable to clients will be our new exterior which we hope will entice an ever-increasing flow of visitors to our salerooms. There has been a transfer of department location – one such is the Book Department which now has its own self-contained saleroom. The move proved highly successful with a record sale total after the first sale in the new location. The introduction of evening wine sales has been enormously successful, enabling many potential buyers to sample and attend these sales out of normal business hours.

During the season, Christie's South Kensington have continued to support many deserving and diverse causes by way of lectures, valuation days and sales held on behalf of various charities such as the NSPCC, RNLI, Cancer Research, The Animal Health Trust and the Council and Care for the Elderly.

A novelty to our salerooms was the recent sale of the residual contents of Gellibrands, home of Laura, the Dowager Duchess of Marlborough. The sale was brought to London for convenience, and it enabled us to transform the saleroom into the various rooms of a private country house, complete with conservatory, much to the surprise of our regular patrons.

South Kensington's ever increasing liaison with St. James's has resulted in what we have called 'tandem sales', whereby both branches hold sales of similar categories on consecutive days, thereby giving a complete spectrum of items offered for sale.

THOMAS BAINES: *The Lion Family among the Granite Hills between Shasha and Macloutsie Rivers, Monday October 9, 1871*
Signed and dated 1872
Oil on canvas
20¼ x 26¼ in.
(51.4 x 66.7 cm)
Sold 27.10.82 for £14,000
($23,660)

RUDOLPH FREIDRICH KURZ: *Indians Fleeing a Prairie Fire*
Dated 6.5.54,
Watercolour and gum arabic on paper
13 x 19¾ in. (33 x 50 cm)
Sold 25.5.83 for £3,200
($5,088)

One of a group of six watercolours by Rudolph Kurz offered in this sale. They were originally in the collection of The Hon. Charles Augustus Murray, author of *Travels in North America, 1834-1836*, to whom they were given by the American artist George Catlin. The top price was £6,500 ($10,335) for *A Group of Indians on a River Bank*.

JEAN THEODORE PERRACHE: *A Gentleman*
Signed and dated 1784
Enamel
1¾ x 1½ in. (4.4 x 3.8 cm)
Sold 11.4.83 for £480 ($744)

ELMYR DE HORY, after RENOIR:
Jeune Fille Coussante
Bears two Renoir signatures
24 x 20 in. (60.9 x 50.8 cm)
Sold 24.1.83 for £1,200
($1,848)

JOHAN ADOLPH RUST: *Dutch Sailing Vessels*
Signed
18 x 24 in. (45.7 x 60.9 cm)
Sold 16.3.83 for £3,000
($4,530)

HELEN ALLINGHAM: *Young Children by a Cottage Gateway*
Signed
Watercolour heightened with white
14 x 10 in. (35.6 x 25.4 cm)
Sold 19.7.82 for £3,000 ($4,620)

HENRY JOHN SYLVESTER STANNARD: *A Surrey Lane*
Signed
Watercolour heightened with bodycolour and white
13 x 20 in. (33 x 50.8 cm)
Sold 28.3.83 for £1,600 ($2,368)

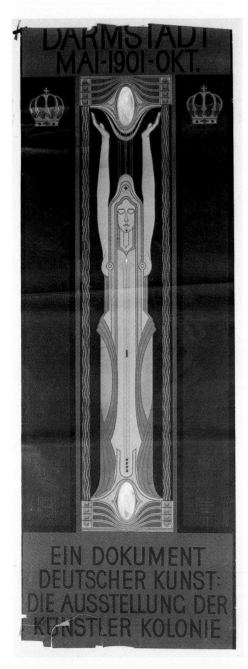

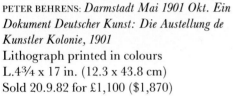

PETER BEHRENS: *Darmstadt Mai 1901 Okt. Ein Dokument Deutscher Kunst: Die Austellung de Kunstler Kolonie, 1901*
Lithograph printed in colours
L.4¾ x 17 in. (12.3 x 43.8 cm)
Sold 20.9.82 for £1,100 ($1,870)

Attributed to WASSILY KANDINSKY: *Chocolate of the 'Chevalier'*
By appointment to the court of His Majesty (in Russian lettering)
1901
Lithograph printed in colours
S.36 x 18½ in. (92.4 x 47.4 cm)
Sold 20.9.82 for £4,000 ($6,800)

Far right

KOLOMAN MOSER:
Frommes Kalendar
Lithograph printed in
colours
L.32¾ x 23 in.
(84 x 58.8 cm)
With another
impression of this
print in different
colours
S.37 x 24¾ in.
(95 x 63,4 cm)
Sold 20.9.82 for £2,800
($4,760)

Right

F. LAZZA: *Circuito di
Milano, Nel Parco Reale
di Monza, 1922*
1922
Lithograph printed in
colours
L.7½ x 5¼ in.
(19.1 x 13.5 cm)
S.7½ x 5¼ in.
(19.1 x 13.5 cm)
Sold 20.9.82 for £850
($1,445)

Posters

Several hundred posters, without doubt one of the largest single collections ever to appear on the open market, were offered for sale at Christie's South Kensington on Monday, 20th September. It was a huge success and set a precedent for a market in posters in this country.

The sale, consigned for sale by an institution, created quite a logistical problem due to their fragility and sheer numbers. The saleroom was filled to capacity, and with keen bidders from Europe and America competition was fierce. A poster attributed to Wassily Kandinsky for chocolate, created great interest and finally went for £4,000 ($6,800) to an American buyer. A poster by Peter Behrens for Darmstadt fetched £1,100 ($1,870). Peter Behrens was surely the best representative of the Succession Movement in this sale. Kolomon Moser's *Fromme Kalendar* (a rare artist in the saleroom), sold for £2,800 ($4,760) and one by Carl

Moos advertising Mode and Sport went for £1,400 ($2,380) to an American buyer. France and Belgium were not so well represented as Germany in this sale, but nonetheless its artists commanded high prices such as Steinlen's *Lait pur de la Vingeanne* for £1,300 ($2,210), Privat Livemont's *Rajah tea and Eau de Cologne* fetched £1,100 ($1,870), while Meunier's delightful poster for *Starlight Savon* went for £280 ($476). Italy too was well represented by F. Lazza with a poster for *Circuito di Milano* which sold to a Swiss collector for £850 ($1,445).

The sale was a near sell-out at £39,000 ($66,300) with only 3 per cent left unsold.

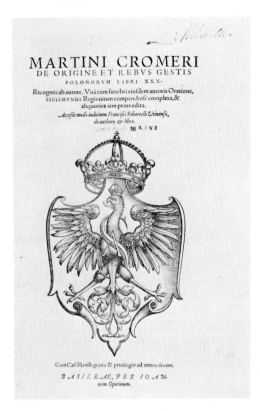

Far left

MARTIN CROMER: *Origine et Rebus Gestis Polonorum*
Basle, 1558
Folio
Sold 15.10.82 for £550
($952)

Left

G. HEYM: *Umbra Vitae*
Munich, 1924
Frontispiece and illustrations by Ernst Ludwig Kirchner, original pictorial cloth
Limited to 510 copies
Sold 21.1.83 for £1,400
($2,170)

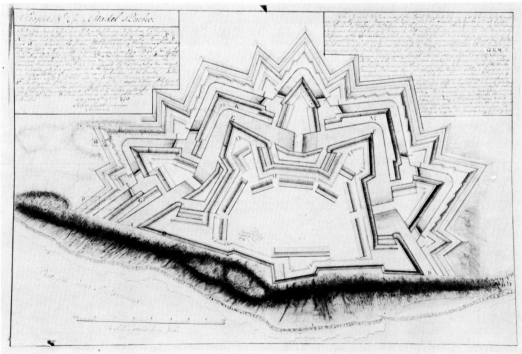

Left

LIEUT. JOHN MARR: *Project No.4, for a Citadel at Quebec*
Manuscript plan, on paper, ink and watercolour
Signed LONDON *8th April 1773, John Marr sub Engineer and Lieutenant*
18¾ x 27 in. (48 x 69 cm)
Sold 2.7.82 for £4,800
($7,392)

One from a set of 12 needlework panels for a room
Early 18th century
Sold 10.5.83 for £40,000 ($61,600)
From the collection of The Lord Trevor

The Trevor Hangings

SUSAN MAYOR

Until this suite of hangings appeared in London late in 1982, it was thought that only one suite of early 18th century English needlework hangings survived – at Wallington in Northumberland. The Wallington set is dated 1717 and is known to have been worked by Julia Lady Calverley and others, for Esholt Hall, Yorkshire, and moved in 1755 to Wallington.

The Trevor set is more elaborate, but less is known of its history. It may have been worked under the supervision of Anne, daughter of Sir John Trevor (1637-1717), Master of the Rolls and briefly Speaker of the House of Commons. Anne Trevor (1658?-1747/8) married firstly Michael Hill of Hilsborough Co. Down who died in 1699 and secondly Alan Broderick, later Viscount Middleton, in 1716. He died in 1727. The tapestries are thought by the family to have been made for Brynkinalt, but it is possible that they were made for one of the Hill-Trevor houses in Ireland: Belvoir, Ros Trevor, and Hilsborough Fort, Co. Down, or for Trevor House, Knightsbridge, now Trevor Square. Another quandary is what the hangings were designed for, some people suggest a screen, but they could have been fitted into the panels of a Jacobean style hall as only two pairs of panels have continuous landscapes. Some day some illustration of a Hill Trevor house may solve the mystery.

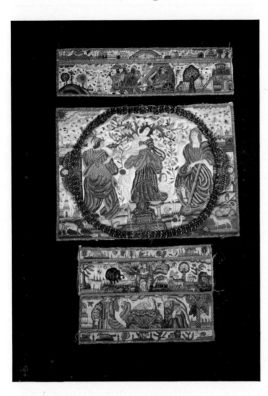

Front panel and border for a needlework casket
English, 17th century
Sold 10.5.83 for £950 ($1,027)

Needlework panel on ivory satin, probably the
lid from a casket which was possibly never made up
English, mid-17th century
11 x 15½ in. (27.9 x 39.4 cm)
Sold 10.5.83 for £4,800 ($7,584)

Two joined side panels and two borders from a
needlework casket
17th century
7½ x 11 in. (19 x 27.9 cm)
Sold 10.5.83 for £600 ($948)

Young girl's waistcoat of wool, embroidered in
green and orange crewels. c.1730
Sold 25.1.83 for £3,200 ($4,928)

Above

Bisque headed bébé, the kid body with
wooden legs
Marked BRU Jne. 10.
25 in. (63.5 cm)
Sold 15.4.83 for £7,800 ($12,090)

Above right

Japanese ivory
brisé fan
c. 1880
12 in. (55.9 cm)
Sold 8.3.83 for £2,400 ($2,198)

Right

Fan
By A. Solde
French, *c.*1865
11 in. (27.9 cm)
Sold 8.3.83 £1,100 ($1,672)

Victorian satinwood and mahogany
Canterbury whatnot
Stamped A.J. Owen & Co.
24 in. (60.9 cm) wide
Sold 2.2.83 for £1,400 ($2,156)

Satinwood Carlton House
writing table inlaid with
mahogany bands, musical
instruments and foliate
arabesques
Stamped Druce & Co.,
Baker Street, Portman Sq.
London W.
53 in. (134.6 cm) wide
Sold 9.2.83 for £5,800
($8,932)

Wootton style desk,
reputedly by E.W. Barnsley
43 in. (109.2 cm) wide
Sold 25.5.83 for £4,500
($7,155)

Victorian mahogany patent extending dining table
By Robert Jupe
66 in (167.6 cm)
82 in. (208.3 cm) diameter half extended; 98 in. (248.9 cm) diameter, fully extended
Sold 26.1.83 for £35,000 ($54,250)

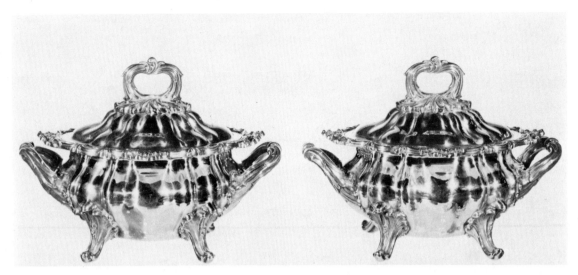

Pair of Victorian silver
sauce-tureens
By Robinson, Edkins
and Aston
Birmingham, 1845
8¼ in. (209 cm)
Sold 31.5.83 for £1,400
($2,212)

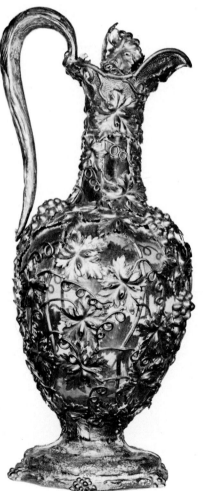

Silver Roman lamp table-lighter
By Omar Ramsden
London, 1937
7½ in. (19 cm) wide
Sold 21.3.83 for £780 ($1,154)

Victorian ruby-glass claret-jug, overlaid with silver trailing
vine decoration
By Reily and Storer
London, 1839
12½ in. (31.75 cm) high
Sold 28.2.83 for £2,600 ($4,004)

Pair of Victorian
silver-gilt cow
creamers
By George Fox
London, 1882 and
1883
6¾ in. (17.1 cm) high
Sold 18.4.83 for £2,200
($3,410)

Victorian silver-
mounted tortoishell
photograph frame
By William Comyns
London, 1895
4½ in. (11.4 cm) high
Sold 7.2.83 for £700
($1,078)

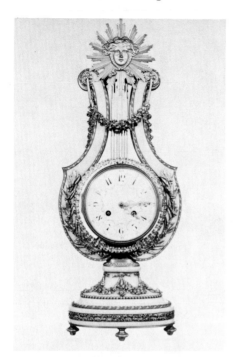

French white marble and ormolu
mounted lyre clock
By Festeau. Le Jeune à Paris
26 in. (66 cm)
Sold 12.1.83 for £2,400
($3,768)

Art Deco green onyx cased clock
flanked by two ivory female figures
By F Preiss
14½ in. (36.8 cm)
Sold 28.1.83 for £1,500
($2,310)

Blue and white cameo glass vase
By Stevens and Williams
6¼ in. (15.9 cm)
Sold 5.5.83 for £950 ($1,501)

One of a pair of Chinese
bronze figures of Kuan Yin
with silver wire inlay
55 in. (139.7 cm) high
Sold 20.12.82 for £7,000
($11,270)

Worcester blue and white
butter boat
c. 1755
4 in. (10.2 cm)
Sold 17.2.83 for £1,000
($1,540)

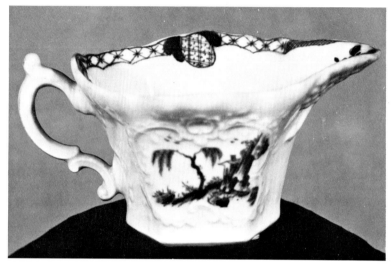

One of a pair of powder-
blue and gilt jars and
covers with metal collars
Sold 7.3.83 for £1,700
($2,618)

Staffordshire figure of Maria Malibran
c. 1836
7¼ in. (18.4 cm) high
Sold 12.5.83 for £2,400 ($3,720)

Whole-plate Chevalier photographe folding
daguerreotype camera outfit
By Charles Chevalier
Paris, *c.* 1840
Sold 7.4.83 for £11,000 ($16,390)

Dubroni wet-plate outfit in fitted walnut carrying case, including
accessories and instructions
Sold 26.5.83 for £3,000 ($4,746)

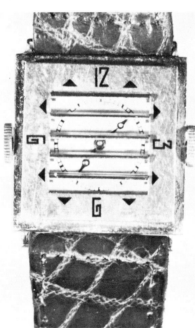

Above left

Berlin ironwork necklace and bracelet
Sold 7.6.83 for £500 ($785)

Above

Head of Ushabti brooch with diamond, onyx, ruby and emerald mounts
Signed Cartier, Paris
Sold 1.2.83 for £9,000 ($13,950)

Left

18 ct gold wrist watch, with button operated shutter cover to reveal dial
The movement signed Vacheron & Constantin
Sold 28.9.82 for £1,150 ($1,989)

Sir Winston Churchill's cigar in wooden case with plaque
This cigar, one of a box given by the Prime Minister in aid of the R.A.F. Benevolent Fund, was auctioned at the Albert Hall on January 26, 1942 by Sir Noel Curtis-Bennett K.C.V.O., and was purchased by John D. Jacoby Esq., for 140 Guineas and presented by him to Sir Noel as a momento of the occasion.
Sold 25.5.83 for £320 ($506)

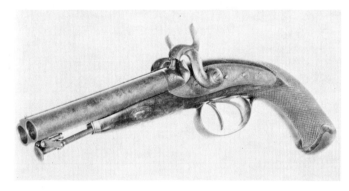

Irish double-barrelled percussion travelling pistol
By W & J Rigby, Dublin
10½ in. (26.7 cm)
Sold 26.1.83 for £400 ($616)

Right

Selection of items from The Adolph Ritter von Sonnenthal Collection relating to human freaks and their role in entertainment.
Sold 3.9.82 in 16 lots for a total of £3,900 ($6,747)

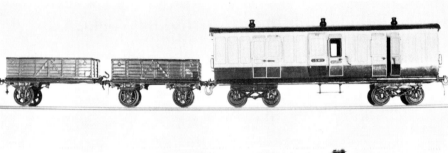

Prince of Wales, the cast brass name plate, London and North Western Railway Prince of Wales Class No. 819, October 1911; and *Princess Mary*, the cast brass nameplate, Great Central Railway Robinson Class No. 510
Sold 24.3.83 for £1,400 each ($2,044)

Mandolin interchangeable cylinder musical box on table with writing drawer
By Nicole Freres
The cylinders 19¼ in. (48.9 cm) long
Sold 23.9.82 for £4,500 ($7,785)

Early 20th century gauge 4 live steam, spirit-fired continental-type 4-4-0 locomotive and tender No E III
By Marklin
Two guage 4 open trucks and a LSWR twin-bogie full brake
By Bing
Sold 9.9.82 for £4,200 ($7,266)

Carette tinplate limousine
1911
12½ in. (31.8 cm) long
Sold 27.1.83 for £1,900 ($2,945)

Historic Aircraft

ROBERT BROOKS

Although Christie's had sold a small number of Historic Aircraft as early as 1969 it was not until the Strathallan and Wings and Wheels Collection sales in 1981 that aviation became a significant factor in the world of fine art auctioneering. The success and interest generated, combined with the ever growing ranks of historic aircraft collectors created considerable demand for a further sale. This was to be the first occasion on which a major auction house would undertake the sale of historic aircraft purely on a consignment basis and with no individual collection as a nucleus. It was particularly significant that we were able to obtain permission from The Imperial War Museum to hold the auction at Duxford. Apart from its geographical advantages, the museum also houses one of the world's finest aircraft collections, and is on the site of one of the most famous wartime fighter bases, from whence Spitfires and Hurricanes were flown during the Battle of Britain. The great co-operation and assistance received from the museum staff was essential to the success of the venture.

An exceptionally strong entry included the MK.IX Spitfire MH434; this was not only in flying condition, but also had a magnificent history including three wartime combat successes. Among the 47 other aircraft offered were a further three Spitfires. A month in advance of the April sale date a highly successful Press Day was organised at Wycombe Air Park, where the Spitfire and four other sale aircraft were demonstrated in flight. Both the preview and sale met with a massive press response: 16 major television companies sent camera crews. Worldwide interest ensured a massive attendance of over 2,000 on April 14th. To add to the atmosphere, a video film of each aircraft in flight was shown on a number of monitors in the marquee before each lot was offered.

Equalling the record £260,000 ($400,500) realised by the Hurricane sold at Strathallan in 1981, the Mk.IX Spitfire was bought by a British based syndicate despite strong overseas opposition. The other aircraft at the top end of the price sector also did extremely well, with only one or two exceptions. Although prices in the lower echelons of the market followed a less balanced pattern, £16,000 ($24,650) for the Stampe and an astonishing £19,000 ($29,300) paid for the De Havilland Chipmunk were auction records.

Plans are already advanced for further similar sales.

1943 Supermarine Spitfire LF Mk. IXB
Sold 14.4.83 at Duxford for £260,000 ($400,500)
Photograph: Arthur Gibson

1943 Hawker Tempest II
Sold 14.4.83 at Duxford for £85,000 ($131,000)
Photograph: David Lee

1951 Fieseler Fil56C (Morane-Saulnier M.S.500) Storch
Sold 14.4.83 at Duxford for £26,000 ($40,100)
Photograph: Air Portraits

1951 De Havilland DHC1 Chipmunk
Sold 14.4.83 at Duxford for £19,000 ($29,300)
Photograph: Clive Norman

1935 De Havilland D.H.90 Dragonfly
Sold 14.4.83 at Duxford for £35,000 ($54,000)
Photograph: Air Portraits

1960 Jaguar XK 150S 3.8 litre roadster
Sold 11.7.83 at Beaulieu for £16,000 ($24,640)

1933 Duesenberg La Grande SJ Phaeton
Coachwork by Union Body Company, Indianapolis
Sold 10.4.83 in Los Angeles for $319,000 (£208,000)

Model of the schooner
rigged single screw
steam yacht
Medusa R.Y.S.
c. 1906
Built by Messrs. Day,
Summers & Co.
Southampton
22¼ x 57 in.
(57 x 146 cm)
Sold on 29.11.82 for
£7,000 ($11,200)

Builder's mirror-
backed half model of
the twin screw steam
yacht *Nahlin*
c. 1930
Built by John Brown
and Co. Ltd.,
Clydebank
13½ x 79 in.
(34.5 x 203 cm)
Sold on 29.11.82 for
£2,600 ($4,150)

Exhibition standard
⅜ in. – 1 ft. scale model
of a triple expansion
surfacing condensing
marine engine and
associated equipment
c. 1932
Built by J.A. Mulhern,
Bootle
19 x 33¾ in.
(48.5 x 86.5 cm)
Sold on 18.4.83 for
£9,000 ($14,400)

Exhibition standard 5 in. guage model of the Great Western Railway Armstrong Queen Class 2-2-2 locomotive and tender No. 1118 *Prince Christian*
c. 1895
Built by P. Rich, Rhewderin
13⅞ x 52 in.
(35.5 x 133.5 cm)
Sold on 18.4.83 for £8,000 ($12,800)

7 mm fine scale two rail electric model of the Highland Railway *Drummond* 0-6-4 Banking Tank No 44
3½ x 10⅜ in.
(9 x 26.5 cm)
Sold on 29.11.82 for £600 ($960)

Contemporary French prisoner-of-war bone and horn model
of a 98 gun Royal Naval Man-of-War
8⅜ x 11¼ in. (21.5 x 29 cm)
Sold on 29.11.82 for £4,500 ($7,200)

Model of the sail/motor RNLI Watson type lifeboat Montrose
No. 1. *John Russell*
24½ x 36⅝ in. (62 x 94 cm)
Sold on 18.4.83 for £1,500 ($2,400)

WINE

From left to right

Ch. Lafite 1844, Ch. Lafite 1876,
Ch. Lafite 1868, Ch. Lafite 1883,
Ch. Lafite 1890

An Outstanding Wine Auction Season

DUNCAN McEUEN

Following the healthy wine auction market amidst surrounding signs of recession in 1982, sales this year have reflected unprecedented demand. Since January, King Street wine sales have averaged a 98 per cent sold total and remarkable new price levels have been achieved.

RECOVERY OF THE MARKET

There are several reasons for this upsurge. First, the trade, having experienced cash-flow problems last year, has now expanded its market and as a result has had to re-stock, with auctions providing the best means of supply. Second, there is a distinct shortage of mature wine and an ever-increasing demand for it. Third, the US dollar has been strong against sterling, and with a still barely tapped American market more and more fine wine is crossing the Atlantic. And fourth, this spring has seen widespread publicity for the 1982 Bordeaux vintage and opening prices from the châteaux have been high enough to make earlier vintages look extremely good value. There is no doubt that the combination of the quality and quantity of the 1982 wines makes them a tempting investment and the market has not been slow to appreciate the fact.

THE NEW POLICY

We have been able successfully to handle this boom through the newly introduced policy of running only two King Street sales a month. This, while leaving alternate Thursdays free to accommodate special sales, has enabled us to concentrate on one top quality Bordeaux sale per month together with a mixed Fine and Rare sale two weeks later. These latter sales have included vintage port, burgundy, champagne and cognac and regularly make over £100,000 ($155,000)

NOTABLE SALES

April 21 witnessed the biggest wine sale in the world since 1976 and a total approaching £500,000 ($780,000) was achieved. No less than 87 cases of Ch Latour 1955 were on offer and realised over £53,000 ($82,680), and there were also 119 cases of 1959 first growths which slaked the thirst of a market greedy for quantities of such an illustrious vintage.

On December 16 we auctioned the stock excess to requirements from Maison Prunier Traktir, the famous fish restaurant in Paris. Over 450 cases were sold which included 20 dozen Ch Margaux 1906 and a prolific quantity of top quality Sauternes from vintages of the 1920's, many in much sought-after half-bottles.

486

The advantage of a spare Thursday was appreciated on May 19 when we offered, at short notice, the cellar of a deceased wine connoisseur whose 325 cases sold for a staggering average of £700 ($1,106) per case. No less than five different wines passed the £2,000 ($3,160) per dozen barrier and a further 13 wines made £1,200 ($1,896) per dozen or more.

Another example of a Christie promotional sale at the request of a grand cru proprietor was evidenced on July 14 when we sold, in the afternoon session, 27 vintages of Ch Beau-Séjour-Bécot, a premier grand cru classé from Saint-Emilion. On offer on June 30 was the private reserve stock of Mme Henry Binaud, the former owner of Château Cantemerle. Twenty vintages from 1905 of that château were sold, together with several pre-phylloxera vintages of Château Lafite, commencing with the 1844.

SOUTH KENSINGTON

Wine sales in the Old Brompton Road continue to prosper and their regular monthly occurrence always draws a large audience intent on purchasing every-day drinking wines spiced with small lots of often fascinating and rare bin-ends. This venue also gives a service to the Trade who dispose of over-stocked lines and, sadly, occasionally sell their stock-in-trade under the auspices of the Receiver.

GENEVA AND AMSTERDAM

We have had the usual bi-annual sales in these centres and while the Swiss results are unspectacular, although dependable, I am glad to report that the reversion to the old format of two sales a year in Amsterdam has paid dividends and a total of £195,000 ($302,250) has been achieved. The market there is strong and enthusiastic and the quality of wine on offer is steadily improving.

CHICAGO

The American market potential is highly encouraging and Michael Broadbent has conducted four auctions in Chicago to illustrate it. They produced a total of over $1¼ million (£806,450) with the sale in November including three exceptional cellars, two from private collectors and the third from Maxims in Chicago, the restaurant faithfully modelled on its Paris namesake. While Chicago auctions offer good *tranches* of mature vintages there is a preponderance of mixed lots and small quantities of the most exceptional rare wines, mostly stored in carefully temperature controlled cellars, and these provide the attraction which draws large audiences and usually upwards of 1,000 written commissions to bid.

CHRISTIE'S WINE PUBLICATIONS

Activity has been maintained on the publication front with *Mouton Baronne Philippe* by Joan Littlewood and Edmund Penning-Rowsell appearing in the autumn and the 1983 edition of *Christie's Price Index of Vintage Wine* in April. This invaluable production lists over 5,000 wines and prices obtained at London and Chicago auctions and now incorporates a new section charting the prices realised over the past 12 years for the leading post-war vintages and châteaux of Bordeaux, and for the top shippers of port covering the best vintages back to 1927.

In June we published, in association with Constables, *Victorian Vineyard – Château Loudenne and the Gilbeys* by Nicholas Faith.

Wine

Some of the outstanding prices of the 1982/1983 season

Red Bordeaux

1844 Ch Lafite	£2,100 ($3,297) (per bottle)
1874 Ch Lafite	£1,150 ($1,886) (per magnum)
1899 Ch Mouton-Rothschild	£290 ($458) (per bottle)
1914 Ch Petrus	£360 ($587) (per bottle)
1928 Ch Latour	£340 ($554) (per magnum)
1945 Ch Mouton-Rothschild	(£7,200) ($11,304) (per dozen bottles)
1945 Ch La Mission-Haut-Brion	£1,500 ($2,220) (per dozen bottles)
1945 Ch Petrus	£560 ($856) (per bottle)
1947 Ch Cheval-Blanc	£1,050 ($1,596) (per 6 bottles)
1953 Ch Lafite	£1,350 ($2,052) (per jeroboam)
1961 Ch Lafite	£2,300 ($3,611) (per dozen bottles)
1966 Ch Petrus	£1,550 ($2,449) (per dozen bottles)
1975 Ch Petrus	£1,000 ($1,580) (per dozen bottles)

White Bordeaux

1890 Ch d'Yquem	£300 ($456) (per bottle)
1921 Ch d'Yquem	£200 ($336) (per bottle)
1967 Ch d'Yquem	£620 ($1,054) (per dozen bottles)

Red Burgundy

1947 La Tache	£740 ($1,162) (per 2 bottles)
1949 Corton Clos du Roi	£370 ($548) (per dozen bottles)
1955 Romanée-Conti	£500 ($760) (per 6 bottles)
1959 La Tache DRC	£960 ($1,565) (per 6 magnums)
1976 Chambertin	£310 ($471) (per 6 magnums)

White Burgundy

1971 Montrachet Latour	£400 ($628) (per 9 bottles)
1976 Montrachet Laguiche	£480 ($730) (per dozen bottles)

Champagne

1964 Dom Perignon	£370 ($625) (per dozen bottles)
1971 Dom Perignon	£330 ($488) (per dozen bottles)

Port

1931 Quinto do Noval	£300 ($462) (per bottle)
1935 Taylor	£740 ($1,169) (per dozen bottles)
1945 Taylor	£720 ($1,137) (per dozen bottles)
1945 Graham	£1,150 ($1,771) (per dozen bottles)
1963 Croft	£165 ($261) (per dozen bottles)

Cognac

1811 Napoleon Grande Fine Champagne	£390 ($593) (per bottle)
1906 Prunier Grande Champagne	£1,400 ($2,268) (per dozen bottles)

STAMPS

Van Diemen's Land
1853 a letter from a soldier with the
99th Duke of Edinburgh's Lanarkshire
Regiment in Tasmania, posted within
the first ten days of issue of Tasmanian
stamps
Sold 4.5.83 for £6,500 ($10,270)

Robson Lowe – Stamps

PETER COLLINS

Results for the season confirmed that there is a strong recovery in the market after the years in the doldrums. The message came through clearly that good material fetches good prices; indifferent material is unsaleable. From mid-season onwards sales frequently showed 80 per cent and upwards of the lots selling, and total realisations generally exceeded valuation, even allowing for the unsold lots.

BOURNEMOUTH

In Bournemouth, good general collections of most countries sold readily enough to confirm the impression that the market has returned to good health; whether it was the collectors or dealers who were buying, there was proof of steady demand. The Scandinavian group of countries continues to be much sought after, the Australian market is recovering and fine Great Britain stamps have again become very saleable. In British Empire, the Georgian High Values of the 1920s and '30s were strong but, above all, it was evident that *condition* is paramount in considering the value of any philatelic item. Postal History remained as popular as ever. Competition for the unusual (as much as rare) items ensured pleasing realisations for good lots.

JOHN O. GRIFFITHS GREAT BRITAIN

In Switzerland, the season opened on 29th September with the collection of Great Britain classics formed by John O. Griffiths which realised a total of Sw.fr. 768,178 (£208,744) with some striking single lots including a notice to postmasters dated 7th May 1840 bearing a pair of Penny Blacks with letters VR (instead of Maltese Cross) in upper corners, which realised Sw.fr. 15,500 (£4,212). A mint block of six 1d. black plate V, formerly in the Caspary collection sold for Sw.fr. 30,000 (£8,152) and a handsome mint block of 2d. blues made Sw.fr. 40,000 (£10,869). A magnificent mint block of 16 1850 10d. embossed, probably the largest mint multiple in existence, and once owned by the Swiss tobacco magnate Burrus, realised Sw.fr. 46,500 (£12,636).

MIDAS BRITISH EMPIRE

On 30th September, the "Midas" collection of British Empire rarities came under the hammer in Zurich, and realised a total of Sw.fr. 878,030 (£238,595). Almost every stamp in this sale had a pedigree or a fascinating history.

With the conquest of Scinde in 1850 Sir Bartle Frere was appointed Governor. His statue stands in Embankment Gardens, London, a memorial to a great Indian administrator. In 1851

Griffiths collection
Mint block of Penny Blacks
Sold 29.9.82 in Zurich for Sw.fr.30,000
(£8,152)

he introduced the horse and camel dawk (post) to supplement the foot runners. This increased the weight of mail that could be carried and cut hours off the time of delivery, but when Frere wanted further improvements to the system the government pointed out that there were more pressing things to spend money on, so Frere ordered his own stamps from De La Rue and issued them to every police officer and native collector of revenues, making every government office in the province of Scinde a post office.

The design of the stamps embodied the Christian Symbol of the Cross and "the mystic sign of 4", invoking Divine protection against the powers of evil. This was a Merchant's Mark used by the East India Company on freight shipped from England on the long, perilous journey round the Cape of Good Hope. The initials of the company appear on the stamp, and also the wording SCINDE DISTRICT DAWK; so Sir Bartle Frere introduced a postal system to Scinde in the words of his report "a complete network of post offices and postal lines all over the country without expence".

The Scinde Dawk stamps were produced locally, first in red sealing wax, secondly with colourless impressions from the die on white paper and, finally, in London from a new die produced by De La Rue.

In 1918 the British Army had moved into the former Turkish territory of Iraq and, to provide stamps quickly, overprinted the stocks of Turkish stamps available with the words IRAQ IN BRITISH OCCUPATION. Some years ago a copy of one of these stamps with the overprint inverted was found. Obviously the sheet had been fed into the printing press upside down but nobody had noticed this, and the stamps were sold and used. Only two used copies of this great rarity are known.

Kut is the Arabian word for a walled village. Kuwait is its diminutive form, with alternative spelling of KOWEIT or KUWET. Kuwait is an important port of Arabia and in 1899 the Sheikh sought British protection against the threat of the Turks. In connection with the wartime operations against the Turks, an Indian post office was established there in 1915 and, from that time, Indian stamps are found used in Kuwait. In 1923 consideration was given to overprinting Indian stamps for use in the Sheikhdom and a series of 15 values was produced overprinted KUWAIT. An official experimental printing of 14 values and 13 "Official" stamps with the overprint spelled Koweit was made. It is believed that only 24 complete sets were printed.

In Acre, a town which was then in the British Mandated territory of Palestine, a Moslem family bought a sheet of stamps at the post office to stamp the invitations to their daughter's wedding. They did not realise that the overprint reading PALESTINE in three languages (Arabic, Hebrew and English) had been applied upside down. The stamps were used and subsequently 11 copies with this inverted overprint were located. Seven of them are damaged. No unused examples are known to exist. A used copy of the 1m. sepia overprinted issue of 1922 made Sw.fr 32,000 (£8,696)

GREAT BRITAIN

On 8th September 1982, two realisations in the Great Britain sale topped £1,000 ($1,728); a Mulready 1d. envelope dated 10th May 1840 (the first Sunday of use), and a selection of 84 Penny Blacks.

LILLYWHITE'S COFFEE HOUSES

During the 17th century Coffee Houses served as post offices, and provided a *poste restante* address for their clients. A fascinating encylopaedic work on the services and usage of the coffee houses was published in 1963 by Bryant Lillywhite after scholarly study of the extensive collection he had acquired over many years. When the collection was sold as a part of the Postal History Auction of 22nd February it realised £3,500 ($5,323)

COLLEGE STAMPS

Towards the end of last year, a family found a parcel which had been long-overlooked, comprising the collection of stamps issued by the Colleges of Oxford and Cambridge. These stamps had been exhibited in an International Stamp Exhibition in London in 1908, where they had won a top award. The owner was the Rev. Hayman Cummings, an Oxford clergyman, who subsequently sold his collection to a north of England philatelist for £200. He had apparently done nothing with it, for it was still on the original leaves on which it had been displayed. Three quarters of a century after its exhibition triumph it came to light again, appearing in the 12th April Great Britain auction where, offered as 60 lots, it realised £10,298 ($15,880). The highlight was an envelope bearing the Hertford College stamp cancelled by the special handstamp of a "Cross Patée Fitchée". It realised £1,700 ($2,621) which is a world record price for any college stamp. One similar cover is in the Royal Collection and a third copy is owned by a collector in Somerset who has specialised in the study of College Stamps since 1916! He is one of the most senior Fellows of the Royal Philatelic Society and it is pleasing to record that he was successful with some of his bids in this sale and able to add one or two pieces to his collection. This auction was of note in that £100,000 ($150,900) worth of Great Britain stamps was sold before lunch.

Another Great Britain "find" was the hoard in a West Sussex garage with early correspondence bearing Penny Blacks. While, in Belgium, a political change brought out a collection of stamp boxes. A wealthy collector was accumulating stamp boxes which he proposed presenting to a museum. A change in government policy meant money to finance the museum was withdrawn and the collector approached Robson Lowe to sell his collection ranging from classic silver stamp cases to modern plastic containers. The collection realised £4,500 ($6,939) when offered in London on 9th November 1982.

Midas
Sold 30.9.82 in Zurich for Sw.fr.21,900
(£5,961)

Sw.fr.1,500 (£408)
Sw.fr.2,600 (£707)
Sw.fr.20,000 (£5,435)

Koweit overprints
Sold 30.9.82 in Zurich for Sw.fr. 32,000
(£8,696)

Rarities of Palestine Mandate Period

Right

(top) Sw.fr.30,000 (£8,152)
(bottom) Sw.fr. 34,000 (£9,240)

Centre

Sw.fr.7,500 (£2,038)

Far right

(top) Sw.fr.4,600 (£1,250)
(bottom) inverted overprint Sw.fr.32,000
(£8,696)

 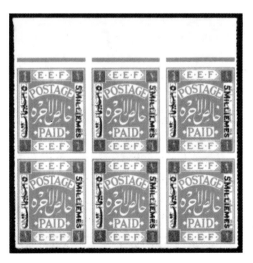 

FOUR LETTERS FROM A SOLDIER SOLD FOR £13,050 ($20,599)

Four letters to a banker in Blairgowrie, Scotland realised on the 14th May for £13,050.

They were dated between 1850 and 1855 from a soldier guarding the convicts in Australasia. The earliest was from Norfolk Island which was colonised by deportees from Botany Bay. The others were from Van Diemens Land (Tasmania), whence the writer's unit of the 99th, Duke of Edinburgh's Lanarkshire Regiment, had been moved. One of the letters bears four copies of the first Tasmania 1d. stamp printed at the local newspaper office and used within the first ten days of its issue.

The writer of these letters would have been rich if he could have had what they realised! The letters were among some old correspondence that was to go as waste paper.

ZURICH MAY/JUNE 1983

The auction held on the 31st May attracted 206 competitors from 30 different countries. The total sales were Sw.fr. 628,126 (£184,743), nearly 16 per cent over the auctioneer's estimate, with 26 per cent of the value unsold.

In this sale, Japan prices averaged 99 per cent over the estimate with less than 10 per cent unsold. The two top covers went to a Zurich connoisseur who was eagerly chased by another collector from Basle and two busy Japanese. The 1871 cover with a pair of 200 mons brought Sw.fr. 15,750 (£4,632) and the 1872 cover with the 1 sen, Sw.fr. 16,875 (£4,963). The Ryukyu mint block of 1952 100y. on 2y. brought Sw.fr. 8,437 (£2,482). There was a strong demand for the mail addressed to Japan.

NEW YORK

Stamp sales in New York for 1982-83 season totalled $1,523,869. An additional $755,595 was generated from two very successful coin and paper currency sales held by the New York Stamp Department. This second year of stamp auctions in New York was marked by discovery and surprise.

The major part of the September 15/16, 1982 sale came from the estate of an American collector, Richard Fay Saffin.

In the 1920s, Richard Saffin had amassed enough wealth to support his collecting pursuits during his remaining sixty years. With a penchant for the unusual, he collected many great philatelic items. But being a recluse, Saffin kept his treasures hidden from the public eye. When his albums were opened by Christie's specialists, the magnitude of his spectacular collection became known.

Of the many extraordinary pieces that Saffin owned, by far the greatest is the envelope illustrated. Mailed in 1856 from Hawaii to San Francisco, by the sailing vessel "Yankee", this envelope bears a unique combination of elements to pay postage. The Hawaiian stamp at upper left is one of the rare "Missionary" stamps, so-called because of their use by missionaries on the islands. The envelope itself is a rarity, as it is imprinted by the California Penny Post Company, a private local mail delivery service which operated briefly during the gold-rush era when government mail service was extremely slow. A 3¢ U.S. stamp is affixed at upper right.

This remarkable item was virtually unknown in philatelic circles. Its history was traced back to the discovery of a file of letters saved by the operator of the California Penny Post, who anticipated a lawsuit with the U.S. Government over his mail service.

The price attained for this unique artefact of postal history was $46,200 (£26.705), paid by New Orleans dealers, Raymond and Roger Weill.

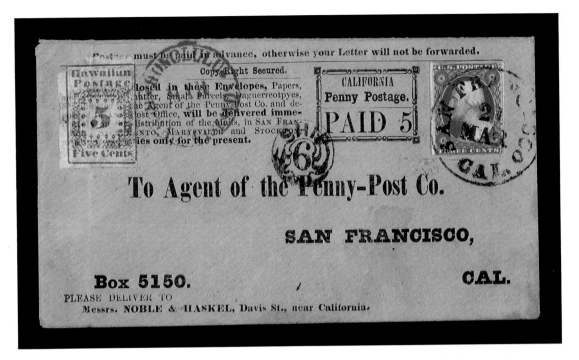

This remarkable 1956 cover bears four different types of postage to carry it on its journey from Hawaii to California U.S.A., producing an extraordinary combination cover.

The cover is an entire of the California Penny Postage Company, to which have been added the 5¢. Missionary to pay the ship-to-shore rate, and the U.S. 3¢. to pay the delivery charges in the U.S.A.. The clamshell design 'SHIP 6' handstamp indicates that the incoming Private Ship Letter Fee to the U.S.A. was charged to the addressee.

The clamshell handstamp is a rarity in its own right.

Persia 1kr. lake-red with two stamps inverted, producing two tête bêche pairs
Sold 30.11.82 in Zurich for Sw.fr.30,000 (£8,746)

Another surprise in the marketplace was the emergence of the Troy collection, which had lain dormant since before World War II. Neatly arranged in five leather-bound albums, the Troy collection was a perfect example of basic stamp collecting on a very grand scale. Its purpose was to show one example of every stamp issued from countries around the world, during the nineteenth century.

While not nearly complete – because completeness is an impossibility – the Troy collection displayed far more stamps than most collectors can ever hope to acquire, especially in rarities.

For example, among the U.S. items was a brilliant yellow stamp picturing Minerva. The stamp was originally issued in large quantities in 1875 to pay postage on newspapers and magazines mailed in bulk. It was reprinted that year for sale at the 1876 Centennial Exposition. Only four of these special printing stamps were actually issued.

The difference between the original and special printings is very slight. But to a collector, it means a great deal. The original stamp is worth a few hundred dollars. The special printing stamp contained in the Troy collection sold for $12,650 (£8,214).

A review of this season shows that Philately is flourishing.

CHRISTIE'S FINE ARTS COURSE

Christie's Fine Arts Course

ROBERT CUMMING

Vienna was the centre for our annual Spring expedition this year. We were a group of 40, young and old, of a wide variety of nationalities, for most of whom Vienna, its museums, its opera and coffee houses was a new discovery. We stayed near Stefansdom in the heart of the city, and in a week explored most of the major monuments with trips out to the Palace of Schonbrunn and along the Danube to the great monastery of Melk. We also saw a splendid performance at the State Opera House of Richard Strauss's Salome. As so much of our teaching stresses the importance of first hand contact with works of art, and the importance of visual values, these annual expeditions, backed up with lectures, are of the greatest importance. We are therefore especially grateful to all those who opened for us collections or buildings which are normally inaccessible. Without the help of our agent in Vienna, Vincent Windisch-Graetz, we would have had a much poorer visit. Dr Fitz Koreni of the Albertina showed us a selection of their finest Durers – a truly memorable experience – Dr Manfred Leithe-Jasper introduced the Kunsthistoriches Museum to us; the curator of the Abbey of Klosterneuburg opened their breathtaking treasury; and the officials of the Post Office took us to the inner rooms of Otto Wagner's brilliant art nouveau building. We thank them all, and also Tobias Meyer, now a student in Vienna, who writes as follows:

"I joined the Christie's Course in 1981 after leaving school. Now I am studying art history at Vienna University and work as a part-time volunteer in the art trade.

The Course gave me the best possible foundation for my present studies and work, both of which reflect the morning lectures and afternoon study groups on which the Course is based. The lectures in the morning were given by experts, many of whom came from outside the Course and Christie's. Subjects of each period were discussed in chronological order and they included historical introductions, painting, sculpture and decorative arts. Lectures about techniques and restoration added to the wide variety of subjects. The organisers of the Course took great trouble to invite a specialist on each subject and when reading after the lecture it happened quite frequently that I found the name of the lecturer on the cover of a book written on the same topic. The immense value of those lectures was that, being provided with the necessary information about a period of its works of art, students saved a lot of time by not having to search for the appropriate book on the subject. Essential points and facts were given in such a way that one never felt lost despite the vast areas of art history which were covered. Students were presented with an accurate easily comprehensible extract of information. This extract could either be directly digested to serve as a basis of general knowledge, or on the other hand could be just the initial motivation for further study.

Having attended those lectures I have found myself well prepared for the scholarly theories about art history I am now confronted with at the University of Vienna. Although I have gained new knowledge from university lectures there was much in them with which I was already familiar. Talking to my colleagues in Vienna I realise how much we were offered at the Course. Many times, especially in classes about 19th/20th century art, I will see a picture and suddenly remember what we were told about it at Christie's. Thus I have found the main advantage of the lectures at the Course is that they have served as an excellent basis for the academic approach to art history at university.

The afternoon classes had a different purpose. In my opinion there were three main lessons to be learned.

1. We learned how to look at a work of art. It was not easy at first to analyse the composition of a painting, to give attention to details and to learn to compare works of art. But under constant guidance it became more and more clear to us how we could develop a "good eye". Only by looking at art are we able to build up a library of works of art in our visual memory. By the end of the Course there would be moments when I knew, being shown a work of art, that I had seen similar works of art before, and could confidently identify what they were.

2. The second lesson learned is best expressed in the words we were told on the first day of the Course in the introductory speech: "learning comes in three stages: first you know nothing; then you think you know everything; and then you think you know nothing. When you reach the third stage you are beginning to get somewhere." Any opinion voiced by a student about a work of art had to be backed up with proof. We had to explain what we saw and what it could mean. We were shown things that did not seem to fit any period or style, and things we did not even know existed. This constant battle with our inadequate knowledge was sometimes frustrating, but today I am very grateful for the sometimes tough treatment we received, for in the art trade one very often comes across works of art that are not museum pieces, and not at all easy to identify.

3. The third lesson was to learn how to catalogue a work of art. We were taught the exact terms for techniques, shapes, decorations and ornaments and the language with which one could identify a work of art without a photograph. This was of great benefit to me when I started working in the art trade.

My main work in the art trade is to catalogue works of art. Besides that I have to write business letters and talk to prospective clients about works exhibited in the gallery. After almost one year in London and having been a frequent, although passive visitor to the saleroom, I am proud to say that I am at intervals sent to London to buy at auction.

When I compare the Christie's Fine Arts Course with my present situation I might come to the conclusion that I am now going through an intensified version of the Course. Half of my day is spent attending lectures at University. The lectures do not change from day to day but give intense and profound information about a more restricted period of art history. The other half of the day I catalogue works of art, I have to talk about them and, inevitably, look at them first hand. The only real difference is that the constant supervision by my tutor on the Course, who also tested my academic knowledge acquired in lectures, is only partially replaced by the supervision of my employer. We do not have direct supervision at the university, so that coming back to Vienna I had to discover that there is nobody to tell me to work hard. Having been looked after for one year, I have had to learn to work on my own.

The Christie's Course has given me the chance of making my hopes for the future become a reality much earlier than I had thought possible and I can say quite confidently that the Christie's Fine Arts Course is the best place to learn about art. However, I confess there is one thing I still find slightly confusing. I have learned a lot of facts about art, and as a student and trainee art dealer I am always studying and handling objects. But what is art? Whenever art reveals itself to somebody it is such a personal experience, and that experience can never be bought or sold. The canvas or the piece of furniture may change hands at a certain price, but the personal experience of looking at a work of art can never be completely transferred from one person to another."

Christie, Manson & Woods Ltd

LONDON
Christie, Manson & Woods Ltd.
8 King Street, St James's, London SW1Y 6QT
Telephone (01) 839 9060   *Telex* 916429
Cables Christiart London SW1

SOUTH KENSINGTON
Christie's South Kensington Ltd
85 Old Brompton Road, London SW7 3JS
Telephone (01)581 2231   *Telex* 922061
Cables Viewing London SW7 England

GLASGOW
Christie's & Edmiston's Ltd
164-166 Bath Street, Glasgow G2 4TG
Telephone (041)332 8134/7 *Telex* 779901

Christie's in the City
Simon Birch
10/12 Copthall Avenue
London EC2R 7D
Telephone (01) 588 4424

Agents in Great Britain and Ireland

INVERNESS
Jack Buchanan
111 Church Street, Invernesss
Telephone (0463) 234603

PERTHSHIRE
Sebastian Thewes
Strathgarry House, Killiecrankie
by Pitlochry
Perthshire
Telephone (079681) 216

ARGYLL
Sir Ilay Campbell, Bt.
Cumlodden Estate Office
Crarae, Inveraray, Argyll
PA 328YA
Telephone (05466) 633

EDINBURGH
Michael Clayton
5 Wemyss Place, Edinburgh
Telephone (031) 225 4757

AYRSHIRE
James Hunter Blair
Blairquhan, Maybole
Ayrshire
Telephone (06577) 239

NORTHUMBRIA
Aidan Cuthbert
Eastfield House, Main Street
Corbridge, Northumberland
Telephone 043471) 3181

NORTH-WEST
Victor Gubbins
St. Andrew's Place, Penrith, Cumbria
Telephone (0768) 66766

YORKSHIRE
Sir Nicholas Brooksbank, Bt.
46 Bootham, York
Telephone (0904) 30911

WEST MIDLANDS
Michael Thompson
Stanley Hall, Bridgnorth, Shropshire
Telephone (07462) 61891

MID-WALES
Sir Andrew Duff Gordon, Bt.
Downton House, New Radnor,
Presteigne, Powys
Telephone (0242) 518999

EAST ANGLIA
Veronica Bowring
Davey House
Castle Meadow
Norwich NR1 3DE
Telephone (0603) 614546

COTSWOLDS
111 The Promenade, Cheltenham, Glos.
Telephone (0242) 518999
Rupert de Zoete *Consultant*

WEST COUNTRY
Richard de Pelet
Monmouth Lodge, Yenston
Templecombe, Somerset
Telephone (0963) 70518

SOUTH DORSET AND SOLENT
Nigel Thimbleby
Wolfeton House, Dorchester, Dorset
Telephone (0305) 68748
and at
Christie's at Robson Lowe
39 Poole Hill, Bournemouth, Dorset
Telephone (0202) 292740

DEVON AND CORNWALL
Christopher Petherick
Treadeague, Porthpean
St. Austell, Cornwall
Telephone (0726) 64672

SOUTH EAST
Kim North
Cotlands, Cowfold,
West Sussex
Telephone (040386) 850

IRELAND
Desmond Fitz-Gerald, Knight of Glin
Glin Castle, Glin, Co. Limerick
Private Residence: 52 Waterloo Road, Dublin 2
Telephone (0001) 68 05 85

NORTHERN IRELAND
John Lewis-Crosby
Marybrook House, Raleagh Road
Crossgar, Downpatrick, Co. Down
Telephone (0396) 830574

CHANNEL ISLANDS
Richard de la Hey
8 David Place, St. Helier, Jersey
Telephone (0534) 77582

Companies and Agents Overseas

Argentina
Cesar Feldman *Consultant*
Libertad 1269, 1012 Buenos Aires
Telephone (541) 41 1616 or 42 2046
Cables Tweba, Buenos Aires

Australia
Sue Hewitt
298 New South Head Road
Double Bay, Sydney 2028
Telephone (612) 326 1422   *Telex* AA26343
Cables Christiart Sydney

Austria
Vincent Windisch-Graetz
Ziehrerplatz 4/22, 1030 Vienna
Telephone (43222) 73 26 44

500

Belgium
Richard Stern, Janine Duesberg
Christie, Manson & Woods (Belgium) Ltd
33 Boulevard de Waterloo
1000 Brussels
Telephone (322) 512 8765 or 8830
Telex Brussels 62042

Brazil
Vera Duvernoy *Consultant*
Caixa Postal 1769
20100 Rio de Janeiro
Cables Christiart Rio de Janeiro

Canada
Murray Mackay
Christie, Manson & Woods International, Inc.
Suite 803, 94 Cumberland Street,
Toronto, Ontario M5R 1A3
Telephone (416) 960 2063   *Telex* 065 23907

Denmark
Birgitta Hillingso
20 Parkvaenget, 2920 Charlottenlund
Telephone (451) 62 23 77

France
Princesse Jeanne-Marie de Broglie
Caroline de Roussy de Sales
Christie's France SARL
17 rue de Lille, 75007 Paris
Telephone (331) 261 12 47   *Telex* 213468

**Monsieur Gérald Van der Kemp,
President d'Honneur of Christie's Europe**
is based in our Paris Office

Italy
Christie's (International) S.A.
Palazzo Massimo Lancellotti
Piazza Navona 114, Rome 00186
Telephone (396) 654 1217   *Telex* Rome 611524
Tom Milnes-Gaskell   Maurizio Lodi-Fè
d.ssa. Luisa Vertova Nicolson *Consultant*

MILAN
Giorgina Venosta
Christie's Italy S.r.l.,
9 via Borgogna
20144 Milan
Telephone (392) 794 712
Telex 316464

TURIN
Sandro Perrone di San Martino
Corso Vittorio 86, 10121 Turin
Telephone (3911) 548 819

Japan
Toshihiko Hatanaka
c/o Dodwell Marketing Consultants
Kowa Building No. 35, 14-14 Akasaka,
1-chome, Minato-ku, Tokyo 107
Telephone (03) 584 2351   *Telex* J23790

Mexico
Ana Maria de Xirau *Consultant*
Callejon de San Antonio 64
San Angel
Delegacion Villa
Alvaro Obregon
0100, Mexico D.F.
Telephone (905) 548 5946

The Netherlands
Christie's Amsterdam B.V.
Cornelis Schuytstraat 57
1071 JG Amsterdam
Telephone (3120) 64 20 11
Telex Amsterdam 15758
Cables Christiart, Amsterdam
Harts Nystad

Norway
Ulla Solitair Hjort
Riddervoldsgt 10 b
Oslo 2
Telephone Oslo (472) 44 12 42

Spain
Casilda Fz-Villaverde de Eraso, Carlos Porras
Edificio Propac
Casado del Alisal 5, Madrid 14
Telephone (341) 228 39 00   *Telex* 43889
Cables Christiart Madrid

Sweden
Mrs Lillemor Malmström
Hildingavägen 19
182 62 Djursholm, Stockholm
Telephone (468) 755 10 92
Telex Stockholm 12916

Baroness Irma Silfverschiold
Klagerups Gard
23040 Bara
Telephone (4640) 440360

Switzerland
Christie's (International) S.A.
8 Place de la Taconnerie, 1204 Geneva
Telephone (4122) 28 25 44
Telex Geneva 423634
Cables Chrisauction Geneva
Dr Géza von Habsburg
Richard Stern
Georges de Bartha

ZÜRICH
Maria Reinshagen
Christie's (International) A.G.
Steinwiesplatz, 8032 Zürich
Telephone (411) 69 05 05
Telex Zürich 56093

West Germany
Jörg-Michael Bertz
Alt Pempelfort 11a, 4000 Düsseldorf
Telephone (49211) 35 05 77   *Telex* 8587599
Cables Chriskunst Düsseldorf

Isabella von Bethmann Hollweg
Wentzelstrasse 21, D-2000 Hamburg 60
Telephone (4940) 279 0866

Charlotte Fürstin zu Hohenlohe-Langenburg
Reitmorstrasse 30, 8000 Munich 22
Telephone (4989) 22 95 39

United States of America
Christie, Manson & Woods International, Inc.
502 Park Avenue, New York, N.Y. 10022
Telephone (212) 546 1000
Cables Chriswoods, New York
Telex (International) New York 620721
(Domestic) 710-5812325
President David Bathurst

CHRISTIE'S EAST
219 East 67th Street, New York, N.Y. 10021
Telephone (212 570 4141   *Telex* 710-581 4211
President J. Brian Cole

CALIFORNIA
Christie, Manson & Woods International, Inc.
342 North Rodeo Drive
Beverley Hills, California 90212
Telephone (213) 275 5534   *Telex* 910 490 4652
Russell Fogarty   Christine Eisenberg
(Automobile and Special Sales)

SAN FRANCISCO
Ellanor Notides
125 Lake Street, San Francisco, California 94118
Telephone (415) 751 2501

FLORIDA
Helen Cluett
225 Fern Street, West Palm Beach, Fla. 33401
Telephone (305) 833 6952

MASSACHUSETTS
Edgar Bingham Jr.
32 Fayette Street, Boston, Mass.02116
Telephone (617) 338 6679

MID-ATLANTIC
Paul Ingersoll
P.O. Box 1112, Bryn Mawr, Pa. 19010
Telephone (215)525 5493

David Ober
2935 Garfield Street, N.W.
Washington D.C. 20008
Telephone (202) 387 8722
Nuala Pell *Consultant*
Joan Gardner *Consultant*

MID-WEST
Frances Blair
46 East Elm Street, Chicago, Illinois 60611
Telephone (312) 787 2765

TEXAS
Linda N. Letzerich
2017 West Gray Houston, Texas 77019
Telephone (713) 529 7777

INDEX

Index